Adorno's Gamble

signale
modern german letters, cultures, and thought

Series Editor: Paul Fleming, Cornell University
Peter Uwe Hohendahl, Founding Editor

Signale: Modern German Letters, Cultures, and Thought publishes new English-language books in literary studies, criticism, cultural studies, and intellectual history pertaining to the German-speaking world, as well as translations of important German-language works. Signale construes "modern" in the broadest terms: the series covers topics ranging from the early modern period to the present. Signale books are published under a joint imprint of Cornell University Press and Cornell University Library. Please see http://signale.cornell.edu/.

Adorno's Gamble

Harnessing German Ideology

Mikko Immanen

A Signale Book

Cornell University Press and Cornell University Library
Ithaca and London

Cornell University Press and Cornell University Library gratefully acknowledge the College of Arts & Sciences, Cornell University, for support of the Signale series.

Copyright © 2025 by Mikko Immanen

All rights reserved. Except for brief quotations in a review, this book, or parts thereof, must not be reproduced in any form without permission in writing from the publisher. For information, address Cornell University Press, Sage House, 512 East State Street, Ithaca, New York 14850.

First published 2025 by Cornell University Press and
Cornell University Library

Library of Congress Cataloging-in-Publication Data

Names: Immanen, Mikko, 1982– author.
Title: Adorno's gamble : harnessing German ideology / Mikko Immanen.
Description: Ithaca : Cornell University Press and Cornell University Library, 2025. | Series: Signale : modern German letters, cultures, and thought | "A Signale book"—title page. | Includes bibliographical references and index.
Identifiers: LCCN 2024015966 (print) | LCCN 2024015967 (ebook) | ISBN 9781501779510 (hardcover) | ISBN 9781501779527 (paperback) | ISBN 9781501779534 (epub) | ISBN 9781501779541 (pdf)
Subjects: LCSH: Adorno, Theodor W., 1903–1969. | Spengler, Oswald, 1880–1936—Influence. | Klages, Ludwig, 1872–1956—Influence. | Philosophy, German—20th century. | Frankfurt school of sociology.
Classification: LCC B3199.A34 I45 2025 (print) | LCC B3199.A34 (ebook) | DDC 193—dc23/eng/20240804
LC record available at https://lccn.loc.gov/2024015966
LC ebook record available at https://lccn.loc.gov/2024015967

Contents

Acknowledgments	vii
Introduction: Repurposing *Zivilisationskritik* for Progressive Ends	1
1. Adorno's Klages Project: The Origin of *Negative Dialectics*	28
2. "Caesarism": Spengler's Master Class in Democracy's Self-Destruction	71
3. "Demystification of Antiquity": Dialectic of Enlightenment	116
Epilogue: Legacies of Adorno's Gamble	156
Bibliography	175
Index	193

Acknowledgments

Early on in this project I asked Richard Wolin for his opinion on whether such a book was worthwhile. Besides his encouraging words, I am grateful to Richard for his precious advice along the way and for his kindness to host me at the CUNY Graduate Center in New York as a Fulbright fellow in 2018–2019. I would also like to express my appreciation to Martin Jay, Olli-Pekka Moisio, Markku Peltonen, and Georgia Warnke for their invaluable comments on my arguments. Finally, discerning criticisms by two anonymous reviewers considerably helped me to further clarify and refine the claims advanced in this book.

The bulk of the book was written in the shadow of the pandemic while I was an Academy of Finland Postdoctoral Researcher at the University of Jyväskylä in 2019–2022. At the Department of Social Sciences and Philosophy, I am particularly indebted to Olli-Pekka Moisio for his insight and encouragement. Discussions with students on critical theory, old and new, count among the most gratifying experiences in Jyväskylä. A warm word of thanks is also due to Seija Paananen and the late Lea Naumanen for their practical help.

Cesare Cuttica, Heikki Haara, Aino Lahdenranta, and Antti Lepistö at the University of Helsinki have been constant sources of intellectual and emotional support. Thanks also to my astute colleagues in the General History Seminar, especially Elise Garritzen, Kaarlo Havu, Markku Kekäläinen, Anna Koivusalo, Kari Saastamoinen, Antti Taipale, Laura Tarkka, Tupu Ylä-Anttila, and Soile Ylivuori.

The "European Narratives of Crisis" conference in 2018, organized by the Centre of Excellence in Law, Identity and the European Narratives (EuroStorie) in Helsinki, offered me one of the first occasions to test the central thesis of *Adorno's Gamble*. It is only fitting that I was able to make the final adjustments to it as a visiting scholar at EuroStorie in 2023. I am grateful for Kaius Tuori for making this visit possible.

I greatly appreciate my outstanding editors at Cornell University Press. Thanks are due to the Signale series editor Paul Fleming for seeing potential in my manuscript and to the Signale managing editor Kizer Walker and the Cornell University Press editor in chief Mahinder Kingra for guiding me through what was, again, a wonderfully pleasant publishing process.

Michael Schwarz at the Theodor W. Adorno Archive was of enormous aid in helping me to steer my way through Adorno's unpublished correspondence. Visiting the Adorno archive and writing this book in Jyväskylä, Helsinki, and New York were enabled by the generous funding of the Research Council of Finland (formerly the Academy of Finland), the Fulbright Finland Foundation, the Finnish Academy of Science and Letters (The Foundations' Postdoctoral Pool), the Ella and Georg Ehrnrooth Foundation, and the Emil Aaltonen Foundation.

"Chief inspectors" Juha Korhonen and Teemu Holmén have been as reliable as one can hope one's best friends to be. I owe thanks also to the following individuals for their feedback, support, company, or inspiration at the time when this book was coming together: Ali Ali, Melike Çakan, Ritva Eskelinen, Senni Eskelinen, Onni Hirvonen, Merja Holmén, Sanna Huhtonen, Andrea Köhler, Sami

Lalou, Petteri Norring, Suurin Pamaus, Candela Potente, Kenneth Quek, Anssi Salminen, Marianne Sandelin, Juha Siltala, Esa Sironen, Raija Sironen, Pamela Slotte, Joona Taipale, Punakiven Traktor, and Erkki Vainikkala.

My most heartfelt gratitude goes to my mother, Leena, and my father, Erkki, as well as my sister Sanna and her family. Hanna, my love, theories may well be relative, but baking is not.

The archival documents from the Theodor W. Adorno Archive are used with permission of the © Hamburg Foundation for the Promotion of Science and Culture. An earlier version of chapter 2 and a section of chapter 3 appeared as "Days of the Cavemen? Adorno, Spengler, and the Anatomy of Caesarism," *New German Critique* 48, no. 2 (2021): 177–204. I am thankful to Duke University Press for permission to republish it here.

Introduction

Repurposing Zivilisationskritik for Progressive Ends

> What is interesting is to read the enemy, because the enemy penetrates the defenses, the weak points.
> —Isaiah Berlin

> Not least among the tasks now confronting thought is that of placing all the reactionary arguments against Western culture in the service of progressive enlightenment.
> —Theodor W. Adorno

In 1969, the Suhrkamp publishing house released *Melancholie und Gesellschaft* (*Melancholy and Society*) by Wolf Lepenies, a study that earned the young sociologist his doctorate two years earlier. In his book, Lepenies put forward a provocative thesis suggesting that Theodor W. Adorno, the leading light of the Frankfurt School and one of the key leftist intellectuals of the twentieth century, and Arnold Gehlen, an influential conservative thinker with a Nazi past, stood intellectually not that far from each other. "Melancholy science," a self-characterization with which Adorno had opened his ponderings on "damaged life" in *Minima Moralia* (1951), and the theological appeal to "the standpoint of redemption" with which he had closed them, emboldened Lepenies to argue that the basic contours of Adorno's thought differed little from Gehlen's despondent anthropology. Their undeniable differences notwithstanding, he contended, both were pessimist elitists with no sincere faith in the prospects of modernity.[1] "It is a quite interesting thing," Adorno, showing considerable sympathy to Lepenies's claim, wrote to Gehlen. "Without question the man is on to something important."[2]

Gehlen (1904–1976) had argued in works such as *Urmensch und Spätkultur* (Prehistorical man and late culture, 1956) that modern democratization had fatefully deprived archaic social institutions, such as state and church, of their function to maintain the stable social order required by a species lacking the guidance of animal instincts.[3] One would think that Adorno (1903–1969), a former émigré of Jewish background who had returned to Germany in 1949, would have found little worth in such conservative anxieties that ran counter to his own efforts to democratize Germany's public sphere. In the 1960s, however, the two developed an unexpectedly close relationship. In their many debates on West German radio and television, Adorno shared Gehlen's misgivings about a form of modern life defined by compulsive consumerism and commodified mass culture. Yet he saw as their cause not excessive but insufficient democratization. While Gehlen drew from these phenomena the conclusion that for the majority of human beings Kant's ideal of autonomy was unattainable, Adorno thought that what kept

---

1. Wolf Lepenies, *Melancholy and Society*, trans. Jeremy Gaines and Doris Jones (Cambridge, MA: Harvard University Press, 1992), 193–96; Theodor W. Adorno, *Minima Moralia: Reflections from Damaged Life*, trans. E. F. N. Jephcott (London: Verso, 2000), 15, 247.

2. Adorno to Gehlen, January 15, 1969, Theodor W. Adorno Archive 453/55, Institute for Social Research, Goethe University Frankfurt. Unless otherwise indicated, all translations are mine.

3. Arnold Gehlen, *Urmensch und Spätkultur: Philosophische Ergebnisse und Aussagen* (Bonn: Athenäum, 1956).

humanity in a "state of immaturity" was not some anthropological deficiency but overpowering economic processes.[4] Still, the warmth between the two politically antagonistic figures did not go unnoticed by contemporaries. Even if "friendship," a characterization made by Helmut Schelsky, Gehlen's conservative colleague, was an overstatement, Adorno's fellow social critics on the Left, such as Günther Anders, saw his dealings with Gehlen as ill-advised fraternizing with a former Nazi.[5]

The question of Adorno's affinities with cultural critics from the opposite end of the political spectrum was taken up in the 1980s by his Frankfurt School heirs, Jürgen Habermas and Axel Honneth. Eager to wrest critical theory free from its bleak interwar origins and update it for merrier times, they claimed that certain elements of Weimar Germany's prophecies of decline had been hardwired into Adorno's thinking. Adorno's preoccupation with radical right-wing critics of modernity, they argued, was a blind spot that had darkened his horizon to such an extent that after 1945 he overestimated the continuing threat of fascism and underestimated the merits of the liberal political tradition and Keynesian welfare state. This preoccupation was in many ways also to blame for the theoretical dead end that the early Frankfurt School had run into in *Dialektik der Aufklärung* (*Dialectic of Enlightenment*, 1947), in which Adorno and Max Horkheimer sought to grasp the relapse of the modern West, proud of its self-image as the beacon of reason, into totalitarianism. For Habermas and Honneth, about to launch their famous paradigm shifts toward unobstructed "communication" and reciprocal "recognition," the prospects of which they judged optimistically, Adorno's worries over the "totally administered society" seemed

---

4. See, for instance, their 1965 debate, "Ist die Soziologie eine Wissenschaft vom Menschen? Ein Streitgespräch zwischen Theodor W. Adorno und Arnold Gehlen," in Friedemann Grenz, *Adornos Philosophie in Grundbegriffen: Auflösung einiger Deutungsprobleme* (Frankfurt: Suhrkamp, 1974), 224–51.

5. Helmut Schelsky, *Rückblicke eines "Anti-Soziologen"* (Opladen, Germany: Westdeutscher Verlag, 1981), 46; Christian Thies, *Die Krise des Individuums: Zur Kritik der Moderne bei Adorno und Gehlen* (Reinbek, Germany: Rowohlt, 1997), 50–51; Stefan Müller-Doohm, *Adorno: A Biography*, trans. Rodney Livingstone (Cambridge: Polity Press, 2009), 340.

outright implausible. "We no longer share this mood, this attitude," Habermas concluded.[6]

With the end of the Cold War Adorno was often deemed an obsolete miserabilist out of tune with the popular Fukuyaman mantra of "the end of history."[7] The global rise of radical right-wing populism in the past decade and the proliferation in public discourse of fake news and conspiracy theories, however, has brought new currency to Adorno's ideas, including concepts such as "culture industry," "authoritarian personality," and "instrumental reason." Fifty years after his passing during the heyday of the New Left, Adorno has also become an unexpected point of reference among younger generations. This can be observed by the success of his only recently published 1967 lecture on right-wing radicalism, which in 2019 stayed on *Der Spiegel*'s list of best-selling books for months.[8] The reason for Adorno's new popularity is not hard to fathom. What is today celebrated as Germany's exemplary "working through the past" after World War II was only beginning in the 1960s, pushed forward by the Eichmann and Auschwitz trials and public interventions by tireless critical voices such as Adorno's. Germany's painful effort to face its Nazi past, which took off in earnest only in the 1970s, has generally been regarded as a success story, especially when compared to Russian attempts to come to terms with Stalinism. Adorno's 1967 lecture resonates today, however, because Germany's laudable culture of remembrance has of late been put on the defensive by "ethnonationalist" think tanks of the country's "New

---

6. Jürgen Habermas, *The Philosophical Discourse of Modernity: Twelve Lectures*, trans. Frederick G. Lawrence (Cambridge, MA: MIT Press, 1990), 106; Jürgen Habermas, "Nachwort," in Max Horkheimer and Theodor W. Adorno, *Dialektik der Aufklärung* (Frankfurt: Fischer, 1986), 277; Axel Honneth, "Anthropologische Berührungspunkte zwischen der Lebensphilosophischen Kulturkritik und der 'Dialektik der Aufklärung,'" in *21. Deutscher Soziologentag 1982. Beiträge der Sektions- und ad hoc-Gruppen*, ed. Friedrich Heckmann and Peter Winter (Opladen, Germany: Westdeutscher Verlag, 1983), 786–92.

7. Francis Fukuyama, *The End of History and the Last Man* (New York: The Free Press, 1992).

8. Theodor W. Adorno, *Aspects of the New Right-Wing Extremism*, trans. Wieland Hoban (Cambridge: Polity Press, 2020); Jan Petter, "Randale, Bambule, Frankfurter Schule: Warum die Generation Greta plötzlich Adorno liest," *Der Spiegel*, August 8, 2019.

Right" (*Neue Rechte*) and the Alternative for Germany Party (and has been accompanied by an alarming increase in antisemitic and anti-Muslim violence), whose leading politicians demand a "U-turn in our remembrance politics."[9]

Moreover, Adorno's critical analyses of Nazism and other forms of right-wing extremism (the topic of his 1967 lecture was Germany's neofascist National Democratic Party) have become topical because they help us to make sense of our wider, indeed global, authoritarian populist predicament. Besides Adorno's own reflections, the pathbreaking mid-century studies on authoritarianism and racial prejudice by the Institute for Social Research, the institutional matrix of the Frankfurt School, have received renewed attention. Today's scholarly discussions on antidemocratic attitudes, xenophobia, sexism, capitalism, and their interconnections, Marc Grimm points out, "are based on questions that could only be asked using the conceptual apparatus derived from the institute's studies."[10] The same goes for the Frankfurt School's pioneering analyses of culture. Although our digitalized social media age may seemingly bear little resemblance to the 1930s world of newspaper and radio, its reflections on a manipulative "culture industry"—characterized by what Adorno called "an extraordinary perfection of certain methods" and "blindness, indeed abstruseness, of the aims"—is, as Volker Weiß suggests, applicable also to our world of "bots, trolls and fake news."[11]

Adorno's new popularity is not restricted to Germany, which makes perfect sense since for him authoritarianism was never a German problem per se but a malady of industrial capitalist modernity

---

9. Quote is from a speech by Björn Höcke in Dresden on January 17, 2017. Höcke is the leader of the Alternative for Germany Party's right-wing extremist faction "Der Flügel" ("The Wing"). Quoted in Volker Weiß, Afterword to Theodor W. Adorno, *Aspects of the New Right-Wing Extremism*, trans. Wieland Hoban (Cambridge: Polity Press, 2020), 58. See also Aleida Assmann, *Das neue Unbehagen an der Erinnerungskultur. Eine Intervention*, 3rd ed. (Munich: C. H. Beck, 2020); Jonathan Bach and Benjamin Nienass, eds., "Myths of Innocence in German Public Memory," Special Issue, *German Politics and Society* 39, no. 1 (2021).

10. Marc Grimm, "Zur Aktualität Kritischer Theorie," *Zeitschrift für Politische Theorie* 8, no. 1 (2017): 116. Translation from Weiß, Afterword, 48.

11. Adorno, *Aspects of the New Right-Wing Extremism*, 13; Weiß, Afterword, 61.

in general. Little wonder, then, that as our current "age of Trump" in some respects resembles more the interwar period than the "golden" postwar decades,[12] many commentators in the United States, Britain, and elsewhere have turned to Adorno's theories to explain these troubling developments—the implication being that, while one should avoid simple analogies between the 1930s and our own time, Habermas's verdict on Adorno's obsolescence is itself outdated.

This renewed interest in Adorno is, I think, well founded. Yet the book at hand is not primarily about Adorno's contemporary relevance. Rather, it asks, where did his critical virtues come from? Adorno's path of thinking is usually seen as a mix of Marxism, psychoanalysis, aesthetic modernism, and Jewish tradition. There is a solid consensus that to understand his intellectual biography one needs to focus on his debts to Georg Lukács's Hegelian-Marxist idea of reification of social institutions, Sigmund Freud's psychoanalytic insight into repression of instincts, Arnold Schönberg's musical expressionism, and Walter Benjamin's peculiar materialism with theological overtones. My intention is not to deny the accuracy of this picture but rather to complicate it by looking at a direction seldom looked at. Taking my cue from Adorno's *Minima Moralia* (the epigraph at the beginning of this chapter),[13] as well as from the suggestions of Habermas and Honneth, I propose that one cannot fully understand Adorno's thought unless one takes into account his ambivalent interest in the German critique of civilization, or *Zivilisationskritik*, a loose current of radical conservative cultural philosophy whose claims about the bankruptcy of reason and progress gained resonance in the wake of World War I.

Despite the openings made in the 1980s by Adorno's heirs, the accepted scholarly wisdom has consigned to the margins the question of his possible intellectual debts to radical right-wing critics of reason. *Adorno's Gamble* overturns this marginalization by demonstrating Adorno's enduring preoccupation, from the late Weimar era through his years in exile to the postwar period, with two

---

12. Thomas Piketty, *Capital in the Twenty-First Century*, trans. Arthur Goldhammer (Cambridge MA: The Belknap Press of Harvard University Press, 2014).
13. Adorno, *Minima Moralia*, 192.

towering figures of early twentieth-century German letters: Oswald Spengler and Ludwig Klages.

Spengler and Klages

Oswald Spengler (1880–1936) needs little introduction. Just months before the end of World War I, in the summer 1918, he burst onto the scene with *Der Untergang des Abendlandes* (*The Decline of the West*, 1918/1922).[14] "After a few weeks of public hesitation," H. Stuart Hughes notes regarding the book's reception, it "started to sell, and it has continued to sell ever since."[15] Indeed, in the aftermath of the Great War, Spengler's book became a bestseller and gained its author a celebrated status in the popular imagination. Ever since it has remained an enduring point of reference whenever the Western world has harbored doubts about its future. *The Decline of the West* famously envisioned for Europe an inevitable withering away of the creative energies of *Kultur* and the rise of a shallow civilization infatuated with material comforts. Against liberal and Marxist visions of progress, Spengler's "cultural morphology"—his equation of human history with the life cycles of plants, or the age-phases of an individual person—argued that the "Faustian" West would out of necessity go through the same stages of childhood, youth, adulthood, and old age as ancient Babylonian, Greco-Roman, Chinese, and other "great cultures" before it. In fact, Europe's downfall, Spengler warned, had been underway for the greater part of the nineteenth century (equivalent in his scheme to the Hellenist period of "Apollonian" antiquity) and it would face its collapse around the end of the twentieth.[16]

---

14. Oswald Spengler, *The Decline of the West*, vol. 1, *Form and Actuality*, trans. Charles Francis Atkinson (New York: Knopf, 1994); *The Decline of the West*, vol. 2, *Perspectives of World-History*, trans. Charles Francis Atkinson (New York: Knopf, 1994).
15. H. Stuart Hughes, *Oswald Spengler: A Critical Estimate* (New Brunswick, NJ: Transaction Publishers, 1992), 1.
16. On Spengler's thought and impact, see Hughes, *Oswald Spengler*; Gilbert Merlio and Daniel Meyer, eds., *Spengler ohne Ende: Ein Rezeptionsphänomen im*

Unlike Spengler, Ludwig Klages (1872–1956), the once-fashionable autodidact from Munich's bohemian district of Schwabing, is today an obscure figure familiar only to students of modern German thought. In the interwar period, however, Klages counted among the most visible critics of liberal modernity and the Enlightenment. Characteristic of his thought, best represented by the monumental *Der Geist als Widersacher der Seele* (The spirit as adversary of the soul, 1929–1932), was an incessant mockery of two millennia of Western "logocentrism," which had allegedly alienated the moderns from vital needs of the "soul" cherished in ancient myths.[17] Klages's antimodern campaign was stimulated early on by a circle, of which he had once been a member, around the charismatic neo-Romantic poet Stefan George, the *George-Kreis*. If Germany was the proverbial land of *Dichter und Denker*, or poets and thinkers, George was extolled as both a *Dichter* and a *Denker*. His lyrical poetry, revered for living up to the ethereal standard of Goethe and Hölderlin, inspired antibourgeois movements as diverse as the prewar German Youth Movement, Munich's short-lived Soviet Republic, and the Hitler Youth. Equally popular, and increasingly so in the Weimar era, was George's educational ideal of holistic *Bildung* (mentoring and cultivation of the country's new spiritual aristocracy), inspired by the ancient Greek example, which he opposed to the sterility and compartmentalization of the modern positivist university.[18]

In Weimar Germany, many of George's protégés acquired academic positions in the humanities and were thus capable of institu-

---

internationalen Kontext (Frankfurt: Peter Lang, 2014); Zaur Gasimov and Carl Antonius Lemke Duque, eds., *Oswald Spengler als europäisches Phänomen: Der Transfer der Kultur- und Geschichtsmorphologie im Europa der Zwischenkriegszeit 1919–1939* (Göttingen, Germany: Vandenhoeck & Ruprecht, 2013).

17. Ludwig Klages, *Der Geist als Widersacher der Seele: Erstes bis Viertes Buch* [The spirit as adversary of the soul: Books one through four], in *Sämtliche Werke, Bd. 1*, ed. Ernst Frauchiger et al. (Bonn: Bouvier Verlag, 1969); *Der Geist als Widersacher der Seele: Fünftes Buch* [The spirit as adversary of the soul: Book five], in *Sämtliche Werke, Bd. 2*, ed. Ernst Frauchiger et al. (Bonn: Bouvier Verlag, 1966).

18. Martin A. Ruehl, "Aesthetic Fundamentalism in Weimar Poetry: Stefan George and His Circle, 1918–1933," in *Weimar Thought: A Contested Legacy*, ed. Peter E. Gordon and John P. McCormick (Princeton, NJ: Princeton University Press, 2013), 240–41. On the George Circle, see Robert Norton, *Secret Germany: Stefan George and His Circle* (Ithaca, NY: Cornell University Press, 2002).

tionalizing the circle's message of intellectual renewal—one thinks, for instance, of Adorno's colleagues at the University of Frankfurt, the historian Ernst Kantorowicz and the historian of literature Max Kommerell.[19] Klages, however, remained an outsider, though an influential one. Since the turn of the century, he had led a bohemian fin-de-siècle circle of his own called the "Cosmics" (*Kosmische Runde*), which in its early days had partly overlapped with the *George-Kreis*. The spiritual renewal the Cosmics pleaded for was more backward-looking than the future-oriented agenda of the George Circle. Its three central figures, Klages, Karl Wolfskehl, and Alfred Schuler, were all enthralled by the prospect of revitalizing a soulless modernity with magical symbols revived from mythic past—among them the ancient Indian symbol of the swastika, rediscovered by Schuler in the 1890s, which the Nazis later adopted as their sign. What ultimately drove the Cosmics and the George Circle apart in 1904 was Klages's growing antisemitism. The George circle, although not immune to anti-Jewish prejudice, counted among its members a number of conservatively oriented Jews, such as Kantorowicz and Wolfskehl. For an unbendable antisemite like Klages, this turned out to be too much to swallow, especially after Wolfskehl's embrace of Zionism. Indeed, adding to the controversial nature of Klages's antimodernism was his steadfast antisemitism. This did not, however, hinder his ideas from reaching large audiences and receiving acclaim from countless notable figures from Sergei Eisenstein and Georg Simmel to Robert Musil and Hermann Hesse. In 1932, Reich President Paul von Hindenburg awarded Klages with the prestigious Goethe Prize of the City of Frankfurt for his contributions to philosophy and psychology. For his literary abilities, Klages was even nominated as a Nobel Prize candidate in literature in 1936 and 1937.[20]

---

19. Ruehl, "Aesthetic Fundamentalism in Weimar Poetry," 241–42, 248.
20. Nitzan Lebovic, *The Philosophy of Life and Death: Ludwig Klages and the Rise of a Nazi Biopolitics* (New York: Palgrave Macmillan, 2013), 39–44, 160. On Klages's thought, see also Michael Grossheim, ed., *Perspektiven der Lebensphilosophie: Zum 125. Geburtstag von Ludwig Klages* (Bonn: Bouvier, 1999); Paul Bishop, *Ludwig Klages and the Philosophy of Life: A Vitalist Toolkit* (New York: Routledge, 2017).

Klages and Spengler had several things in common. Both resided for years in Munich, the epicenter of Germany's antibourgeois, neo-Romantic counterculture. Both sought to make their mark as private scholars working free of the constraints of academia. And both wrote massive multivolume tomes encompassing well over one thousand pages. Besides being immensely popular writers, Klages and Spengler also counted as stalwarts of the so-called conservative revolutionary movement of Weimar Germany, a term coined by the Austrian poet Hugo von Hofmannsthal in 1927. These latter-day representatives of "German ideology," or the Counter-Enlightenment, differed from traditional guardians of German *Kultur* in their apocalyptic visions and dreams of what one of their leading voices, Hans Freyer, titled *Die Revolution von Rechts* (Revolution from the right, 1931). Like Spengler, most of them, including the militant novelist Ernst Jünger and the legal theorist Carl Schmitt, were what Jeffrey Herf labels "reactionary modernists."[21] That is, unlike traditional pastoral conservatives, they had no qualms embracing modern technology as an element of their radical nationalism. By contrast, others, among them Klages and Arthur Möller van der Bruck, the author of *Das dritte Reich* (*Germany's Third Empire*, 1923), abhorred militarism and modern technological civilization. The core tenets shared by all in the movement, however, were elitist antipathy toward the "ideas of 1789," the Weimar Constitution, cosmopolitan mass culture, and communism. After World War II, the conservative revolutionaries were stamped as intellectual forerunners of Nazism, although the Nazis were often unsuccessful, as in the cases of Spengler and Klages, in luring them to espouse Hitler's version of Germany's "national awakening."[22]

Many of these authors drew on and radicalized the current known as *Lebensphilosophie*, or philosophy of life. With roots in Romanticism and such later nineteenth-century critics of the

---

21. Jeffrey Herf, *Reactionary Modernism: Technology, Culture, and Politics in Weimar and the Third Reich* (Cambridge: Cambridge University Press, 1986).
22. Roger Woods, *The Conservative Revolution in the Weimar Republic* (New York: Palgrave Macmillan, 1996); Stefan Breuer, *Anatomie der konservativen Revolution* (Darmstadt, Germany: Wissenschaftliche Buchgesellschaft, 1993).

Enlightenment as Wilhelm Dilthey, Johann Jakob Bachofen, and Friedrich Nietzsche, *Lebensphilosophie* blossomed in the half century between 1880 and 1930.[23] The life philosophers questioned what they mocked as the eighteenth century's overemphasis on analytic reason and discursive thought. Rather than focus on Kant's sober notion of the understanding (*Verstand*), they anchored their search for truth in more elusive stimuli such as feeling and intuition, or what they called "lived experience" (*Erlebnis*). In the realm of communal life, they tended to disapprove of modern industrial society (*Gesellschaft*), for them an epitome of shallow civilization (*Zivilisation*), and juxtaposed to its atomism more firmly rooted collective ties of the community (*Gemeinschaft*), purportedly a vital guardian of genuine *Kultur*.[24] In the hands of the interwar conservative radicals, however, nineteenth-century *Lebensphilosophie*'s careful balancing act between wholeness, immediacy, and creativity on one side and intellectual sobriety on the other gave way to antitheses of a more Manichean variety. Hence, Spengler dismissed the conventional cause-effect reasoning of academic historians as superficial compared to his privileged "physiognomic" illumination and Klages replaced life-denying scientific abstractions with dreams and other ecstatic states that he cherished as gateways to archaic truths about life-affirming Eros.[25]

Around the time that Adorno was taking his first steps in philosophy, *Lebensphilosophie* was the vogue of the day. "Every age finds its own redeeming word," one astute observer remarked in

---

23. Herbert Schnädelbach, *Philosophy in Germany, 1831–1933*, trans. Eric Matthews (Cambridge: Cambridge University Press, 1984), 139.

24. On *Lebensphilosophie* and its role in modern German culture and thought, see Gudrun Kühne-Bertram, *Aus dem Leben—zum Leben: Entstehung, Wesen und Bedeutung populärer Lebensphilosophien in der Geistesgeschichte des 19. Jahrhunderts* (Frankfurt: Peter Lang, 1987); Anne Harrington, *Reenchanted Science: Holism in German Culture from Wilhelm II to Hitler* (Princeton, NJ: Princeton University Press, 1996); Robert J. Richards, *The Romantic Conception of Life: Science and Philosophy in the Age of Goethe* (Chicago: University of Chicago Press, 2002).

25. Spengler, *The Decline of the West*, vol. 1, 26 and vol. 2, 47; Ludwig Klages, *Vom kosmogonischen Eros*, in *Sämtliche Werke, Bd. 3*, ed. Ernst Frauchiger et al. (Bonn: Bouvier, 1974), 353–497. On the conservative revolutionary appropriation of *Lebensphilosophie*, see Lebovic, *The Philosophy of Life and Death*, chap. 5.

1928. If the watchword of the eighteenth century, the century of the Enlightenment, had been "reason," and if the nineteenth century, the forward-looking epoch of liberalism and industrialism, had marched under the banner of "progress," the twentieth century had set its hopes on the notion of "life." Suspicious of "blind faith in progress," exhausted by "civilization fatigue," and cynical about "the creative potential of socialism," the early twentieth century expressed a profound disillusionment with the ideals of its predecessors. It understood itself instead as an era of "awakening," yet one that "brought with it a longing for a new dream, a new enchantment."[26]

In dominant readings of Adorno's path of thinking, as already mentioned, the question of his possible debts to the conservative revolutionaries has been sidestepped. Stressing the critical Marxism of Lukács and Benjamin on one hand and Freudian psychoanalysis on the other, the major early studies on Adorno and the Frankfurt School by Martin Jay, Susan Buck-Morss, and Gillian Rose had little to say about Adorno's interest in right-wing critique of civilization.[27] Much of this neglect likely resulted from the fact that these studies were written in the wake of the New Left and its Marxist presumption of a clear-cut divide between Romantic irrationalism and progressive rationalism, a presumption strengthened by the then-prevalent interpretation among historians of the conservative revolution as nothing but a pernicious progenitor of Nazism.[28] With initial suggestions by Habermas and Honneth, however, in the 1980s this image of Adorno began to change. Jay, the leading

---

26. Helmut Plessner, *Levels of Organic Life and the Human: An Introduction to Philosophical Anthropology*, trans. Millay Hyatt (New York: Fordham University Press, 2019), 1–2.
27. Martin Jay, *The Dialectical Imagination: A History of the Frankfurt School and the Institute of Social Research, 1923–1950* (Boston: Little, Brown and Co., 1973); Susan Buck-Morss, *The Origin of Negative Dialectics: Theodor W. Adorno, Walter Benjamin, and the Frankfurt Institute* (New York: The Free Press, 1977); Gillian Rose, *The Melancholy Science: An Introduction to the Thought of Theodor W. Adorno* (London: Macmillan Press, 1978).
28. George L. Mosse, *The Crisis of German Ideology: Intellectual Origins of the Third Reich* (New York: Grosset & Dunlap, 1964); Fritz Stern, *The Politics of Cultural Despair: A Study in the Rise of the Germanic Ideology* (Berkeley: University of California Press, 1961).

historian of the Frankfurt School, acknowledged conservative cultural criticism as one element in Adorno's thought, and in his grand history of the Frankfurt School Rolf Wiggershaus recognized Klages's presence in *Dialectic of Enlightenment*.[29] The theme also received attention in the dispute over Carl Schmitt's impact on the Frankfurt School and in Hermann Mörchen's study on the peculiar "refusal of communication" between Adorno and Martin Heidegger.[30]

The scholarship on Adorno's relationship to Spengler and Klages, however, is still very limited. In 1982, Axel Honneth called attention to "the profound intellectual connections" between Klages and *Dialectic of Enlightenment*, connections that had "sporadically" been mentioned every now and then but had never been properly scrutinized.[31] Honneth's reading was followed by half a dozen more or less brief takes of the topic, written mainly in the 1980s and 1990s.[32] Scholarly assessments of Adorno and Spengler, initiated in 1981 by George Friedman, are even fewer in number and shorter in length.[33] Indicative of this far-from-ideal situation in Adorno scholarship is the

---

29. Martin Jay, *Adorno* (Cambridge, MA: Harvard University Press, 1984), 17–19; Rolf Wiggershaus, *The Frankfurt School: Its History, Theories, and Political Significance*, trans. Michael Robertson (Cambridge: Polity Press, 1994), 327.

30. "Special Section on Carl Schmitt and the Frankfurt School," *Telos* 71 (1987): 37–109; Hermann Mörchen, *Adorno und Heidegger: Untersuchung einer philosophischen Kommunikationsverweigerung* (Stuttgart: Klett-Cotta, 1981).

31. Honneth, "Anthropologische Berührungspunkte," 786.

32. Albrecht Wellmer, *The Persistence of Modernity: Essays on Aesthetics, Ethics and Postmodernism*, trans. David Midgley (Cambridge: Polity Press, 1991), 3–4; Georg Stauth and Bryan S. Turner, "Ludwig Klages (1872–1956) and the Origins of Critical Theory," *Theory, Culture & Society* 9 (1992): 45–63; Georg Stauth, "Critical Theory and Pre-Fascist Social Thought," *History of European Ideas* 18, no. 5 (1994): 714–23; Michael Grossheim, "'Die namenlose Dummheit, die das Resultat des Fortschritts ist.'—Lebensphilosophische und dialektische Kritik der Moderne," *Logos. Zeitschrift für systematische Philosophie* 3, no. 2 (1996): 97–133; Michael Pauen, *Dithyrambiker des Untergangs. Gnostizismus in Ästhetik und Philosophie der Moderne* (Berlin: Akademie Verlag, 1994), 366–69; Richard Wolin, *Walter Benjamin: An Aesthetic of Redemption* (Berkeley: University of California Press, 1994), xxx; Stefan Breuer, "Materialistische Erkenntniskritik," in *Adorno Handbuch: Leben—Werk—Wirkung*, ed. Richard Klein et al., 2nd ed. (Berlin: J. B. Metzler, 2019), 432–36; Stefan Breuer, *Kritische Theorie: Schlüsselbegriffe, Kontroversen, Grenzen* (Tübingen: Mohr Siebeck, 2016), 243–53.

33. George Friedman, *The Political Philosophy of the Frankfurt School* (Ithaca, NY: Cornell University Press, 1981), 79–86, 214–18; David Roberts, *Art and*

fact that if the Klagesian provenance of Walter Benjamin's ideas has come under increasing scholarly attention, in Adorno's case we still rely on tentative first steps. Concerning Benjamin, it has been argued, for example, that his grandiose lifework on the nineteenth-century Paris shopping arcades drew on Klages's theory of archaic images, or *Urbilder*.[34] In contrast, if standard presentations of Adorno mention Klages's name at all, they simply cite Adorno's criticism of Benjamin's fascination with the life philosopher, the implication being that Adorno himself had no investment in Klages's ideas.

Exemplary of this stance are comments by Rolf Tiedemann, Adorno's former student and the editor of his collected works. Criticizing Adorno's Frankfurt School heirs—explicitly Albrecht Wellmer's reading of *Dialectic of Enlightenment* as a "Marxist appropriation of Klages' radical critique of civilization and reason"[35] —Tiedemann complains that Adorno "has been 'situated' rather bizarrely by certain later would-be representatives of the Frankfurt School somewhere in the vicinity of Klages." For Tiedemann, *Dialectic of Enlightenment* expresses Adorno's unqualified rejection of Klages.[36] Undoubtedly, Tiedemann is right to emphasize the gulf separating Adorno from Klages's antidemocratic, antisocialist, and antisemitic agenda. Indeed, it bears emphasizing that Adorno neither

---

Enlightenment: Aesthetic Theory after Adorno (Lincoln: University of Nebraska Press, 1991), 73–81; Pauen, *Dithyrambiker des Untergangs*, 357–61.

34. See, for instance, Lebovic, *The Philosophy of Life and Death*, chap. 3; Joseph Mali, "The Reconciliation of Myth: Benjamin's Homage to Bachofen," *Journal of the History of Ideas* 60, no. 1 (1999): 165–87; John McCole, *Walter Benjamin and the Antinomies of Tradition* (Ithaca, NY: Cornell University Press, 1993), 236–52; Miriam Bratu Hansen, "Benjamin's Aura," *Critical Inquiry* 34, no. 2 (2008): 336–75; Irving Wohlfahrt, "Walter Benjamin and the Idea of a Technological Eros: A Tentative Reading of *Zum Planetarium*," *Benjamin Studies* 1, no. 1 (2002): 65–109; Matthew Charles, "Secret Signals from Another World: Walter Benjamin's Theory of Innervation," *New German Critique* 45, no. 3 (2018): 39–72.

35. Wellmer, *The Persistence of Modernity*, 3.

36. Rolf Tiedemann, editor's note in Theodor W. Adorno, *Ontology and Dialectics (1960/61)*, ed. Rolf Tiedemann, trans. Nicholas Walker (Cambridge: Polity Press, 2019), 300–301n14. See also Georg Stauth's recollection of the very cold welcome that his remarks, in an undergraduate seminar in 1964, on "Klages's theory of cognition" received from Horkheimer's assistants, in Stauth, "Critical Theory and Pre-Fascist Social Thought," 724n18.

minced words about Klages's and Spengler's protofascist scorn for the "ideas of 1789" nor took seriously their neo-Romantic metaphysics, whether it was Klages's dichotomy of spirit and soul or Spengler's cultural morphology. "The works on the Cosmogonic Eros and kindred mysteries," Adorno wrote in *Minima Moralia*, indicated the liability of nonacademic outsiders to fall prey to "crackpot religion" and "half-educated sectarianism."[37] He was adamant that Klages's "agitatory cult of primordial powers" had paved way for Nazism and that "Spengler and his like are not so much prophets of the course the *Weltgeist* will take as its diligent promoters."[38]

Nevertheless, Tiedemann's argument does not hold up upon closer scrutiny. Adorno commented on Klages positively in his public works more than once. In the above-cited passage from *Minima Moralia*, he argued, with an implicit reference to Klages, that intellectual outsiders, although prone to nonscientific alternative truths, could occasionally better see through the prejudices of their time than their more mainstream contemporaries: "A gaze averted from the beaten track, a hatred of brutality, a search for fresh concepts not yet encompassed by the general patterns, is the last hope for thought." Unsurprisingly then, in 1941, when he and Horkheimer set out write *Dialectic of Enlightenment*, Adorno listed Klages and Spengler among a handful of "theoreticians of extreme reaction whose criticism of liberalism proved superior in many respects to that which came from the left wing."[39] Finally, in *Dialectic of Enlightenment* Adorno and Horkheimer stated that Klages (together with Nietzsche and Stefan George) had "recognized the nameless stupidity which is the result of progress."[40]

---

37. Adorno, *Minima Moralia*, 66–68.

38. Theodor W. Adorno, "The George-Hofmannsthal Correspondence, 1891–1906," in *Prisms*, trans. Samuel Weber and Shierry Weber (Cambridge, MA: MIT Press, 1981), 206n17; "Spengler after the Decline," in *Prisms*, 66.

39. Theodor W. Adorno, "Spengler Today," *Studies in Philosophy and Social Science* 9, no. 2 (1941), 318.

40. Max Horkheimer and Theodor W. Adorno, *Dialectic of Enlightenment: Philosophical Fragments*, trans. Edmund Jephcott (Stanford, CA: Stanford University Press, 2002), 194.

Learning from One's Enemies

Why do I claim that Adorno owed something crucial to Klages and Spengler? Why do I want to associate Adorno with such radical conservative writers, who not only despised his emancipatory aspirations but who, moreover, have of late become household names among the European and American "new right"?[41] To begin with, unlike Nitzan Lebovic, I am not after a rehabilitation of early twentieth-century vitalist discourse. Lebovic has recently proposed that this discourse should not be viewed as a mere trailblazer of radical nationalism and fascism, but ought to be considered, especially in what he sees as its rebellious and unpoliticized manifestations up until the early 1920s, as a serious philosophical orientation and a valuable tool in making sense of the discontents of our own time as well.[42] Such reconsiderations of modern German intellectual history certainly make it easier to entertain the hypothesis that Adorno, too, could have learned something from thinkers from the opposite political camp.[43] The main motive behind my argument, however, is quite simply that this is what Adorno's writings seem to say.

My argument has been in the making for some years. Had I been presented with it, say, eight years ago when I was writing my first book on Martin Heidegger's role in the emergence of the early Frankfurt School, I would have been skeptical.[44] I would have countered by insisting, much in the spirit of Rolf Tiedemann, that reactionary charlatans like Spengler and Klages could hardly have preoccupied a thinker of Adorno's caliber. With Heidegger, I would have argued, things were different. For, notwithstanding his shocking attempt in

---

41. Volker Weiß, *Die autoritäre Revolte: Die Neue Rechte und der Untergang des Abendlandes* (Stuttgart: Klett-Cotta, 2018); George Hawley, *Making Sense of the Alt-Right* (New York: Columbia University Press, 2017), 36–37.
42. Lebovic, *The Philosophy of Life and Death*, 1–19.
43. For an argument against oversimplified divisions of Weimar thought into right-wing and left-wing camps, see Manfred Gangl and Gérard Raulet, eds., *Intellektuellendiskurse in der Weimarer Republik: Zur politischen Kultur einer Gemengelage*, 2nd ed. (Frankfurt: Peter Lang, 2007).
44. Mikko Immanen, *Toward a Concrete Philosophy: Heidegger and the Emergence of the Frankfurt School* (Ithaca, NY: Cornell University Press, 2020).

his *Schwarze Hefte* (*Black Notebooks*) to give antisemitism a philosophical basis, Heidegger was, at least before 1933, a philosopher of the first rank and, more importantly, was held to be by Adorno despite his resistance to Heidegger's ontological manner of philosophizing. In contrast, Adorno was deeply suspicious of the neo-Romantic nonsense put forward by *Zivilisationskritiker*, or critics of civilization (and could not, in fact, find a worse thing to say about Heidegger than that his later notion of "forgetfulness of being" was a species of "demonology" not far from Klages's "most obscure speculations"[45]). Or so I maintained at the time. But little by little, cracks in this image began to appear, and I came to consider the possibility that maybe there was more to Adorno's remarks on Klages and Spengler than had previously been recognized. I may have sensed something of this while writing my first book, but the present one is an attempt to tackle this question head-on.

Adorno's preoccupation with Spengler and Klages, I believe, was about what Isaiah Berlin (1909–1997) once described as the virtue of learning from one's enemies. "I am bored by reading people who are allies, people of roughly the same views," Berlin declared in a late interview, contrasting his fellow liberals with ideological opponents both on the right and on the left. Berlin, one of the most vocal defenders of liberalism and pluralism in the twentieth century, noted that "a brilliant enemy," such as Joseph de Maistre on the far right or Karl Marx on the far left, had the gift of making one aware of "the weak points" of one's most cherished beliefs. The latter, Berlin noted, were often a mere "collection of platitudes," and therefore thinkers politically at the furthest remove from us, thinkers who do not share our ideas, can nonetheless "make one think."[46] Berlin's remarks seem to me immensely instructive in making sense of the attention Adorno gave to the writings of Spengler and Klages. In a comparable manner to Berlin, Adorno contended that to strengthen the Enlightenment tradition in its struggle against superstition and

---

45. Theodor W. Adorno, *Ontology and Dialectics (1960/61)*, ed. Rolf Tiedemann, trans. Nicholas Walker (Cambridge: Polity Press, 2019), 225.
46. Isaiah Berlin, "Isaiah Berlin: In Conversation with Steven Lukes," *Salmagundi* 120 (Fall 1998): 90–91.

myth and its effort to improve the lot of humanity, one had to be alert to its blind spots.[47]

What were these blind spots? To understand Adorno's ambivalent stance toward conservative *Zivilisationskritik* it is imperative at the outset to differentiate between two notions of enlightenment: one historical, the other *geschichtsphilosophisch*, or pertaining to the philosophy of history. Spengler and Klages loathed the heritage of the eighteenth-century Enlightenment and the French philosophes, whereas for Adorno this heritage, with its intellectual and political ideals, was of enormous importance. Notwithstanding this ideological gulf, what intrigued Adorno in the two radical conservatives was their pessimistic philosophy of history, the view that Western history, driven by science and technology, was anything but that linear and unambiguous progress that liberals and Marxists believed it to be. *Dialectic of Enlightenment*'s ambivalent narrative of the demythologization process from Homeric epics to the modern era is likewise concerned with this larger civilizational tendency of emancipatory reason to turn into mythic domination. Hence, although Adorno shared the Enlightenment's dream of a just and free society, he saw in the critiques of civilization of Spengler and Klages a healthy antidote to a naive belief in progress.

To do justice to Adorno's reasoning and to avoid severe misunderstandings, we need to underscore the critical nature of his reception of Spengler and Klages. It would be erroneous to view Adorno's relationship with these figures in terms of simple influence. To be influenced by someone means passively adopting their ideas rather than critically appropriating them. Adorno should in-

---

47. It is an interesting biographical fact that when Adorno moved to Oxford in 1934 after Hitler's seizure of power, he got to know Isaiah Berlin, whose Russian Jewish family had moved to Britain after the October Revolution of 1917. In Oxford, Adorno and Berlin would frequent the same academic circles and often converse with each other, though mostly about music and literature rather than philosophy. See Evelyn Wilcock, "Adorno in Oxford 1: Oxford University Musical Club," *Oxford Magazine* 127 (1996): 11–13; "Adorno in Oxford 2: A Merton Circle," *Oxford Magazine* 143 (1997): 10–12; Andreas Kramer and Evelyn Wilcock, "'A Preserve for Professional Philosophers': Adornos Husserl-Dissertation 1934–37 und ihr Oxforder Kontext," *Deutsche Vierteljahrsschrift für Literaturwissenschaft und Geistesgeschichte* 73 (October 1999): 150–51.

deed be seen as an active reader of the theories of Spengler and Klages. As he put it in *Minima Moralia*, the task was to put conservative theories in the service of enlightenment, a task inconceivable without a considerable remolding of them. This active repurposing, one could say, expresses Adorno's general attempt to capture the "truth content" of a given idea, whether philosophical, political, or aesthetic. That is, what critical theory in Adorno's view recovers from these ideas through "dialectical" or "immanent" critique is never identical to those ideas themselves or to the stated intentions of their authors.[48]

To say that Adorno learned from Spengler and Klages is to say, following Berlin's insight, that they made him think. Influence in the sense of passive adoption does not entail thinking or learning, whereas critical reception does. It is in this sense that the word "harnessing" in the title of this book is used.

Another central point in my argument is that Adorno's demand in *Minima Moralia* to appropriate reactionary arguments for progressive ends was not something that he planned to tackle only after World War II. Rather, it was something that one can trace to his formative years in the early 1930s, well over a decade before *Dialectic of Enlightenment* and its petition not to leave "consideration of the destructive side of progress to its enemies."[49] To support my argument, and to advance beyond previous scholars' overt focus in the 1980s and 1990s on *Dialectic of Enlightenment*, I will make use of Adorno's subsequently published correspondence. This shows, for example, that after the appearance of the last volume of Klages's *Spirit as Adversary of the Soul* in 1932, Adorno planned a lengthy review essay on it in an attempt to, as he described it to his erstwhile mentor, Siegfried Kracauer, "come to grips with the mythical."[50] For some commentators, even evidence like this is not enough to accept Adorno's possible borrowings from *Zivilisationskritik* as legitimate.

---

48. On Adorno's concept of truth, see Owen Hulatt, *Adorno's Theory of Philosophical and Aesthetic Truth* (New York: Columbia University Press, 2016).
49. Horkheimer and Adorno, *Dialectic of Enlightenment*, xvi.
50. Adorno to Kracauer, March 14, 1933, in Wolfgang Schopf, ed., *Theodor W. Adorno/Siegfried Kracauer: Correspondence 1923–1966*, trans. Susan Reynolds and Michael Winkler (Cambridge: Polity Press, 2020), 207.

Rolf Tiedemann does acknowledge Adorno's "significant interest in Klages in his correspondence." Yet he is reluctant to put much weight on such "private documents not intended for publication."[51] I would argue, in contrast, that such private statements should be considered and that they indeed express Adorno's genuine opinions. For contrary to Tiedemann's view, there is no real difference between Adorno's private and public statements on the critics of civilization. Both his private and public comments convey an ambivalent and anything but simply dismissive opinion of Klages as well as of Spengler, whose short anthropological treatise from 1931, *Der Mensch und die Technik (Man and Technics)*, he reviewed in 1932 in the journal of the Institute for Social Research.[52] In any case, these examples should assure skeptical readers that the interpretations advanced in this book try their best to base themselves on "sound argument" rather than cheap "insinuation," a caution Richard Wolin once voiced regarding some earlier takes on the topic.[53]

Adorno's Gamble offers a new account of Adorno's path of thinking from his first steps as an independent thinker in the late Weimar era through his exile years in Oxford, New York, and Los Angeles to his return to Germany. John Abromeit has recently reconstructed Max Horkheimer's intellectual biography up to *Dialectic of Enlightenment*, which starts to converge with Adorno's only in the late 1930s after the latter's arrival in New York and the darkening of the world-political situation.[54] While nowhere near as comprehensive in its scope, my book adds an important dimension to this new picture of the "foundations of the Frankfurt School" by looking at it from Adorno's perspective. This perspective has been admirably charted before by Martin Jay, Susan Buck-Morss, and Gillian Rose, as well as by major biographies by Detlev Claussen

---

51. Tiedemann, editor's note in Adorno, *Ontology and Dialectics*, 300–301n14.
52. Theodor W. Adorno, review of *Der Mensch und die Technik. Beitrag zu einer Philosophie des Lebens*, by Oswald Spengler, *Zeitschrift für Sozialforschung* 1, nos. 1–2 (1932): 149–51.
53. Wolin, *Walter Benjamin*, xxxi.
54. John Abromeit, *Max Horkheimer and the Foundations of the Frankfurt School* (Cambridge: Cambridge University Press, 2011).

and Stefan Müller-Doohm.⁵⁵ However, my reading, by setting the modern advocates of "German ideology" at its center, complicates our image of Adorno, the history of the Frankfurt School, and modern German thought more generally. *Zivilisationskritik*, I contend, does not offer *the* key to Adorno's thought. Rather, what it offers is *a* key, yet one that has remained too far from the lock for too long. That such a work is long overdue is evident from the fact that in three recent companion volumes on Adorno and the Frankfurt School, comprising approximately two thousand pages, Spengler and Klages are mentioned on only four.⁵⁶

Why focus only on Spengler and Klages and not on other conservative revolutionaries? In the already cited 1941 remark on rightwing critics of liberalism, Adorno also praised Arthur Möller van der Bruck and Ernst Jünger. The list of candidates does not end here. Stefan George, the revered lyric poet and protector of "Secret Germany," was a generational figure whose critique of commodified language Adorno, too, appreciated. Rudolf Borchardt, translator of Pindar, intrigued Adorno to the extent that in 1969 he accepted the invitation from the Borchardt society to become a board member. Adorno's interest in Martin Heidegger and Arnold Gehlen is by now beyond question. Yet Heidegger's case has already received considerable attention.⁵⁷ And while Adorno's dialogue with Gehlen in the 1960s would no doubt benefit from closer scrutiny, it took place after the basic coordinates of Adorno's thought had found their place.⁵⁸

---

55. Detlev Claussen, *Theodor W. Adorno: One Last Genius*, trans. Rodney Livingstone (Cambridge, MA: Harvard University Press, 2008); Müller-Doohm, *Adorno: A Biography*.

56. Peter E. Gordon, Espen Hammer, and Max Pensky, eds., *A Companion to Adorno* (Hoboken, NJ: Wiley-Blackwell, 2020); Peter E. Gordon, Espen Hammer, and Axel Honneth, eds., *The Routledge Companion to the Frankfurt School* (New York: Routledge, 2019); Richard Klein et al., eds., *Adorno Handbuch: Leben—Werk—Wirkung*, 2nd edition (Berlin: J. B. Metzler, 2019).

57. Peter E. Gordon, *Adorno and Existence* (Cambridge, MA: Harvard University Press, 2016); Immanen, *Toward a Concrete Philosophy*, Part 2; Iain Macdonald and Krzysztof Ziarek, eds., *Adorno and Heidegger: Philosophical Questions* (Stanford, CA: Stanford University Press, 2008).

58. On Adorno and Gehlen, see Thies, *Die Krise des Individuums*. On Adorno's relationship to George and Borchardt, see Paul Fleming, "The Secret Adorno," *Qui Parle* 15, no. 1 (2004): 97–114.

What about the spiritual forefather of all these figures, Friedrich Nietzsche? Nietzsche, it seems quite evident, left his imprint on Adorno's thought, as Habermas and others have argued. His critique of psychological renunciation and repressive morality were important for Adorno, as was his critique of Western rationalism.[59] I would argue, however, that the "genealogical proviso" that Axel Honneth designates as the emblematic Nietzschean feature of Adorno's variety of critical theory can be traced to the early 1930s and his readings of Klages and Spengler.[60] Indeed, I have chosen to focus on the latter two because they demonstrably troubled Adorno at critical junctures of his development and because their ideas can throw several crucial aspects of Adorno's thought into sharper relief.

I will argue that the lessons Adorno took away from his engagement with Klages and Spengler—in the sense of the active repurposing accentuated above—were no side issues but concerns that touched the very core of his philosophy. In his 1966 magnum opus, *Negative Dialektik* (*Negative Dialectics*), Adorno summed up this core as the attempt "to use the strength of the subject to break through the fallacy of constitutive subjectivity," a goal that had guided him "ever since he came to trust his own mental impulses."[61] By constitutive subjectivity Adorno meant both intellectual and practical domination of nature enabled by instrumental reason, or "identity thinking," whose focus on measurable aspects of objects ignored their unique qualities. But when exactly did Adorno learn to "trust his own mental impulses"? In other words, when did he find his own philosophical voice? World War II is often offered as the turning point. After the Holocaust Adorno famously deemed it barbaric to write poetry and saw humanity confronted with "a new categorical imperative . . . to

---

59. Habermas, *The Philosophical Discourse of Modernity*, 106–30; David Owen, "Nietzsche and the Frankfurt School," in *The Routledge Companion to the Frankfurt School*, ed. Peter E. Gordon et al. (New York: Routledge, 2019), 251–58.

60. Axel Honneth, *Pathologies of Reason: On the Legacy of Critical Theory*, trans. James Ingram (New York: Columbia University Press, 2009), 43, 45. See also Seyla Benhabib, *Critique, Norm, and Utopia: A Study of the Foundations of Critical Theory* (New York: Columbia University Press, 1986), 166, 171.

61. Theodor W. Adorno, *Negative Dialectics*, trans. E. B. Ashton (New York: Continuum, 2007), xx.

arrange their thoughts and actions so that Auschwitz will not repeat itself."⁶² Equally often, however, Adorno's path is presented as a striking continuum. One can with little difficulty divide paths of other notable twentieth-century philosophers into periods of "before" and "after." Heidegger underwent his legendary "turn" after *Sein und Zeit* (*Being and Time*) and Wittgenstein gave up on his early *Tractatus Logico-Philosophicus*. Adorno's path, however, appears as a sharper enunciation of themes adopted early on. But where does its *Ur*-moment lie?

The perceived wisdom would no doubt, and with good reasons, stress certain publication events in the final years of the Weimar Republic. Walter Benjamin introduced his idiosyncratic materialism in *Ursprung des deutschen Trauerspiels* (*Origin of the German* Trauerspiel) in 1928 and in the early drafts of his *Das Passagen-Werk* (*The Arcades Project*) a year later; it is not an overstatement to say that both were nothing short of revelations to Adorno. In 1930, *Das Unbehagen in der Kultur* (*Civilization and Its Discontents*) introduced a darker Freud ever more skeptical about the capacities of industrial civilization to foster peaceful coexistence; this work was familiar to Adorno, who at the time watched Max Horkheimer and Erich Fromm develop the Frankfurt School's Freudo-Marxist program. The appearance in 1932 of Marx's youthful *Ökonomisch-philosophische Manuskripte* (*Economic-Philosophical Manuscripts*) encouraged "Western Marxists," Adorno among them, to take capitalism to task not only for violating distributive justice but also for alienating human beings from themselves. If we add to this picture Jewish theology with its mistrust of graven images and rationalist systems, a motif adopted from Benjamin, and Arnold Schönberg's "new music" with its emphasis on dissonance, which already fascinated Adorno in the 1910s, the canonical image of Adorno is complete.⁶³ Recently,

---

62. Theodor W. Adorno, "Cultural Criticism and Society," in *Prisms*, trans. Samuel Weber and Shierry Weber (Cambridge, MA: MIT Press, 1981), 34; Adorno, *Negative Dialectics*, 365.

63. On the role of the Jewish tradition in Adorno's thought, see Peter E. Gordon, *Migrants in the Profane: Critical Theory and the Question of Secularization* (New Haven, CT: Yale University Press, 2020), chap. 3; Hent de Vries, *Minimal Theologies: Critiques of Secular Reason in Adorno and Levinas*, trans. Geoffrey

as was already noted, this image has received a "Heideggerian" coloring that stresses the powerful presence of Heidegger's *Being and Time* (1927) in that philosophical atmosphere in which Adorno's critical theory took shape.

But the turn of the 1930s also saw the publications of Klages's *Spirit as Adversary of the Soul* and Spengler's *Man and Technics*, an anthropological grounding of the cultural morphology introduced in *The Decline of the West* a decade earlier. Adorno certainly found the official doctrines of Klages and Spengler to be outright irrational. And yet, I would like to argue that he did not dismiss Spengler and Klages as intellectually fruitless prophets of reaction but sought to distill, through critical appropriation, truths in their suspicion of modern beliefs in reason, democracy, and progress. This distillation, *Adorno's Gamble* seeks to demonstrate, decisively nurtured key elements of Adorno's thought: his peculiar aesthetic, or "mimetic," form of reason in *Negative Dialectics* (chapter 1), his life-long sensitivity to the fragility of democracy (chapter 2), and his dark philosophy of history in *Dialectic of Enlightenment* (chapter 3).

Chapter Outline

Negative Dialectics, in which Adorno articulated his notion of "mimetic" reason, is usually, and rightly so, seen as informed by Benjamin and aesthetic modernism. Yet in chapter 1 I argue that this notion also owed a great deal to Adorno's overlooked "Klages project," which he began in the early 1930s and which consumed his energies during his Oxford exile in the mid-decade. The intention of this project, I will show, was to interpret *The Spirit as Adversary of the Soul* as a discerning criticism of the idea of constitutive

---

Hale (Baltimore, MD: Johns Hopkins University Press, 2005). On Adorno and aesthetic modernism, see Peter Uwe Hohendahl, *The Fleeting Promise of Art: Adorno's Aesthetic Theory Revisited* (Ithaca, NY: Cornell University Press, 2013); Peter E. Gordon, ed., "Adorno's *Aesthetic Theory* at Fifty," Special Issue, *New German Critique* 48, no. 2 (2021): 1–220; Samir Gandesha et al., eds., *The "Aging" of Adorno's Aesthetic Theory: Fifty Years Later* (Milan: Mimesis International, 2021).

subjectivity, an idea that would figure prominently in *Negative Dialectics*. The Klages project, I argue, was a key step in the process that led Adorno to find his own philosophical voice—that is, to formulate an aesthetically sensitive form of reason attuned to what *Negative Dialectics* would call the "non-identical." While this process only came into its own in the 1960s, I argue that it was forged three decades earlier as a critical rejoinder to Klages's critique of "logocentrism."

As for Adorno's sensitivity to the frailty of democracy, it is often claimed, again very plausibly, that this sensitivity was fed by Marxist distrust of liberalism and Freud's skepticism of peaceful coexistence. Chapter 2 contends, however, that it derived also from Spengler's neglected analysis of "Caesarism" in *The Decline of the West*. Although Adorno denounced Spengler's cultural morphology as utter nonsense, in his 1941 essay "Spengler Today," written in New York, he praised Spengler's observations of certain undemocratic trends of Weimar Germany: bureaucratization of the party system, the rise of manipulative mass media, and the concomitant emergence of a personality type susceptible to propaganda. Spengler's analysis of Caesarism, I will show, stimulated Adorno's own subsequent analyses of the "culture industry" in *Dialectic of Enlightenment* and authoritarianism in *The Authoritarian Personality* (1950).

Finally, one frequently finds Freud's idea of "the return of the repressed," Benjamin's theological "angel of history," or Max Weber's notion of "disenchantment" named as inspirations for *Dialectic of Enlightenment*'s thesis of the entwinement of myth and reason. Each of these interpretations has its indisputable merits. Yet chapter 3 views Adorno and Horkheimer's thesis as an outgrowth and consummation of Adorno's prior struggles with Klages and Spengler. In 1936, Adorno called for a "demystification of antiquity" that would differentiate a progressive "critique of hypostatized reason" from Klages's complete "abandonment of reason."[64] And shortly before Adorno and Horkheimer began working on *Dialectic of Enlightenment* in

---

64. Adorno to Horkheimer, November 28 and December 15, 1936, in *Briefe und Briefwechsel—Bd. 4: Theodor W. Adorno—Max Horkheimer, Briefwechsel*

California, Adorno conceded that Spengler was aware of "the dual character of enlightenment," while to Horkheimer he expressed his hope that his reflections on Spengler would form "a real preparatory work for our things."[65]

Methodologically, *Adorno's Gamble* is a work of intellectual history. The epilogue, however, weighs the legacy of Adorno's "gamble" from today's perspective. In the 1980s, Habermas and Honneth judged Adorno's interest in thinkers of the "conservative revolution" as a lapse of judgment; while Adorno sought to decipher the "truth content" of *Zivilisationskritik*, in his heirs' estimation he came to mimic some of its most problematic prejudices, most notably its civilizational pessimism.[66] My book, written in a less optimistic era of severe political, societal, and environmental crises, complicates this account. Did Adorno's "gamble" only serve to cloud his horizon? Was it only something to be regretted? I do *not* pose these questions out of any kind of sympathy for the conservative revolution, which has its defenders in numerous "new right" think tanks on both sides of the Atlantic, but for logical reasons. For if my argument about Adorno's indebtedness to Spengler and Klages is plausible, then the following questions inevitably ensue: Was it not partly this gamble that nurtured Adorno's critical virtues, virtues valued again today? Was it not partly his daring effort to learn from his conservative opponents and their "reactionary arguments against Western culture" that now gives him an edge over other progressive, but too optimistic, social theorists—such as Habermas as well as those countless commentators who in the 1990s bought into Francis Fukuyama's notion of "the end of history"? The epilogue enters a dialogue with recent assessments of Adorno's

---

1927–1969, Bd. I: 1927–1937, ed. Christoph Gödde and Henri Lonitz (Frankfurt: Suhrkamp, 2003), 235, 263.

65. Adorno, "Spengler Today," 309; Adorno to Horkheimer, May 3, 1941, in *Briefwechsel 1927–1969, Bd. II: 1938–1944*, 109.

66. Ironically, in 1956 the young Habermas still claimed that Klages's insights into "anthropology and philosophy of language" should not be left "hidden behind the veil" of his "anti-intellectualist metaphysics and apocalyptic philosophy of history." These insights were "not outdated" but ahead of their time. Jürgen Habermas, "Ludwig Klages—überholt oder unzeitgemäß? Zum Tode des deutschen Philosophen," *Frankfurter Allgemeine Zeitung*, August 3, 1956.

topicality and entertains the possibility that Adorno's effort to harness German ideology, rather than becoming a burden, served to sharpen his critical virtues.[67]

---

67. In engaging with such "presentist," or more philosophico-political concerns, I am guided by the conviction that intellectual history can disclose enormously important dimensions of philosophical texts, but equally by the belief that one can be a rigorous historian and still expect the best historiography to address not only the past but also the present. This fusion of intellectual history and more presentist concerns is informed by Peter E. Gordon's methodological reflections in "Contextualism and Criticism in the History of Ideas," in *Rethinking Modern European Intellectual History*, ed. Darrin M. McMahon and Samuel Moyn (Oxford: Oxford University Press, 2014), 32–55.

1

Adorno's Klages Project

The Origin of Negative Dialectics

Theodor W. Adorno's main work, *Negative Dialectics* (published in 1966), is famous for its bleak view of Western history as a path "from the slingshot to the megaton bomb," for its indictment of Western philosophy as continuation of this "rage" against nature on a conceptual level, and for its plea for a "mimetic," aesthetically informed reason attentive to the particularity of objects. Adorno's dialectics differs from earlier versions in its emphasis on objects' reluctance to fit smoothly into any conceptual totality such as Plato's "ideas" or Hegel's "spirit." "The cognitive utopia," Adorno suggests instead, "would be to use concepts to unseal the nonconceptual with concepts, without making it their equal."[1] Adorno's tour de force counts among numerous twentieth-century works concerned with

---

1. Theodor W. Adorno, *Negative Dialectics*, trans. E. B. Ashton (New York: Continuum, 2007), 10, 22, 320, 373–74.

the "uses and abuses" of reason. With a varying sense of urgency, this concern animated much of European philosophy in the first half of the century, and Henri Bergson, Max Weber, Edmund Husserl, and Ludwig Wittgenstein are only the most renowned thinkers to scrutinize the epistemic premises and cultural worth of a rationality reduced to abstractions and means-ends calculations.

Alongside these sophisticated critiques, however, the early decades of the century also witnessed countless assaults on reason that could not list conceptual rigor or evenhandedness as their virtues. Perhaps the most infamous of these came from the pen of Ludwig Klages, who in *The Spirit as Adversary of the Soul* (1929–1932) conceived Western history as a Manichean antagonism between life-denying intellect (or spirit) and life-affirming soul. While Klages condemned capitalist industrialism and Judeo-Christian monotheism as central expressions of the former, he laid the ultimate blame on the emergence of reason at the dawn of civilization. If Adorno's antidote to the perils of modernity was a better form of reason, Klages waved off the entire "logocentric" history of the West and envisioned a return to mythic sources of life. These sources, "archaic images" (*Urbilder*) as Klages called them, could be revived in dreams, drug-related ecstasies, or other states that loosened the grip of the intellect and allowed the soul to beat to the rhythm of the cosmos.

How are these two critiques of reason, one written in the 1960s and the other thirty years earlier, related? Usually they are not, as Adorno's critical theory is kept at the furthest remove from Klages's philosophy of life, for understandable reasons. Klages's proto-fascist and antisemitic valorization of primeval, "chthonic," forces carried to its extreme the dream of cultural regeneration of the neo-Romantic poet Stefan George and his circle. A one-time member of this circle, Klages's teachings represented just the kind of prophetic re-enchantment that Weber had famously derided after World War I. Adorno and Klages never met or corresponded. And when Adorno looked back at the early century reassessments of reason shortly before the appearance of *Negative Dialectics*, he applauded Husserl's and Bergson's openings toward "micrology."

Klages's related efforts, however, he dismissed as "merely a matter of *Weltanschauung*."[2]

If something has previously been made of the Adorno-Klages connection, this has happened almost exclusively by pointing out parallels between Klages's ideas and *Dialectic of Enlightenment*, Adorno's other key work, coauthored with Max Horkheimer in the 1940s. This observation was first made by Axel Honneth in the early 1980s. Honneth proposed that Adorno and Horkheimer's tracing of the ills of enlightened modernity to Homeric times bore a resemblance to Klages's bleak narrative of occidental "logocentrism."[3] Honneth's proposition, which was taken up by other commentators in the 1980s and 1990s,[4] was not as implausible as dominant interpretations of Adorno claimed. In *Dialectic of Enlightenment*, Klages served as one interlocutor in the authors' examination of myth and enlightenment in Homer's *Odyssey*. And while they were decidedly against Klages's vitalism, they acknowledged that he had "recognized the nameless stupidity which is the result of progress."[5] Honneth and others were, I believe, onto something important with their suggestion about Klages's presence in *Dialectic of Enlightenment*, and we shall return

---

2. Theodor W. Adorno, *Lectures on Negative Dialectics: Fragments of a Lecture Course 1965/1966*, ed. Rolf Tiedemann, trans. Rodney Livingstone (Cambridge: Polity Press, 2008), 70.

3. Axel Honneth, "Anthropologische Berührungspunkte zwischen der Lebensphilosophischen Kulturkritik und der 'Dialektik der Aufklärung,'" in *21. Deutscher Soziologentag 1982. Beiträge der Sektions- und hoc-Gruppen*, ed. Friedrich Heckmann and Peter Winter (Opladen, Germany: Westdeutscher Verlag, 1983), 786–92.

4. Albrecht Wellmer, *The Persistence of Modernity: Essays on Aesthetics, Ethics and Postmodernism*, trans. David Midgley (Cambridge: Polity Press, 1991), 3–4; Michael Grossheim, "'Die namenlose Dummheit, die das Resultat des Fortschritts ist.'— Lebensphilosophische und dialektische Kritik der Moderne," *Logos. Zeitschrift für systematische Philosophie* 3, no. 2 (1996): 121–30; Georg Stauth and Bryan S. Turner, "Ludwig Klages (1872–1956) and the Origins of Critical Theory," *Theory, Culture & Society* 9 (1992): 51–55; Georg Stauth, "Critical Theory and Pre-Fascist Social Thought," *History of European Ideas* 18, no. 5 (1994): 719–22; Michael Pauen, *Dithyrambiker des Untergangs. Gnostizismus in Ästhetik und Philosophie der Moderne* (Berlin: Akademie Verlag, 1994), 366–69; Richard Wolin, *Walter Benjamin: An Aesthetic of Redemption* (Berkeley: University of California Press, 1994), xxx.

5. Max Horkheimer and Theodor W. Adorno, *Dialectic of Enlightenment: Philosophical Fragments*, trans. Edmund Jephcott (Stanford, CA: Stanford University Press, 2002), 194.

to this question in chapter 3. My contention, however, is—and here I have benefited from the brief readings offered by Michael Grossheim, Michael Pauen, and more recently Stefan Breuer, the only scholars to have paid any attention to Adorno's interest in Klages as early as the early 1930s[6] —that the Frankfurt School's most famous book only culminated Adorno's preoccupation with Klages that had started over a decade earlier with the appearance of *The Spirit as Adversary of the Soul*.

Adorno earned his PhD in 1931 from Frankfurt University with a study on Kierkegaard. In his subsequent inaugural address in May, "Die Aktualität der Philosophie" ("The Actuality of Philosophy"), he rejected Klages's theory of archaic images. The task of critical theory, Adorno stated, was to critically illuminate its time with "constellations," montages of societal, psychological, and cultural phenomena. These constellations, he stressed, "divorce themselves centrally from the archaic, the mythic archetypes" that "Klages hopes to preserve as categories of our knowledge."[7] Remarkably, however, only months later in November, Adorno praised Klages as a sharp critic of bourgeois ideology,[8] and the following year he began working on a review of *The Spirit as Adversary of the Soul*.

What are we to make of what looks like a sudden turnaround in Adorno's assessment of Klages? A lot, I argue. For what Adorno meant by bourgeois ideology, I believe, was not just about acquisitive impulses, an ascetic work ethic, or other "decadent" modern phenomena scorned by turn-of-the-century Romantic anticapitalists of Klages's bent. Rather, at issue was a philosophical concern at the very heart of Adorno's own thought. "To use the strength of the

---

6. Grossheim, "'Die namenlose Dummheit,'" 103–4, 120; Pauen, *Dithyrambiker des Untergangs*, 369; Stefan Breuer, *Kritische Theorie: Schlüsselbegriffe, Kontroversen, Grenzen* (Tübingen: Mohr Siebeck, 2016), 244–46; Stefan Breuer, "Materialistische Erkenntniskritik," in *Adorno Handbuch: Leben—Werk—Wirkung*, ed. Richard Klein et al., 2nd ed. (Berlin: J. B. Metzler, 2019), 432–33.

7. Theodor W. Adorno, "The Actuality of Philosophy," trans. Benjamin Snow, in *The Adorno Reader*, ed. Brian O'Connor (Oxford: Blackwell, 2000), 36.

8. Adorno's contribution to "Wissenschaft und Krise. Differenz zwischen Idealismus und Materialismus. Diskussionen über Themen zu einer Vorlesung Max Horkheimers," in Max Horkheimer, *Gesammelte Schriften, Bd. 12: Nachgelassene Schriften 1931–1949*, ed. Gunzelin Schmid Noerr (Frankfurt: Fischer, 1985), 354.

subject to break through the fallacy of constitutive subjectivity" was the goal, Adorno wrote in the preface to *Negative Dialectics*, that had guided his thinking "ever since he came to trust his own mental impulses."[9] Adorno's early interest in Klages in the last years of the Weimar Republic, I will argue in this chapter, played an important role in his finding his own philosophical voice and becoming that critic of constitutive subjectivity he described three decades later in his main work, *Negative Dialectics*. By reconstructing the previously overlooked first stages of Adorno's struggle with Klages's philosophy of life, this chapter lays a foundation on which to better revisit Klages's role in *Dialectic of Enlightenment* in chapter 3.

Our reconstruction of what I shall call Adorno's "Klages project," however, seems to run into insurmountable obstacles from the start. Adorno never completed his Klages review, and whatever drafts there may have been are lost. Yet my principal goal in this chapter is to show that tremors of Adorno's preoccupation with Klages can be felt in a manuscript he wrote in Oxford exile in 1934–1937. This manuscript is a highly significant text in Adorno's oeuvre. Adorno later incorporated it into his 1956 *Metakritik der Erkenntnistheorie (Against Epistemology)*; moreover, he once described the latter as a crucial "ramp leading up to" *Negative Dialectics* that was "indispensable" to understanding it.[10] Rolf Tiedemann, the editor of Adorno's collected works, highlights the Oxford manuscript as a rare illustration of Adorno's expressly philosophical development between his Kierkegaard book and *Dialectic of Enlightenment*.[11] What this manuscript accomplished was Adorno's first articulation of that "mimetic" reason that he would

---

9. Adorno, *Negative Dialectics*, xx.
10. Theodor W. Adorno, *Against Epistemology: A Metacritique. Studies in Husserl and the Phenomenological Antinomies*, trans. Willis Domingo (Cambridge: Polity Press, 2013); Adorno to Kracauer, September 28, 1966, in *Theodor W. Adorno/Siegfried Kracauer: Correspondence, 1923–1966*, ed. Wolfgang Schopf, trans. Susan Reynolds and Michael Winkler (Cambridge: Polity Press, 2020), 490.
11. Rolf Tiedemann, editor's afterword to Theodor W. Adorno, *Gesammelte Schriften, Bd. 20.2: Vermischte Schriften II*, ed. Rolf Tiedemann (Frankfurt: Suhrkamp, 1986), 828.

seek to refine for the rest of his life. Klages, I argue in detail in the following sections, gave a powerful impetus to this attempt.

However, before going into Adorno's "Klages project," its inception in Frankfurt, and its continuation by other means in Oxford, we must spend some time with his early Kierkegaard book. The latter was written during a stage in Adorno's development that Stefan Müller-Doohm fittingly calls "A *Privatdozent* in the shadow of Walter Benjamin."[12] The story of Adorno and Benjamin has of course been told many times.[13] But it serves as a good, indeed necessary, starting point for our story as well, for it has become increasingly evident that Benjamin's ideas emerged to no small degree in the shadow of Klages.

"By the Strength of an Image"

Kierkegaard: Konstruktion des Ästhetischen (*Kierkegaard: Construction of the Aesthetic*) appeared on February 27, 1933, the day following the Reichstag fire in Berlin. A revised version of Adorno's habilitation, written in 1929–1930 at the University of Frankfurt for Paul Tillich, the book argued that the idealist dream of capturing reality as a meaningful whole was bankrupt. Such totality was to be found neither in the eternal realm of ideas, as Plato had thought, nor in history, as Hegel had assumed with his belief in "the rationality of the real." As it was written in the wake of the 1920s German Kierkegaard revival, one would expect Adorno's book to have extolled existentialism as a fruitful step from the heights of idealism to concrete reality. But Adorno judged existentialism as idealism in disguise. How he made this surprising claim was no less unusual. Instead of arguing

---

12. Stefan Müller-Doohm, *Adorno: A Biography*, trans. Rodney Livingstone (Cambridge: Polity Press, 2009), 145.
13. See Alexander Stern, "Guilt and Mourning: Adorno's Debt to and Critique of Benjamin," in *A Companion to Adorno*, ed. Peter E. Gordon et al. (Hoboken, NJ: Wiley-Blackwell, 2020), 51–66; Eugene Lunn, *Marxism and Modernism: A Historical Study of Lukács, Brecht, Benjamin, and Adorno* (Berkeley: University of California Press, 1982), part 3.

conceptually against Kierkegaard's doctrine of the "stages of life's way"—which ranked aesthetic and eudaemonistic concerns as inferior to ethical and religious ones—Adorno demonstrated its failure by way of a detour of metaphors and images that Kierkegaard frequently relied on. By constructing "constellations" out of these seemingly secondary elements, Adorno aimed to disclose a deeper societal truth behind existentialism, one not in accord with its stated intents.

Adorno's attempt to shatter Kierkegaard's existentialism, as he described it, "by the strength of an image,"[14] laid special emphasis on imagery related to the *intérieur* of the nineteenth-century bourgeois home. Repeated use of such imagery, Adorno claimed, bespoke the need for a rentier like Kierkegaard to hold onto something solid amid rapid societal change. The image of the bourgeois home as a safe haven from ebbs and flows of capitalism, Adorno argued, served as an unconscious model for Kierkegaard's notion of spiritual inwardness, in which the latter claimed to have found the bedrock that previous idealism had sought in the outside world. This belief, however, was a bourgeois illusion that shifted the spotlight from pressing social questions to bombastic introspection. Besides capitalist reification, Kierkegaard's elevation of spiritual over eudaemonistic motives betrayed existentialism's archaic "enmity to nature." For, notwithstanding his inflated emphasis on the individual, Kierkegaard's belittling of sensual gratification was a sign of mythic self-sacrifice. Ironically, the repressed sensuality returned in the bodily metaphors that Kierkegaard used to depict his purportedly authentic, spiritual individual. Contrary to its intentions, then, existentialism disclosed truth where it officially denied it most resolutely, in the aesthetic realm of sensuality, which in its nonconceptual character lay closer to the particularity of nature than the universality of thought.[15]

---

14. Theodor W. Adorno, *Kierkegaard: Construction of the Aesthetic*, trans. and ed. Robert Hullot-Kentor (Minneapolis: University of Minnesota Press, 1989), 131.

15. Adorno, *Kierkegaard*, 40–53. See also Robert Hullot-Kentor, "Critique of the Organic: Kierkegaard and the Construction of the Aesthetic," in *Things beyond Resemblance: Collected Essays on Theodor W. Adorno* (New York: Columbia University Press, 2006), 77–93; Marcia Morgan, "Adorno's Reception of Kierkegaard: 1929–1933," *Sören Kierkegaard Newsletter* 46 (2003): 8–11.

Kierkegaard was Adorno's first attempt to charge idealism with the conceptual continuation of the domination of nature. Not for nothing has the book been interpreted as an initial version of *Dialectic of Enlightenment*'s thesis about the entwinement of myth and reason.[16] The book was also Adorno's first attempt to pay heed to what *Negative Dialectics* would call "the non-identical" or "the preponderance of the object," the dependence of ostensibly timeless philosophical truths on somatic and social phenomena. Or, as Adorno put it in his inaugural address (with a reference to Freud), on the "refuse of the physical world."[17]

How did Adorno come up with this peculiar form of philosophical criticism? By the late 1920s, Adorno, the only child of an assimilated Jewish father and a Catholic mother, already had a wealth of philosophical experience under his belt. He had earned his doctorate in 1924 with a dissertation on Husserl, though he found little to his liking in the academic rationalism of the times. Besides Kierkegaard, Adorno's imagination had been fed by Georg Lukács and Ernst Bloch, whose works joined romantic anticapitalism with philosophically informed Marxism. A still better source used to answer the question of the origins of Adorno's thought would be his readings in 1918, at the age of fifteen, of Kant with his mentor Siegfried Kracauer, who "impelled" his young protégé to interpret the seemingly sterile architectonics of pure reason as a peephole to the discontents of eighteenth-century Europe.[18]

Most decisive, however, was Adorno's zealous imbibing, ten years later, of Walter Benjamin's idiosyncratic materialism. Adorno's concern with the domination of nature was prefigured by the negative philosophy of history of Benjamin's *Origin of the German* Trauerspiel

---

16. Hullot-Kentor, "Critique of the Organic," 78; Susan Buck-Morss, *The Origin of Negative Dialectics: Theodor W. Adorno, Walter Benjamin, and the Frankfurt Institute* (New York: The Free Press, 1977), 59.

17. Adorno, "The Actuality of Philosophy," 32.

18. Theodor W. Adorno, "The Curious Realist: On Siegfried Kracauer," in *Notes to Literature*, vol. 2, trans. Shierry Weber Nicholsen (New York: Columbia University Press, 1992), 58–59. On Adorno's early development, see Detlev Claussen, *Theodor W. Adorno: One Last Genius*, trans. Rodney Livingstone (Cambridge, MA: Harvard University Press, 2008), 65–114; Müller-Doohm, *Adorno: A Biography*, 37–109. On Kracauer's role, see Hullot-Kentor, "Critique of the Organic," 83–84.

(1928), which viewed the path of civilization as mythic "natural-history" and philosophy's systematic aspirations as its repetition. The theme also surfaced palpably in the final aphorism to Benjamin's *Einbahnstraße* (*One-Way Street*, 1928), "To the Planetarium," which deplored the shaken equilibrium between modern humanity and the cosmic forces of nature.[19] Again, Benjamin anticipated Adorno's pictorial criticism by replacing idealist categorizations with "constellations," or "dialectical images." On one point, however, the two diverged. Whereas Adorno was suspicious of the presence of mythic elements in modernity and sought their dismantling, inherent in Benjamin's criticism was also, in Jürgen Habermas's words, a "rescuing" motif that stemmed from his fascination with Kafka, Proust, and surrealism. This motif impacted Benjamin's understanding of politics as well. Doubtful of Marxists' ability to match alluring Nazi myths with prosaic economic arguments, Benjamin strove to channel mythic energies into left-wing ends. The grand expression of this turning of "the energies of intoxication for the revolution" was his decoding, begun in 1927, of Parisian shopping arcades as an allegory of modernity in all its ambivalence.[20]

Despite their differences, Benjamin's openings are echoed on every page of Adorno's *Kierkegaard*. This much is uncontroversial about Adorno's intellectual roots. But as the accepted wisdom on Benjamin has recently come under new scrutiny, that on Adorno needs reassessment as well. This wisdom, canonized in the 1960s by the New Left, stressed the Marxist nature of Benjamin's *Das Passagen-Werk* (*The Arcades Project*), which supposedly bid farewell to his youthful metaphysical concerns with myth. In subsequent decades, however, this reading was challenged, and it was argued

---

19. Walter Benjamin, *Origin of the German* Trauerspiel, trans. Howard Eiland (Cambridge, MA: Harvard University Press, 2019); *One-Way Street*, trans. Edmund Jephcott (Cambridge, MA: The Belknap Press of Harvard University Press, 2016), 93–96.
20. Walter Benjamin, "Surrealism: The Last Snapshot of the European Intelligentsia," in *Reflections: Essays, Aphorisms, Autobiographical Writings*, trans. Edmund Jephcott (New York: Schocken Books, 1978), 189; Jürgen Habermas, "Walter Benjamin: Consciousness-Raising or Rescuing Critique," in *On Walter Benjamin: Critical Essays and Recollections*, ed. Gary Smith (Cambridge, MA: MIT Press, 1988), 90–128.

that Benjamin's redemptive interest in myth stayed intact throughout his life. The latest, and perhaps most provocative, reinterpretation has emphasized Benjamin's debt to Ludwig Klages.[21] In 1926, a year before Benjamin embarked on his *Arcades Project*, he called for a confrontation with Klages, the "great philosopher and anthropologist." Four years later, in 1930, he praised *The Spirit as Adversary of the Soul* as "a great philosophical work" that had astonished him with its "really new and wide-ranging conceptions."[22]

John McCole and Irving Wohlfarth argue that Klages inspired Benjamin's "To the Planetarium" and its lament on the technological domination of nature. They also contend that Benjamin's criticism of idealism as conceptual domination followed the lead of Klages, who denounced "the entire occidental logistics after Plato" as "false reification."[23] Benjamin's attraction to Klages goes back as far as the eve of World War I, when in 1913 Klages's speech "Mensch und Erde" ("Man and Earth") was read at the legendary Hoher Meissner gathering of the German Youth Movement. Klages's speech, which quickly received authoritative status in the youth movement, denounced the "annihilation of life" by progress, which "levels forests, eradicates animal species, eliminates primitive peoples," and "reduces everything that remains to a mere commodity."[24] Benjamin, the

---

21. On the reception history of Benjamin's thought, see John McCole, *Walter Benjamin and the Antinomies of Tradition* (Ithaca, NY: Cornell University Press, 1993), 10–21; Nitzan Lebovic, *The Philosophy of Life and Death: Ludwig Klages and the Rise of a Nazi Biopolitics* (New York: Palgrave Macmillan, 2013), 8–11.

22. Walter Benjamin, "Review of Bernoulli's *Bachofen*," in vol. 1 of *Selected Writings*, ed. Marcus Bullock and Michael W. Jennings (Cambridge, MA: The Belknap Press of Harvard University Press, 1996), 426; Benjamin to Scholem, August 15, 1930, in *The Correspondence of Walter Benjamin, 1910–1940*, ed. Gershom Scholem and Theodor W. Adorno, trans. Manfred R. Jacobson and Evelyn M. Jacobson (Chicago: University of Chicago Press, 1994), 366.

23. McCole, *Walter Benjamin*, 178–80, 187; Irving Wohlfarth, "Walter Benjamin and the Idea of a Technological Eros: A Tentative Reading of *Zum Planetarium*," *Benjamin Studies* 1, no. 1 (2002): 76; Ludwig Klages, *Der Geist als Widersacher der Seele: Erstes bis Viertes Buch* [The spirit as adversary of the soul: Books one through four], in *Sämtliche Werke, Bd. 1*, ed. Ernst Frauchiger et al. (Bonn: Bouvier Verlag, 1969), 115.

24. Ludwig Klages, "Mensch und Erde," in *Sämtliche Werke, Bd. 3*, ed. Ernst Frauchiger et al. (Bonn: Bouvier Verlag, 1974), 621.

then-president of the Berlin branch of the youth movement, paid a visit to Klages in Munich the following year and invited him to lecture in Berlin. In 1915, as Benjamin moved to Munich to study, he hoped to establish more solid contact with Klages, but to his disappointment the latter had moved to Switzerland in protest against the war. Benjamin never adopted Klages's "clumsy metaphysical dualism" of reason and life or his wholesale dismissal of modernity and technology.[25] Yet the neo-Romantic autodidact left a lasting impression on him, as evinced, for instance, by Benjamin's commendatory letter to Klages after the appearance of the latter's *Vom kosmogonischen Eros* (*Of Cosmogonic Eros*) in 1922.[26]

By 1926 at the latest, however, Benjamin had become aware of Klages's darkest side, his antisemitism.[27] The life-destroying principle of the "intellect," or "the vampire will to power," Klages declared, had one of its roots in the "world-historical mistake" that was the "victorious 'monotheism' of the Israeli prophets."[28] While especially brazen in his main work, antisemitic stereotypes, widespread in the Central European cultural milieu at the turn of the century, had already infected Klages's thinking early on. Nitzan Lebovic describes Klages as a "cultural antisemite" who did not see Jews as a biological race. This view is supported by the fact that Klages had Jewish friends. Yet his reliance on biological vocabulary, as Lebovic notes, brought him close to racial antisemitism, as did his attempt to rationalize his racist prejudices with his theory of "graphology"—which had gained him prestige in the anti-Freudian camp of German psychology—by claiming that handwriting disclosed something of a

---

25. Benjamin to Scholem, August 15, 1930, in *The Correspondence of Walter Benjamin*, 366. See also, for instance, Walter Benjamin, "Johann Jakob Bachofen," in vol. 3 of *Selected Writings*, trans. Edmund Jephcott et al., ed. Howard Eiland et al. (Cambridge, MA: The Belknap Press of Harvard University Press, 2002), 19.

26. Benjamin to Klages, February 28, 1923, in *Gesammelte Briefe, Bd. 2: 1919–1924*, ed. Christoph Gödde and Henri Lonitz (Frankfurt: Suhrkamp, 1996), 319; Wolin, *Walter Benjamin*, xxxi.

27. Benjamin to Scholem, January 14, 1926, in *The Correspondence of Walter Benjamin*, 288.

28. Ludwig Klages, *Der Geist als Widersacher der Seele: Fünftes Buch* [The spirit as adversary of the soul: Book five]. *Sämtliche Werke, Bd. 2*, ed. Ernst Frauchiger et al. (Bonn: Bouvier Verlag, 1966), 1266.

person's ethnic "type." Even though Klages never became a Nazi himself, his antisemitic jargon of life exerted a powerful influence on the racial theories of the National Socialists. To redeem his reputation after World War II, Klages removed antisemitic passages from his letters and other texts. His disciple Hans Eggert Schröder later did the same for his entire literary estate.[29]

Cognizant as Benjamin was of the veneration accorded to Klages by Germany's *völkisch* youth—those "habitués of the chthonic forces of terror, who carry their volumes of Klages in their packs," as he noted in 1930[30]—and repugnant as he must have found Klages's antisemitism, it did not prevent him from appreciating Klages's ideas. Besides Benjamin's sensitivity to the destructive side of Western history, Klages also inspired the pivotal notion of his *Arcades Project*, the "dialectical image." By the latter, Benjamin referred to textual montages of urban life whose unexpected arrangements tried to shake the reified everyday perception of things. In *The Arcades Project*, Benjamin used these images to convey what he saw as the paradoxical nature of nineteenth-century Parisian shopping quarters. The latter were expressions both of myth and utopia. On the one hand, they demonstrated the disconcerting longevity of mythic patterns of thought and perception—for example, in fashion, which, dictated by market incentives, offered the same things time and again under the guise of novelty. On the other hand, the arcades radiated unfulfilled hopes for a better world. To account for this ambivalence, Joseph Mali and John McCole argue, Benjamin drew on Klages. While Benjamin praised the surrealists and other interwar neomythologists for welcoming the presence of mythic energies in disenchanted modernity—and not in prehistory, where Klages falsely searched for them—they lacked the conceptual tools

---

29. Lebovic, *The Philosophy of Life and Death*, 18, 29–30, 121. On Klages's contributions to debates on psychology in Germany, see chap. 4 in Lebovic's book, as well as Anthony D. Kauders, *Der Freud Komplex. Eine Geschichte der Psychoanalyse in Deutschland* (Berlin: Berlin Verlag, 2014), 137–50.

30. Walter Benjamin, "Theories of German Fascism: On the Collection of Essays *War and Warriors*, edited by Ernst Jünger," in vol. 2, pt. 1 of *Selected Writings*, trans. Rodney Livingstone et al., ed. Howard Eiland et al. (Cambridge, MA: The Belknap Press of Harvard University Press, 1999), 321.

to explain this. These tools Benjamin found in Klages's theory of "dream consciousness."[31]

"Irrational" sequences of events that moderns experienced in dreams and other states free of the hold of consciousness, Klages claimed, were remnants of the prehistorical "mythical consciousness" of so-called primitives. The "primitives" perceived mythic figures and deities as self-evident constituents of reality. The moderns, however, could still reach these vigorous, life-enhancing "images" by loosening the grip of their rational capacities, a conviction (akin to Carl Gustav Jung's "archetypes") Klages owed to the nineteenth-century scholar of ancient symbols, Johann Jakob Bachofen.[32] Klages's theory was crucial for Benjamin's notion of the "dialectical image." While Klages used the theory of "dream consciousness" to back his antimodern adoration of the archaic past, Benjamin applied it to accentuate the persistence of salvific mythical energies in modernity. In contrast to Klages, for Benjamin history was no simple degeneration from ancient wisdom. The relationship was more reciprocal. The present, rather than having forgotten the wisdom of the past, was in a position to fulfill the past's unredeemed potential, something that had never yet been realized. Or, as Benjamin put it in what would be his last work: "Like every generation that preceded us, we have been endowed with a *weak* messianic power, a power on which the past has a claim."[33]

Such, then, is the intellectual—or rather anti-intellectual—background of Adorno's first book. Adorno knew about Benjamin's fascination with Klages, as their correspondence a couple of years later shows. Nothing suggests that Adorno himself would have drawn

---

31. McCole, *Walter Benjamin*, 178–80, 236–52; Joseph Mali, "The Reconciliation of Myth: Benjamin's Homage to Bachofen," *Journal of the History of Ideas* 60, no. 1 (1999): 170–76. See also Miriam Bratu Hansen, "Benjamin's Aura," *Critical Inquiry* 34, no. 2 (2008): 336–75.

32. Ludwig Klages, "Vom Traumbewusstsein," in *Sämtliche Werke, Bd. 3*, ed. Ernst Frauchiger et al. (Bonn: Bouvier Verlag, 1974), 155–238.

33. Walter Benjamin, "On the Concept of History," trans. Harry Zohn, in vol. 4 of *Selected Writings*, ed. Howard Eiland and Michael W. Jennings (Cambridge, MA: The Belknap Press of Harvard University Press, 2003), 390. Emphasis in the original.

on Klages while writing his *Kierkegaard* in 1929–1930. The book does not mention him. And in his inaugural address, as we have already seen, Adorno unequivocally rejected Klages's thought. Even if the constellations, or "historical images," built by critical theory, Adorno noted, might resemble Klages's archaic images in "a hundred characteristics," one ought not to overlook the differences. Klages's images "describe their fatalistic orbit in the heads of human beings," whereas those of critical theory are "instruments of human reason." This was the case even when critical theory came up with images— such as Marx's figure of "the commodity structure" as an overpowering supra-individual feature of capitalism—that "seem to align themselves objectively as magnetic centers of objective being."[34]

Such criticisms of Klages enable the accepted wisdom in Adorno scholarship to dismiss the question of Klages's impact as nonsense, a dismissal further backed by the fact that Adorno, in editing Benjamin's correspondence and collected "Schriften" in the 1950s, removed some of his friend's remarks on Klages (as well as those on the other "conservative revolutionaries" Carl Schmitt and Ernst Jünger).[35] That the story does not go quite like this, however, is indicated by Adorno's embarking, shortly after his inaugural address, on a Klages project of his own.

The Unrealized Klages Project

In the summer of 1932, Max Horkheimer, who two years earlier had assumed the directorship of the Institute for Social Research, wrote to Adorno, a close associate but not yet an official member of the institute, of a need to discuss some practical matters in the coming weeks. Among these was a plan for a review in the institute's journal, *Zeitschrift für Sozialforschung*, of Klages's *Spirit as Adversary*

---

34. Adorno, "The Actuality of Philosophy," 36, 33.
35. Bernhard Kraller and Heinz Steinert, Editorial remarks on Theodor W. Adorno and Lotte Tobisch, *Der private Briefwechsel*, ed. Bernhard Kraller und Heinz Steinert (Vienna: Literaturverlag Droschl, 2003), 283.

of the Soul, whose last volume had just appeared.³⁶ The following spring, two weeks after the publication of Adorno's *Kierkegaard,* and with the Nazi destruction of the Weimar Republic rapidly advancing, we find Adorno immersed in the project. Adorno wrote to Siegfried Kracauer from Berlin that he was writing "a major piece taking issue with Klages." A month later he reported the expansion of the project into "a more extensive study" (that now included Bachofen as well).³⁷

Why did Adorno choose to spend time on such a study on Klages? Horkheimer, we can surmise, was eagerly expecting to see a highly critical review of Klages's book. Some years earlier he had acknowledged that Klages was an "extremely important" figure in contemporary German thought.³⁸ Yet the planned review, Horkheimer in all likelihood hoped, would attempt to demarcate the institute's progressive neo-Marxist criticism of capitalism and liberalism from various irrational attacks, such as Klages's, that seemed to have won the day in 1933. Horkheimer's brief criticism of Klages in 1934 speaks to this conclusion. Not only did he accuse Klages of blurring the "distinction between fantasy and correct theory," he also took exception to Klages's defamation of technology. Klages overlooked the undeniable fact, Horkheimer pointed out, that while machines certainly "can 'destroy life,'" they "also contribute to maintaining, easing, and promoting it."³⁹

Adorno certainly shared Horkheimer's caution. And yet for him, more was involved than just criticism: this was an opportunity to learn. This is indicated by his discussion with Kracauer, his erstwhile mentor, on the Kierkegaard book. In an otherwise endorsing

---

36. Horkheimer to Adorno, June 30, 1932, in *Briefe und Briefwechsel—Bd. 4: Theodor W. Adorno—Max Horkheimer, Briefwechsel 1927–1969, Bd. I: 1927–1937,* ed. Christoph Gödde and Henri Lonitz (Frankfurt: Suhrkamp, 2003), 13–14.

37. Adorno to Kracauer, March 14 and April 10, 1933, in Adorno, *Correspondence 1923–1966,* 207, 209.

38. Max Horkheimer, "Einführung in die Philosophie der Gegenwart," in *Gesammelte Schriften, Bd. 10: Nachgelassene Schriften 1914–1931,* ed. Alfred Schmidt (Frankfurt: Fischer, 1990), 332.

39. Max Horkheimer, "The Rationalism Debate in Contemporary Philosophy," in *Between Philosophy and Social Science: Selected Early Writings,* trans. G. Frederick Hunter et al. (Cambridge, MA: MIT Press, 1993), 230.

review of it, Kracauer made one critical observation: the book's "undifferentiated concept of the mythical."[40] "I can already tell you," Adorno replied, welcoming the criticism, "that I am very much inclined to acknowledge your reservations about the scope of the concept of the mythical and the way in which it is applied, and that I am endeavoring very energetically to come back to this point to make advances as far as these issues are concerned." To this effect, Adorno continued, he had already added to the book's published version a section that tried to concretize the notion of the mythical through an analysis of Kierkegaard's reading of Plato's allegories. Yet more was required, he admitted, and "this is where the real problems lie." Adorno was working on Klages, "most of all, to come to grips with the mythical."[41]

This was unlikely to have been their first exchange on Klages. As Nitzan Lebovic notes, in 1922, Kracauer had published passages and a brief overview of Klages's *Vom kosmogonischen Eros* in the *Frankfurter Zeitung*, whose feuilleton section he oversaw. Two years later, he had reviewed Klages's talk on the same paper's radio hour.[42] Adorno was thus likely to have been familiar with Klages's earlier book, which anticipated many of the themes of *The Spirit as Adversary of the Soul*. If he was, then he had had time to digest Klages's ideas for years. It seems likelier, however, especially in light of the fact that Adorno does not mention Klages in his Kierkegaard study, that it was only in the early 1930s that Klages's ideas began to arouse his imagination.[43]

As noted above, another thinker whom Adorno mentioned to Kracauer in his letter was Johann Jakob Bachofen, a long-forgotten

---

40. Siegfried Kracauer, "Der enthüllte Kierkegaard," in *Werke, Bd. 5.4: Essays, Feuilletons, Rezensionen*, ed. Inka Mülder-Bach (Berlin: Suhrkamp, 2011), 491.

41. Adorno to Kracauer, March 14, 1933, in Adorno, *Correspondence 1923–1966*, 207. On the new section, "The Mythical Content," see Adorno, *Kierkegaard*, 53–57.

42. *Frankfurter Zeitung*, June 14, 1922, feuilleton section, 1–2; *Frankfurter Zeitung*, October 25, 1924, feuilleton section, 2; Lebovic, *The Philosophy of Life and Death*, 85.

43. In 1933, Adorno also reviewed a 1931 *Festschrift* for Klages: Review of *Charakterkunde der Gegenwart*, ed. Hans Prinzhorn, *Zeitschrift für Sozialforschung* 2, no. 1 (1933): 110–11.

nineteenth-century scholar of Greco-Roman antiquity. In his lifetime, Bachofen's reinterpretations of ancient symbols and myths had been met with skepticism by the academic guardians of German classical studies. In the 1920s, however, Bachofen's iconoclastic ideas, especially his theory of primeval matriarchal societies, gained considerable attention among both learned circles and laypeople. The person most responsible for this "Bachofen renaissance" was Klages, who edited a new edition of Bachofen's collected works and showed frequent admiration for the unduly forgotten Swiss. With their antimodern accent, Bachofen's theories resonated among various quarters of the German intelligentsia that were uneasy with the materialism, liberalism, and soullessness of secularized modernity. While it was mostly the *völkish* right—both in its openly fascist and more aesthetic-vitalist, Klagesian shapes—that Bachofen's theories managed to captivate, he also attracted less orthodox left-wing critics of modernity (who could cite Friedrich Engels's discussion of Bachofen as an example); none more so than Walter Benjamin, who modeled his exploration of Parisian arcades on Bachofen's excavations of ancient ruins.[44]

Adorno's review of Klages's *Spirit as Adversary of the Soul*, together with Erich Fromm's article on Bachofen's *Das Mutterrecht* (*The Mother Right*, 1861), indicated that the Institute for Social Research was well aware of what was going on in German thought in the early 1930s.[45] Adorno's Klages project, however, came to an abrupt halt only a few weeks later in April 1933. Faced with the looming Nazification of the German civil service (*Gleichschaltung*), decreed on April 7, and an end to his young academic career, Adorno was at pains to secure an alternative career path by preparing himself for "the state examination for private music teachers." "Things are going far from well as regards my health," he lamented to

---

44. Mali, "The Reconciliation of Myth," 179–80; Lebovic, *The Philosophy of Life and Death*, chap. 3. For more on Bachofen, see Peter Davies, *Myth, Matriarchy and Modernity: Johann Jakob Bachofen in German Culture 1860–1945* (Berlin: De Gruyter, 2010).

45. Erich Fromm, "Die sozialpsychologische Bedeutung der Mutterrechtstheorie," *Zeitschrift für Sozialforschung* 3, no. 2 (1934): 196–227.

Kracauer, and because of this, "the Klages business is in abeyance."⁴⁶ In subsequent years, as it turned out, Adorno was unable to finish his Klages essay as other tasks and the gloomy political situation weighed heavily on him. The urgency of the project remained, however, as evinced by Adorno's correspondence in the mid-1930s.

This urgency is palpable in Adorno's 1936 letter from Oxford to Horkheimer in New York. Reminding the latter of their earlier Klages plan, which had not been realized for "psychological reasons alone," Adorno underlined its topicality. They should, he proposed, interpret Klages not only as a "romantic reactionary," but also as "a radical critic of the bourgeois ideology of labor."⁴⁷ Significantly, we find Adorno making a similar claim as early as November 1931 in an internal discussion of the institute in Frankfurt. "In the postwar metaphysics," he stated, "the bourgeoisie had at one point seen through its ideology and sought its revision, albeit in a distorted way. More important than the great [Max] Scheler and [Nicolai] Hartmann [are] thereby more radical ones like Klages."⁴⁸ Anticipating his later observation in *Minima Moralia* on Klages as an outsider with occasionally discerning insights,⁴⁹ Adorno here singled him out as someone who had seen deeper into bourgeois prejudices than the esteemed academic philosophers Scheler, a leading light of phenomenology, and Hartmann, a major spokesperson of 1920s neo-ontology. Uttered just months after Adorno's dismissal of Klages in his inaugural address, "The Actuality of Philosophy," this praise, repeated to Horkheimer in 1936, is noteworthy.

What did Adorno mean by "bourgeois ideology"? What had Klages seen through? Klages's vitalism contained an anticapitalist side with its condemnation of the rule of money, industrial

---

46. Adorno to Kracauer, April 26, 1933, in Adorno, *Correspondence 1923–1966*, 211–12.
47. Adorno to Horkheimer, December 15, 1936, in Adorno, *Briefwechsel, Bd. I: 1927–1937*, 263.
48. Adorno's contribution to "Wissenschaft und Krise," 354.
49. Theodor W. Adorno, *Minima Moralia: Reflections from Damaged Life*, trans. E. F. N. Jephcott (London: Verso, 2000), 66–68.

mechanization, acquisitive impulses, and ascetic work ethic.[50] I would surmise, however, that a more profound phenomenon was at play, older than capitalism and wider than mere economic issues. This is indicated by the contexts of Adorno's remarks. The 1931 discussion revolved around a philosophical debate over idealism and materialism, and Adorno juxtaposed Klages favorably against other philosophers. Again, the context of the 1936 letter was a discussion of a chance to understand Klages's "spirit" in more historical terms rather than as some dark anthropological constant of the human condition. In 1936, Adorno, unable to carry out the Klages project himself, was entertaining the possibility of delegating it to someone else. His top candidate was Alfred Sohn-Rethel, an old friend from Frankfurt and a fellow émigré. Upon reading the latter's manuscript on the societal underpinnings of ancient Greek philosophy, Adorno was convinced that his friend was up to the task. Sohn-Rethel, Adorno believed, could both recognize Klages's legitimate criticisms of Western philosophy and replace his neo-Romantic speculation with serious social-historical insights.

We shall come back later to an exchange between Adorno and Horkheimer on Sohn-Rethel. But what has already been said quite clearly shows that by "bourgeois ideology" Adorno had in mind nothing less than the seminal problem of his later *Negative Dialectics*: the idea of "constitutive subjectivity." This idea is essentially about two things. It means, first, the intellectual domination of nature through "identity thinking," which by reducing reality to its lowest common denominator prepares it for instrumental purposes. In this view, concepts are pragmatic tools that serve the utilitarian self-preservation of the human animal. Secondly, this phenomenon has a societal dimension in the dominance of capitalist commodity form, which reduces qualitatively different things to abstract exchange-value. What makes the idea of constitutive subjectivity an illusion or ideology, however, is that it is not what it claims to be. The refusal of objects to fit into abstract categorizations without remainder gives

---

50. See, for instance, Klages's *Der Geist als Widersacher der Seele: Fünftes Buch*, 1204; "Mensch und Erde," 623; *Vom kosmogonischen Eros*, in *Sämtliche Werke, Bd. 3*, ed. Ernst Frauchiger et al. (Bonn: Bouvier Verlag, 1974), 396, 468–69.

the lie to the subject's insistence on being the lawmaker to reality. And the refusal of overpowering societal forces to bow before the subject's desire for autonomy makes futile its Promethean self-image as the engine of history. Moreover, as a phenomenon, constitutive subjectivity, Adorno claims, is much older than European modernity and the latter's key philosophical expression, Kant's "Copernican turn" to the subject. Its roots reach as far back as the "archaic" period of Greek antiquity and pre-Socratic philosophy.

This brings us back to the exchange between Adorno and Kracauer in the spring of 1933. Adorno's coming to a better understanding of "the mythical," I believe, had everything to do with this problem complex. What Kracauer had found problematic in Adorno's *Kierkegaard* was not a lack of historical illustrations of "the mythical," although Adorno's adding a section on Kierkegaard and Plato would suggest this. The above considerations on "bourgeois ideology" and "constitutive subjectivity" suggest a problem of another kind. Instead of a onetime phenomenon of a distant Greek past—the fight between pre-Socratic *Logos* and Homeric *Mythos* in the seventh and sixth centuries BCE—Adorno's concept of the mythical, Kracauer complained, looked like an ahistorical invariant suited to every phase of history. This, however, was precisely Adorno's point. Mythical delusions were very much alive in the modern era. Adorno had demonstrated this with respect to existentialism in his first book, and the political events of 1933 made this all the more painfully clear. Thus, instead of abandoning his sweeping notion of the mythical, Adorno sought to sharpen it. This is what his Klages essay was about. But Adorno's attempt, as noted, did not materialize. Nor did his wish to have Sohn-Rethel take over the task (for reasons that will be discussed later). Let us next turn to what I take to be Adorno's attempt to carry out the Klages project by other means in Oxford exile.

The Klages Project by Other Means

The Nazi seizure of power in 1933 drastically changed the lives of Adorno and his Frankfurt School companions. In 1934, the

Horkheimer-led Institute for Social Research emigrated to Columbia University in New York, while Adorno, not yet an official member of the institute, ended up at Merton College in Oxford.[51] In his years in England (1934–1937), Adorno directed his energies to a manuscript on Edmund Husserl's phenomenology, which did not once mention Klages's name. Nevertheless, I think the impression that Klages had made on Adorno is visible in between the lines of his Husserl study. In this study, I argue, Adorno continued to process the problem complex associated with "the mythical" introduced in the previous section. This is important for our understanding of Adorno's intellectual development and the emergence of his central idea of "constitutive subjectivity." As noted earlier, in 1956 Adorno incorporated his Oxford manuscript in a revised form into one of his key works, *Against Epistemology*, a work that he later regarded as a crucial "ramp leading up to" *Negative Dialectics*.[52]

On the face of it, Adorno's Oxford draft served two functions. It was supposed to become his doctoral thesis (DPhil), which would enable him to meet the requirements of the British academic system. Husserl's phenomenology had already been the theme of Adorno's first academic thesis in 1924.[53] At Oxford, his work on "The Principle of Intentionality and Categorial Intuition" under the supervision of Gilbert Ryle, a famed English expert on German philosophy, proceeded productively despite their markedly different philosophical backgrounds. But the Husserl study served another purpose as well. Adorno wished to convince Horkheimer, who had been skeptical of his earlier work on Kierkegaard, of his ability to advance the program of the Institute for Social Research. In 1934, Horkheimer invited Adorno to work on a project on "dialectical

---

51. On the Frankfurt School's emigration, see Thomas Wheatland, *The Frankfurt School in Exile* (Minneapolis: University of Minnesota Press, 2009), chap. 1.

52. Adorno to Kracauer, September 28, 1966, in Adorno, *Correspondence 1923–1966*, 490.

53. Adorno's 1924 thesis is titled *Die Transzendenz des Dinglichen und Noematischen in Husserls Phänomenologie* and appears in *Gesammelte Schriften, Bd. 1: Philosophische Frühschriften*, ed. Rolf Tiedemann (Frankfurt: Suhrkamp, 1973), 7–77.

logic," essentially about the philosophical premises of Frankfurt School critical theory. Hence the unofficial name of Adorno's Oxford draft was a "Prolegomena to Dialectical Logic." Adorno's draft, however, failed on both of its assignments. His hopes of publishing an article on phenomenology and modern capitalism in the institute's journal was obstructed by Horkheimer himself, who still had reservations about Adorno's version of critical materialism. Adorno's draft did not turn into an academic thesis either. In 1937, Horkheimer succeeded in securing Adorno a position in a research project on music in Princeton University, and he also invited Adorno to become an official member of the institute. Given this situation, Adorno saw no reason to stay in England and complete his thesis.[54]

The third, unspoken Klagesian layer of Adorno's Oxford manuscript is visible in its view of the essential continuity of Western philosophy as "lordship of spirit." From Parmenides's doctrine of "the One and the Many" and Plato's mathematization of thought to Husserl's bracketing of empirical elements from philosophy, Adorno maintained, Western philosophy had always been *prima philosophia*, or first philosophy: a methodical search for "an absolutely first . . . as the doubt-free and certain point of departure." By reducing reality to mere thought categories, "which can always be reliably and constantly used"—and which characterized the history of philosophy long before Descartes introduced the term "method"— Western philosophy had deprived "itself of any relation to things." The "liquidation of idealism" that Adorno pursued in his Oxford manuscript claimed that, from antiquity to modernity, Western thought had always tried to ease its insecurity in the face of transient and unpredictable reality by reducing, or formalizing, objects to their measurable aspects.[55]

---

54. On Adorno's Oxford years, see Andreas Kramer and Evelyn Wilcock, "'A Preserve for Professional Philosophers': Adornos Husserl-Dissertation 1934–37 und ihr Oxforder Kontext," *Deutsche Vierteljahrsschrift für Literaturwissenschaft und Geistesgeschichte* 73 (October 1999): 115–61. On the "dialectical logic" project, see John Abromeit, *Max Horkheimer and the Foundations of the Frankfurt School* (Cambridge: Cambridge University Press, 2011), chap. 8.

55. Adorno, *Against Epistemology*, 5, 9–14.

Stefan Breuer is the first and as far as I know the only person to suggest that Adorno's Oxford manuscript was filled with Klagesian themes. Klages's presence, Breuer argues, is palpable in Adorno's expansion of the problem of domination beyond the Marxist focus on societal domination to the domination of nature, in his tracing of the latter to the pre-Socratic dawn of Western philosophy, and in his conviction about the continuity of Western thought from Parmenides to phenomenology. Breuer underlines the "powerful impression made on Adorno by the determination with which Klages's critique of the world-destroying effects of modern science and of the technology based on it came to a head in his attack against" the pre-Socratics. Adorno was "deeply impressed," Breuer suggests, "by the radicalism of a thinking that did not waver to extend the vitalist critique of the world-relationship of the natural sciences to the relation between humanity and nature as such and to come to a head in an attack against identifying thought as well as the labor process as a purposive activity."[56]

Breuer is correct to stress Klages's presence in Adorno's Oxford draft. To be sure, a critique of idealism and Platonism had already animated Adorno's *Kierkegaard*, as had the concern with the domination of nature, as Adorno emphasized in a later preface to his first book.[57] However, the "liquidation of idealism" that Adorno sought in the Oxford draft goes more explicitly beyond Marxism to the question of the domination of nature, and its time span reaches not just to Plato but all the way to the pre-Socratics. One could, of course, question whether Adorno had already made these extensions to his position in the mid-1930s in Oxford, for the remarks on the domination of nature, the pre-Socratics, and the mathematization of thought pop up only in the introduction to *Against Epistemology*, which was not written until the 1950s.[58] By this reasoning, these extensions would be later insights gained only in the 1940s in

---

56. Breuer, "Materialistische Erkenntniskritik," 432–33; Breuer, *Kritische Theorie*, 245.

57. Theodor W. Adorno, *Gesammelte Schriften, Bd. 2: Kierkegaard. Konstruktion des Ästhetischen*, ed. Rolf Tiedemann (Frankfurt: Suhrkamp, 1979), 262.

58. On the chronology of the different chapters of the book, see Adorno, *Against Epistemology*, 2.

Dialectic of Enlightenment. Speaking strongly against this claim, however, are Adorno's comments in 1936 on Klages, Sohn-Rethel, and "bourgeois ideology" as well as already in 1933 on Klages and "the mythical." It is safe to conclude, then, that Klages's critique of "logocentrism" stimulated Adorno's critique of constitutive subjectivity, and that Adorno discovered his own philosophical voice partly as a result of his struggle with Klages in the first half of the 1930s.

At this point, one may wonder how this argument about Klages's centrality in the development of Adorno's thought stands in relation to recent attributions of this role to phenomenology. Adorno's stance toward phenomenology was long viewed as hostile, thanks to his rather rough treatments of Husserl in *Against Epistemology* and Heidegger in *Jargon der Eigentlichkeit* (*Jargon of Authenticity*, 1964). Nevertheless, this one-sided view has been challenged in recent years. Peter E. Gordon argues that, beginning with his 1931 inaugural address, Adorno forged his own materialist philosophy in a lifelong conversation with Heidegger's "failed attempt to break free of idealism." I have, for my part, interpreted Adorno's programmatic lecture as a contribution to the so-called Frankfurt discussion, in which Adorno, pressed by his Heideggerian-minded university colleagues, attempted to articulate his own position in a dialogue with *Being and Time*. Lambert Zuidervaart sees both Heidegger's existential ontology and the Frankfurt School as "offspring" of Husserl's effort to set philosophy on a new, nonidealist footing.[59]

There is much truth to all of these readings. As we have seen, however, in 1931, shortly after his inaugural address, Adorno praised Klages's critical potential over that of phenomenology. Despite their claims to the contrary, the phenomenologists were stuck in the same identity thinking, or "bourgeois ideology," that they criticized. Thus, Adorno described the "basic intention" of Nicolai Hartmann's thought as the "preservation of the autonomy of spirit with the concomitant concession of its 'groundedness' in extra-spiritual

---

59. Peter E. Gordon, *Adorno and Existence* (Cambridge, MA: Harvard University Press, 2016), x–xi, 127; Mikko Immanen, *Toward a Concrete Philosophy: Heidegger and the Emergence of the Frankfurt School* (Ithaca, NY: Cornell University Press, 2020), Part 2; Lambert Zuidervaart, *Truth in Husserl, Heidegger, and the Frankfurt School: Critical Retrieval* (Cambridge, MA: MIT Press, 2017), 13.

being."⁶⁰ Max Scheler and Martin Heidegger, he claimed, operated with categories of subjective idealism no matter how much temporal dynamics these categories, such as Heidegger's "historicity," were supposed to contain.⁶¹ All these efforts built on Husserl's attempt, "in which the bourgeois spirit strives mightily to break out of the prison of the immanence of consciousness, the sphere of constitutive subjectivity, with the help of the same categories as those implied by the idealistic analysis of the immanence of consciousness."⁶² Klages, who had no qualms about forsaking conceptual thought as such, did not carry such a "bourgeois" bias. He could thus see through the blind spots of the philosophical tradition, even as he obviously succumbed to other, neo-Romantic delusions of his own.

Adorno always considered phenomenology a serious philosophical movement, as is shown by his lifelong dialogue with Husserl and Heidegger, and it is not that he would have considered Klages a serious philosopher of their caliber. But precisely because he was an outsider—a point Adorno made in 1931 and repeated twenty years later in *Minima Moralia*—Klages held an advantageous perspective on the prejudices of the philosophical tradition, none of them more deep-seated than the idea of the primacy of the subject. On this basis, we can conclude that, as important as phenomenology was for Adorno's finding his own philosophical voice during the final years of the Weimar Republic, Klages decisively nurtured his view of Western philosophy as sublimated self-preservation, with phenomenology as its latest stage.

So far we have read Adorno's Oxford draft as evidence of Klages's impression on him. But this draft was by no means simply about Adorno's adoption of Klages's themes, as Breuer claims. It was in equal measure—and this is crucial—about Adorno's critical repurposing of them. In other words, as much as the draft expresses

---

60. Theodor W. Adorno, Review of *Das Problem des geistigen Seins*, by Nicolai Hartmann, *Zeitschrift für Sozialforschung* 2, no. 1 (1933): 110.

61. Adorno, "The Actuality of Philosophy," 27–28; Theodor W. Adorno, "The Idea of Natural-History," trans. Robert Hullot-Kentor, in *Things beyond Resemblance: Collected Essays on Theodor W. Adorno*, ed. Hullot-Kentor (New York: Columbia University Press, 2006), 254–59.

62. Adorno, *Against Epistemology*, 189.

Adorno's appreciation of Klages's concerns, it demonstrates with equal clarity that Adorno held dialectical reason, not irrational vitalism, as their guardian of greatest potential. Let us, therefore, move to explore this latter side of Adorno's Oxford draft.

"With the Strength of the Subject"

This is where Breuer's interpretation of the Oxford draft requires qualification. Breuer recognizes Adorno's espousal of Klages's concerns as his own, but he fails to see Adorno's draft simultaneously as a sign of his new appreciation of conceptual thought. Initially, Adorno had planned to criticize Husserl in the same way he had criticized Kierkegaard earlier, via "a kind of retranslation of an eminently 'philosophical' language back into a language of images," as he described his "original idea."[63] But ultimately Adorno opted for another approach. While still aiming to illuminate a larger historical truth through a close reading of an individual thinker, he now focused (as we will see in greater detail in the next section) on philosophical arguments themselves rather than a thinker's haphazard use of metaphors and images.

What motivated this change in Adorno's approach in the mid-1930s was his dissatisfaction with what he now saw as the antirational excesses of his *Kierkegaard* and Walter Benjamin's left-wing Klagesianism. In the late 1920s, Adorno had endorsed the original plan of Benjamin's *Arcades Project* as an interpretation of modern capitalism as a repetition of mythical compulsions of the archaic past.[64] He was not pleased, however, with how Benjamin had come to understand his project by the mid-1930s, in the so-called Arcades Exposé of 1935. In contrast to the original plan, Benjamin now

---

63. Adorno to Benjamin, November 6, 1934, in Theodor W. Adorno, *The Complete Correspondence, 1928–1940: Theodor W. Adorno and Walter Benjamin*, ed. Henri Lonitz, trans. Nicholas Walker (Cambridge, MA: Harvard University Press, 1999), 55.

64. For these early Königstein drafts, see Walter Benjamin, *The Arcades Project*, trans. Howard Eiland and Kevin McLaughlin (Cambridge, MA: Harvard University Press, 2002), 873–87.

underscored the arcades' redemptive, or utopian, dimension—and downplayed, at least in Adorno's estimation, their negative aspects—by viewing them as reflections of the "collective unconscious" and its yearning for a more meaningful world.[65] This interpretation, Adorno complained, resulted in a number of problems. First, it created a false image of the archaic past as a "Golden Age" against which modernity falsely appeared in too negative a light. This undialectical understanding of the mythical, Adorno maintained, played into the hands of Klages's black-and-white rejection of modernity. Second, Benjamin's invocation of the "collective unconscious," a theme central to Klages as well as to Jung, not only blurred class divisions but also betrayed an unhealthy antisubjectivism that found no way around the ills of modernity other than irrational "powers of intoxication." Third, the very idea of a "dialectical image" was distorted if it was understood to express a content of consciousness rather than a societal state of affairs that produced false consciousness.[66]

This intellectual estrangement from Benjamin was a pivotal step for Adorno in the process of finding his own self-understanding as a philosopher. Equally crucial, however, was Adorno's concurrent and related awakening to the potential of dialectical thought—or, as he wrote to Benjamin in 1936, his "renewed and extremely fruitful study of Hegel."[67]

If running through Adorno's *Negative Dialectics*, as Robert Hullot-Kentor notes, is "the Hegelian dialectic, passed through Benjamin's" micrological teachings,[68] then it is here in Adorno's Oxford study that the second Hegelian component enters his thought. Previously, Adorno had viewed modern art as an exemplary site of critical self-reflexivity in the twentieth century, whereas philosophy, whether as neometaphysics or scientific positivism, was an inferior, less self-conscious, form of cultural expression. Adorno's Kierkegaard book,

---

65. Walter Benjamin, "Paris, the Capital of the Nineteenth Century," in vol. 3 of *Selected Writings*, 32–49.
66. Adorno and Gretel Karplus to Benjamin, August 2–4, 1935, in *The Complete Correspondence*, 104–14.
67. Adorno to Benjamin, September 6, 1936, in *The Complete Correspondence*, 147.
68. Hullot-Kentor, "Critique of the Organic," 89.

as Hullot-Kentor observes, had followed this Benjaminian assumption by presenting "montages of images" that were supposed "to speak for themselves" without much conceptual explication.[69] But now, with a nod to Hegel, Adorno began to appreciate philosophy's capacity for critical self-awareness. Adorno's goal was still to construct "constellations" or "dialectical images," but the emphasis was now on the side of dialectics.

It seems to me that this discovery of Hegel marks the consequential moment in Adorno's finding his own philosophical voice, or in learning to "trust his own mental impulses," as he wrote in *Negative Dialectics*. Increasingly suspicious of the antisubjectivist excesses plaguing Benjamin's thought, in his critique of idealism Adorno no longer relied, as he still had in *Kierkegaard*, on "the strength of an image," but rather on what he would call in *Negative Dialectics* "the strength of the subject."[70] This meant that Adorno no longer criticized "bourgeois ideology," or "constitutive subjectivity," by nonconceptual, pictorial means. Instead, he tried to illustrate the shortcomings of conceptual abstractions through conceptual means, by surrendering faulty concepts to immanent conceptual criticism in the manner of Hegel's *Phänomenologie des Geistes* (*Phenomenology of Spirit*, 1807). Not for nothing is the German original of Adorno's *Against Epistemology* (a misleading translation, as is often noted) called *Metakritik der Erkenntnistheorie*, or "metacritique of epistemology." It does not dismiss epistemology so much as tries to cure it of its blind spots.[71]

---

69. Hullot-Kentor, "Critique of the Organic," 284n28.
70. Adorno, *Kierkegaard*, 131; Adorno, *Negative Dialectics*, xx.
71. Adorno's turn to Hegel was a gradual process that occurred between his works on Kierkegaard and Husserl. One can, however, see its first signs in the difference between Adorno's habilitation thesis, submitted in 1930, and the book published as *Kierkegaard* in 1933. The latter, as Robert Hullot-Kentor points out, was "more self-assuredly Hegelian" than the earlier version. Adorno made the revisions in less than two months in the fall of 1932. He worked intensively to make all the desired changes, the number of which ultimately surprised even Adorno himself. Hullot-Kentor suggests that what happened during Adorno's revision process was "the unexpected emergence of what became his mature style" ("Critique of the Organic," 90–91). The birth pangs of this emergence can be seen in Adorno's vacillation between two positions in his lecture on "natural-history" in July 1932, shortly before he began the revision process. Here Adorno defended

What stimulated Adorno's turn to Hegel? One likely source was criticisms of *Kierkegaard* by Adorno's colleagues at the University of Frankfurt. Inspired by Heidegger's existential phenomenology, they accused Adorno (as he described it) of turning philosophy "into an aesthetic picture game" that threatened to expel from it "every permanent standard."[72] Early reviewers of the Kierkegaard book echoed these criticisms. F. J. Brecht complained that "to discuss this book is difficult; to sum it up without distorting it, impossible," whereas Helmut Kuhn bemoaned that because the book's "energetic and adroit thought does not solidify into binding and definitive concepts," it "rolls by in expressive and polished formulations that are frequently overwhelmingly successful but also hovering and fragile." Another commentator lamented the book's "peculiarly swirling and swimming" character, while Karl Löwith took exception to what he called Adorno's "dictatorial, ranting and mannered style." Robert Hullot-Kentor points out that by judging *Kierkegaard* in such terms, these reviewers seemed helpless to figure out the reason behind its unconventional style: namely, that to overcome philosophy's idealist practice of reducing reality to ready-made categories required a thoroughly new focus on language and representation.[73] Only thus transformed, as Adorno emphasized in his 1931 inaugural address,

---

Benjamin's constellation as a different logical form against the discursive logic of idealism. Yet at the same time he called for, and to an extent executed, an immanent conceptual criticism of the neo-ontology of Heidegger's *Being and Time* (Adorno, "The Idea of Natural-History," 256–60, 263–66). Interestingly from the perspective of the Klages question, the *Ur*-moment of Adorno's new Hegelian outlook in fall 1932 coincided with the beginning of his Klages project. This suggests that very early on in this Klages project, Adorno conceived of Hegelian dialectic, when sufficiently modified, as a suitable rejoinder to Klages's critique of reason.

72. Adorno, "The Actuality of Philosophy," 37. For the context, see Immanen, *Toward a Concrete Philosophy*, 149–51.

73. F. J. Brecht, review of *Kierkegaard: Konstruktion des Ästhetischen*, by Theodor W. Adorno, *Kant Studien* 40 (1935): 327; Helmut Kuhn, review of *Kierkegaard: Konstruktion des Ästhetischen*, by Theodor W. Adorno, *Zeitschrift für Ästhetik und allgemeine Kunstwissenschaft* 28, no. 1 (1934): 104; Anonymous, Review of *Kierkegaard: Konstruktion des Ästhetischen*, by Theodor W. Adorno, *Kölner Vierteljahrsschrift für Soziologie* 12 (1934): 198; Karl Löwith, review of *Kierkegaard: Konstruktion des Ästhetischen*, by Theodor W. Adorno, *Deutsche Literaturzeitung* 4 (1934): 28. All of these reviews are quoted in Hullot-Kentor, "Critique of the Organic," 80–81.

was philosophy able "to construct keys, before which reality springs open," whereas traditional metaphysics "chose categories too large; so they did not even come close to fitting the keyhole."[74]

No matter how poorly Adorno's colleagues or early reviewers of *Kierkegaard* grasped this nonargumentative pictorial strategy, their misunderstandings may have pushed Adorno to rethink his approach. Another likely push came from the Hegel renaissance in Germany, inaugurated by Wilhelm Dilthey in the early 1900s, the ontological second wave of which was led by Adorno's supervisor, Paul Tillich, and his Frankfurt School colleague, Herbert Marcuse. Adorno criticized these ontological readings, in essence projections of Heidegger's *Dasein* into Hegel's notion of "life," as yet another instance of "identity thinking," the reduction of reality to subjective categories no matter how sensitive these purportedly were to "concreteness." Nevertheless, these neo-ontological readings may well have stimulated Adorno to take a fresh look at Hegel. What most certainly did were the impulses of the left-wing camp of the Hegel revival. In Marx's footsteps, Georg Lukács and Max Horkheimer sought to reinterpret Hegel's dialectics materialistically with the goal of making originally idealist notions, such as the concept of "totality," useful in understanding and criticizing the workings of capitalism.[75]

---

74. Adorno, "The Actuality of Philosophy," 35.
75. On the Hegel renaissance, see Immanen, *Toward a Concrete Philosophy*, 56–60. On Adorno's debt to Lukács and Horkheimer, see Breuer, "Materialistische Erkenntnikritik," 430–32; Abromeit, *Max Horkheimer*, 378–82. Horkheimer had also been skeptical of Adorno's early pictorial approach. As John Abromeit has shown, as professor of social philosophy in 1931, Horkheimer wrote an official report on the original version of Adorno's *Kierkegaard*, which Adorno had submitted to the philosophy faculty as a habilitation thesis. Although Horkheimer praised Adorno's criticism of Kierkegaard's notion of interiority and recommended the approval of the thesis as a habilitation, he did not hold back his reservations regarding Adorno's approach: "The direction of the philosophical interests as well as the method of thought and the linguistic formulation of this *Habilitationsschrift*," Horkheimer wrote, "are not related to my own philosophical aims. If Wiesengrund [Adorno] believes he has rescued hope and reconciliation in Kierkegaard's thought, in so doing he has expressed a fundamental theological conviction, which points to a philosophical intention that is radically different from my own and this intention is palpable in every sentence." Max Horkheimer, "Bemerkung in Sachen der Habilitation Dr. Wiesengrund," Archiv des Dekanats der Philosophischen Fakultät der J. W.

Adorno did not, of course, become a Hegelian in any orthodox sense. Hegel's notion of spirit—his reduction of history and nature to logic—was idealism at its extreme that climaxed in his rationalization of human suffering on the "slaughter bench" of history.[76] Adorno had already in *Kierkegaard* criticized these aspects of Hegel. Yet in the Oxford draft he took crucial steps toward *Negative Dialectics*, which, as Jay M. Bernstein notes, exemplifies what it means to be Hegelian after the critiques of idealism by Marx and Nietzsche, and after the horrors of modern history.[77] I would qualify this by saying that Adorno's Oxford draft is Hegelianism pressed through the specifically Klagesian mangle, Hegelianism that in its utter negativity—allergic even to materialist renderings à la Lukács and Horkheimer, to whom Adorno otherwise owed a great deal—is at pains to safeguard Klages's concerns about the perils of "logocentrism."[78] (Horkheimer, as we will shortly see, was not happy with the excessive negativity of Adorno's position, which in his view went far beyond what was required to give dialectics a materialist push and in so doing came dangerously close to Klagesian irrationalism.)

With such a negative interpretation of Hegel, however, Adorno did not think he was necessarily committing a major injustice. As he stated at the time of writing *Negative Dialectics*, "of the ideas that I am presenting to you, there is not a single one that is not contained, in tendency at least, in Hegel's philosophy."[79] In the preface to *Negative Dialectics*, Adorno recounted Benjamin's reactions to this Hegelian turn in his thinking. Benjamin, after reading a part of Adorno's Oxford manuscript in 1937, was amazed at his

---

Goethe Universität, Frankfurt am Main (section 134, number 4), 5. Cited in Abromeit, *Max Horkheimer*, 352.

76. Adorno, *Against Epistemology*, 44; Georg Wilhelm Friedrich Hegel, *Lectures on the Philosophy of World History. Introduction: Reason in History*, trans. H. B. Nisbet (Cambridge: Cambridge University Press, 1975), 69.

77. Jay M. Bernstein, "Negative Dialectic as Fate: Adorno and Hegel," in *The Cambridge Companion to Adorno*, ed. Tom Huhn (Cambridge: Cambridge University Press, 2004), 20.

78. On Adorno's distance from Lukács and Horkheimer, particularly regarding the concept of "totality," see Martin Jay, *Marxism and Totality: The Adventures of a Concept from Lukács to Habermas* (Berkeley: University of California Press, 1984).

79. Adorno, *Lectures on Negative Dialectics*, 21.

friend's determination to "cross the frozen waste of abstraction"—Husserl's phenomenology—"to arrive at concise, concrete philosophizing."[80] If in *Negative Dialectics* Adorno mapped this "crossing in retrospect," in the Oxford manuscript we find him making it for the first time.

I acknowledge that my interpretation, which places heavy emphasis on Adorno's appropriation of Hegel since c. 1935, may be guilty of downplaying the role played by another giant of classical German philosophy, Immanuel Kant, in the emergence of Adorno's "negative dialectics." Brian O'Connor argues that in *Negative Dialectics* and his other mature works Adorno saw Kant's notion of things-in-themselves "as a realist position." Adorno's purpose is to recruit this (for him) quasi-materialist notion for his critique of more transcendental or idealist elements of Kant's thought as well as for his own wider anti-idealist campaign against constitutive subjectivity. It is difficult to answer, O'Connor remarks, when exactly Adorno adopted this approach of going against Kant with Kant. It may go back, he surmises, to Adorno's youthful decoding with Kracauer of the *Critique of Pure Reason* as a contradictory work brimming with "fissures and flaws" (as Adorno himself later recalled). On the other hand, Adorno's academic theses form the 1920s, written for the neo-Kantian Hans Cornelius, seem occasionally to anticipate his mature readings of Kant. O'Connor concludes, however, that considering their ultimately Cornelian, idealist thrust, one cannot yet take these early works as a sign of Adorno's philosophical independence.[81] What this means is that even if Kant was crucial to Adorno's finding his own philosophical direction, which I do not dispute, this hardly happened before the 1930s and his "Klages project."

---

80. Adorno, *Negative Dialectics*, xix.
81. Brian O'Connor, *Adorno's Negative Dialectic: Philosophy and the Possibility of Critical Rationality* (Cambridge, MA: MIT Press, 2004), 19–20, 101–6. For more on Adorno's appropriation of Kant, see Peter Uwe Hohendahl, *The Fleeting Promise of Art: Adorno's Aesthetic Theory Revisited* (Ithaca, NY: Cornell University Press, 2013), chap. 1; Hauke Brunkhorst, *Adorno and Critical Theory* (Cardiff: University of Wales Press, 1999). On Adorno's early readings of Kant with Kracauer, see Adorno, "The Curious Realist," 58–59.

In this section, we have probed the basic coordinates of Adorno's new dialectical approach. But how did this approach function in practice? How did Adorno show that conceptual thought did not have to lead to "identity thinking" or a system, but could engage in self-reflection? How did he concretely demonstrate that reason could pay heed to the unique, or mimetic, side of objects? If Adorno wished to show that Klages's *Spirit as Adversary of the Soul* had not cast the final verdict on Western philosophy, he had to answer these questions.

Concepts as "Imageless Images"

When released from the idealist architectonics of Hegel's system, Adorno believed, the dialectical method of "determinate negation" contained the seeds of a nondominative, mimetic form of reason. Adorno expressed this belief beautifully in a late essay, where he wrote that Hegel's *Phenomenology of Spirit* deposes "individual concepts" by using "them as though they were the imageless images of what they mean."[82] This implied that seemingly timeless philosophical categories were not understandable in themselves (i.e., identical), but pointed beyond themselves. Not, Adorno qualified, to self-identical Spirit as Hegel erroneously thought, but to what *Negative Dialectics* called the "non-identical." Thinking was unavoidably embedded in the material world (both natural and social) it had to cope with. Unlike idealist attempts to fix philosophical truth in abstracto, dialectical truth was "a constellation of moments," or "a field of force," the understanding of which required immersion in historical concreteness.[83]

This emphasis on the affective and societal preconditions of thought, or what *Negative Dialectics* called "the preponderance of the object,"[84] went against most past and current philosophy, for

---

82. Theodor W. Adorno, *Hegel: Three Studies*, trans. Shierry Weber Nicholsen (Cambridge, MA: MIT Press, 1993), 123.
83. Adorno, *Against Epistemology*, 72.
84. Adorno, *Negative Dialectics*, 184. On this notion, see O'Connor, *Adorno's Negative Dialectic*, chap. 2.

which the opposite, the primacy of the subject—or what Adorno at other times called constitutive subjectivity or bourgeois ideology—was the founding bedrock. In *Against Epistemology*, Adorno surrendered this subjectivist position to severe criticism by focusing on its latest representative, Edmund Husserl, and his view of consciousness as a "sphere of absolute origins." This criticism, as we have already seen, dates from the mid-1930s. To demonstrate this in greater detail, I will draw on Adorno's two Husserl articles that emanated from his Oxford exile in the 1930s.[85] It bears emphasizing that what is essential here is not the object of Adorno's criticism, Husserl, but rather the form of this criticism. Adorno no longer sought to criticize idealism's totalizing pretensions through aesthetic, pictorial means, but conceptual ones. If this attempt was to turn out a success, it ought to express mimetic qualities. It should not, in other words, approach its objects abstractly from the outside, as classifying thought did, but immanently, beginning with the objects' own premises. Let us see how Adorno carried out this criticism and how he decoded Husserl's phenomenological concepts as "imageless images."

Adorno saw phenomenology as a paradoxical attempt to safeguard the individuality and uniqueness of things from idealist classification using idealism's own logic. Husserl's doctrine of "categorial intuition" maintained that "given" to thought were not only empirical facts but also essential aspects of reality, or the "things themselves," as Husserl's famous battle cry put it. This simple intuitability of essences, Husserl believed, avoided identifying this essential, extrafactual dimension of things with their universal, or measurable, features (the guilt of older idealism). Instead, Husserl argued, it allowed one to identify the essence of things with their unique aspects. Yet somehow these essences still resided in a nonmaterial realm of their own, untouched by any empirical circumstances. This "logical absolutism," Adorno lamented, restored idealism rather than surpassing

---

85. Although Horkheimer vetoed the appearance of Adorno's planned Husserl article in the institute's journal, Adorno managed to publish two articles elsewhere. "Zur Philosophie Husserls" (1937) appeared in *Archiv für Philosophie* in 1938 and "Husserl and the Problem of Idealism" (1939) in the *Journal of Philosophy* in 1940. Both can be found in *Gesammelte Schriften, Bd. 20.1: Vermischte Schriften I*, ed. Rolf Tiedemann (Frankfurt: Suhrkamp, 1986), on pp. 46–118 and 119–34, respectively.

it. Husserl's faith in the givenness of essences overlooked that thinking necessarily needs the empirical. Concrete reflections and theorizing were crucial in the generation, and critical evaluation, of concepts. What Husserl overlooked, in other words, was the dialectical relation between subject and object.[86]

Husserl's errors began, then, with his neglect of the somatic elements of life, such as pain and desire, which showed that subjectivity was no pure immanence but a worldly creature.[87] Equally fateful, however, was his neglect of social reality. Adorno contended that Husserl's need for absolute certainty, essences untouched by history, reflected bourgeois insecurities at a time of profound economic transformation. The resemblance of Husserl's concepts—such as endowment, judgment, and demesne—to modern legal terminology betrayed the bourgeoisie's need for secure property relations. "Security," Adorno observed, "is left as an ultimate and lonely fetish like the number, one million, on a long deflated banknote."[88] In Adorno's view, phenomenology reproduced the contradictions of late capitalism. The turn of the twentieth century witnessed the displacement of the individual initiative of nineteenth-century liberal capitalism by monopolies, yet paradoxically this era still clung to the ideology of heroic entrepreneurship. The static nature of Husserl's essences, which knew nothing of earlier idealism's dynamic aspects—Kant's spontaneity of thought or Hegel's consciousness of freedom—signified self-renunciation in the face of overpowering social forces. At the same time, Husserl's conviction that no historical circumstances could undo these essences reproduced bourgeois self-delusions.[89]

Bespeaking the dialectical nature of this critique of Husserl, Adorno praised Hegel as the first and the only person to understand the aporetic character of idealist concepts.[90] Later he elaborated on what was going on in this critique. It was about pushing

---

86. Adorno, "Husserl and the Problem of Idealism," 120–29, 133; "Zur Philosophie Husserls," 76–77, 82–83, 96.
87. Adorno, "Zur Philosophie Husserls," 60, 66–67.
88. Adorno, "Zur Philosophie Husserls," 95.
89. Adorno, "Zur Philosophie Husserls," 84–90, 95–96.
90. Adorno, "Zur Philosophie Husserls," 84.

phenomenology, "with the latter's own force," to where it "cannot afford to go." The model derived from *Phenomenology of Spirit*, whose procedure consisted both of "passively following the movement of the concept and actively directing this movement, thus transforming the object."[91] Adorno viewed Husserl's concepts as just the kind of "imageless images" that, when "passively" followed according to their own logic, exposed themselves as sediments of historical experience: psychological renunciation, societal turbulence, and cognitive domination. To show this, Adorno had to "actively direct" Husserl's reasoning on one crucial point: in rejecting the very assumption of constitutive subjectivity. As a result, phenomenology was "transformed." Crucially, it was not just false consciousness. Husserl's flawed attempt to overcome idealism disclosed a larger truth, one akin to what Adorno had earlier demonstrated with respect to Kierkegaard. Husserl was an "unconscious but faithful historiographer of the self-alienation of thought."[92] As "imageless images," his concepts narrated the history of the decline of the individual in capitalism.

With this immanent critique of phenomenology, Adorno had shown that conceptual thought did not necessarily forfeit the uniqueness of its objects. Adorno's nascent negative dialectics, as Jay M. Bernstein notes, aspired "to rescue, in the medium of the concept," the mimesis repressed by idealist classifications.[93] In so doing, Adorno believed he had revealed dialectical reason as a potential guardian of the concerns raised by Klages's critique of reason.

What about the other seminal goal of Adorno's Klages project, namely, to reach a better understanding of "the mythical"? How far had Adorno advanced in understanding this problem complex, closely linked to the problem of constitutive subjectivity, or "bourgeois ideology," tackled in the Husserl manuscript? To answer this question, we need to take a closer look at Adorno's already cited letters to Horkheimer, especially their discussion of Alfred Sohn-Rethel's investigations of ancient Greek thought.

---

91. Adorno, *Against Epistemology*, 5, 25.
92. Adorno, *Against Epistemology*, 63.
93. Bernstein, "Negative Dialectic as Fate," 43–44.

"My work is making it increasingly clear to me," Adorno told Horkheimer in 1936, "just how little in principle bourgeois thinking has ever changed and how all the much ballyhooed difference of standpoints is merely an illusion."[94] But where did the roots of this thinking, what Klages called logocentrism and Adorno idealism, lie? In his 1930s Husserl articles, Adorno had argued that phenomenology reflected modern capitalism. With this reading, Adorno sought to contribute to Horkheimer's "dialectical logic" project, which tried to connect the developments of modern philosophy to the twists and turns of the European bourgeoisie from c. 1500 to 1900. As we have already seen, however, for Adorno "identity thinking" was not a modern problem. Klages had helped him to see how far back in history it reached and how it encompassed not only social domination but the domination of nature as well. Further, Klages had reinforced his fear that "the mythical" was no onetime struggle between *Logos* and *Mythos* in a distant Greek past, but a problem that was very much alive in modern society and thought.

But Klages's neo-Romantic speculation erred in viewing logocentrism as a mysterious spiritual force sui generis that just happened to enter the scene sometime in the seventh century BCE. A more plausible historical account of the origin of "the mythical" was required. This was provided by Sohn-Rethel, who in 1936 sent Adorno his manuscript (which he wished to publish in the institute's journal) on the societal factors behind the emergence of Greek philosophy, on the basis of which Adorno thought Sohn-Rethel was a potential candidate to take over his Klages project.

Sohn-Rethel sought to take Georg Lukács's pioneering Marxist reading of philosophy from 1923 further. Lukács had argued that Marxist ideology critique should focus not only on political economy but also on epistemology. Modern natural science and its epistemological consummation, Kant's critique of reason, marked the reification of thought. Their third-person perspective obstructed human beings from realizing that while nature may be thus observed from the outside, the same approach to history would relegate

---

94. Adorno to Horkheimer, May 26, 1936, in Adorno, *Briefwechsel, Bd. I: 1927–1937*, 147. Translation from Abromeit, *Max Horkheimer*, 388.

human beings to passive bystanders of societal development. Lukács laid the blame for this reified consciousness on capitalism. The replacement of use-value with abstract exchange-value favored a contemplative attitude that forgot human agency, a fateful situation for Marxists who dreamed not only of understanding but also of changing of the world.[95]

Sohn-Rethel's novelty lay in taking Lukács's reading a step forward—or rather backward—by tracing reification to Greek antiquity. With his interpretation of pre-Socratic philosophy of nature as an outgrowth of what he viewed as ancient Greece's protocapitalism, Sohn-Rethel was in a position to show, as Adorno explained to Horkheimer, that Klages's "spirit" was "nothing but the mythologized concept of labor."[96] Sohn-Rethel suggested that the capacity of thought to abstract conceptually from concrete historical circumstances, as happened for the first time in pre-Socratic rationalism, had its roots in the money-mediated economy of the "archaic" seventh-century Greece, whose abstract exchange relations (embodied by the introduction of coinage) and exploitation of slave labor formed the concrete societal basis—"real abstraction"—for the emergence of the pre-Socratic doctrines—abstraction in thought.[97]

Adorno was overwhelmed by Sohn-Rethel's effort to "deduce logical categories from exploitation," an effort that both confirmed his own assumptions and clarified their murky points.[98] Jokingly, Adorno compared the situation to the controversy between Leibniz and Newton over the invention of calculus.[99] To another friend

---

95. Georg Lukács, *History and Class Consciousness: Studies in Marxist Dialectics*, trans. Rodney Livingstone (London: Merlin Press, 1971), 110–49.

96. Adorno to Horkheimer, December 15, 1936, in Adorno, *Briefwechsel, Bd. I: 1927–1937*, 263.

97. Sohn-Rethel would publish his theory in book form only in 1970, as *Geistige und Körperliche Arbeit: Zur Theorie der gesellschaftlichen Synthesis*. For the English translation, see *Intellectual and Manual Labor: A Critique of Epistemology*, trans. Martin Sohn-Rethel (London: Macmillan Press, 1978), 1–29.

98. Adorno to Horkheimer, January 25, 1937, in Adorno, *Briefwechsel, Bd. I: 1927–1937*, 278.

99. Adorno to Sohn-Rethel, November 17, 1936, in *Theodor W. Adorno und Alfred Sohn-Rethel: Briefwechsel 1936–1969*, ed. Christoph Gödde (München: text + kritik, 1991), 32.

Adorno wrote that Sohn-Rethel had come, albeit from a different perspective, "to the same conclusions" as he in his Oxford study—"that in the depths of validity, the genesis can be found in 'praxis' or, as I put it in my Husserl book: truth is not in history, history is in the truth."[100] What Adorno meant by this was what *Negative Dialectics* would call "the preponderance of the object": the subtle historical inscription of ostensibly ahistorical idealist concepts. What this view of concepts as "imageless images," as sediments of historical reality, meant, however, was that Klages was mistaken in treating "identity thinking" as some dark anthropological invariant of the human condition. Rather, it had its societal roots in the nascent capitalism of ancient Greece. As Adorno stated when he paid homage to his friend in *Negative Dialectics*: "Alfred Sohn-Rethel was the first to point out that hidden in this principle" of logical identity "lies work of an inalienably social nature."[101]

Horkheimerian Headwinds

To Adorno's great disappointment, his hopes of seeing an article published on Klages in *Zeitschrift für Sozialforschung* were vetoed by none other than Horkheimer. Notwithstanding Horkheimer's initial interest in a review of *The Spirit as Adversary of the Soul*, eventually he came to turn down all suggestions for such a text, whether written by Adorno, Sohn-Rethel, or Benjamin. Richard Wolin suggests that it was Klages's antisemitism that made Horkheimer reluctant to accept texts that were even slightly favorable to him.[102]

---

100. Adorno to Leo Löwenthal, November 19, 1936, in Adorno, *Briefwechsel, Bd. I: 1927–1937*, 524. Translation from Abromeit, *Max Horkheimer*, 383–84.

101. Adorno, *Negative Dialectics*, 177. For recent explanations of the emergence of philosophy in ancient Greece (which emphasize the societal context yet are critical of Sohn-Rethel's theory), see Othmar Franz Fett, *Der undenkbare Dritte: Vorsokratische Anfänge des eurogenen Naturverhältnisses* (Tübingen, Germany: Edition Diskord, 2000) and Tobias Reichardt, *Recht und Rationalität im frühen Griechenland* (Würzburg, Germany: Königshausen & Neumann, 2003).

102. Wolin, *Walter Benjamin*, xxxviii.

Indeed, the review plan for Klages's book had been made before the Nazis' rise to power, and Horkheimer may very well have changed his mind after 1933.

This *political* interpretation of Horkheimer's rejection, however, cannot explain why, at around the same time, he rejected Adorno's Husserl article, which nowhere mentioned Klages. This rejection was quite a blow to Adorno. He complained that he had "never worked on anything with such great investment" and that he regarded this text as his "first philosophical work, at least the first with which I am more or less satisfied."[103] My contention is that what Horkheimer saw as major *theoretical* defects of Adorno's Husserl article—and thereby of Adorno's nascent "negative dialectics"—namely its insufficient faith in reason, goes a long way to explaining his uneasiness with the Klages plans as well.

In their exchanges over the Atlantic, Horkheimer raised several objections to Adorno's Husserl article. He questioned, for example, Adorno's view of phenomenological concepts, such as the categorial intuition, as inherently contradictory. Phenomenologists, Horkheimer claimed, would never accept this line of criticism as an immanent one. What bothered him the most, however, was Adorno's wider anti-idealist campaign. Even if one were to agree with Adorno's critique of Husserl, how could this, Horkheimer wondered, attest to "the fiasco of idealism" as such?[104] It was one thing to interpret phenomenological abstractions as reflections of modern capitalism. Horkheimer could wholeheartedly endorse this historically specific ideology critique. Indeed, his own materialist interpretation of modern philosophy emphasized the changing ideological function of idealism in different phases of capitalism. Hence, even though phenomenology—the idealism of the era of monopoly capitalism—had a quietist, accommodating effect, German idealism one hundred years earlier—the idealism of the liberal

---

103. Adorno to Horkheimer, August 7, 1937, in Adorno, *Briefwechsel, Bd. I: 1927–1937*, 388. Translation from Abromeit, *Max Horkheimer*, 385.

104. Horkheimer to Adorno, October 13, 1937, in Adorno, *Briefwechsel, Bd. I: 1927–1937*, 423–30.

capitalist period—had had a very different function. Even if Hegel, Fichte, and Schelling, as Marx had famously derided, had sought to engender changes only in thought, their doctrines served emancipatory interests.[105]

Yet it was quite another thing to claim, as Adorno seemed to being doing, that conceptual abstractions as such were somehow damaging to social criticism, or to insist that the societal structures and thought patterns of Greek antiquity and modern capitalist Europe were somehow identical. Horkheimer had already directed similar criticisms against Sohn-Rethel, even as he acknowledged that the latter's effort to establish a connection between pre-Socratic rationalism and societal exploitation could fruitfully "illuminate the Klagesian concept of spirit."[106]

Although in 1934 Horkheimer had invited Adorno to collaborate on his "dialectical logic" project, and thereby to clarify the philosophical premises of the Institute for Social Research, the notion of dialectics that Adorno created in the process was not to his liking. The philosophical foundation of Horkheimer's own position, and thereby of the "classic" Frankfurt School of the 1930s, was a materialist reinterpretation of Hegel's dictum that "the true is the whole."[107] Empirical facts discovered by psychology, sociology, and history achieved their true meaning only when referred to the larger social totality, what Marx and Engels called "the social life process." To lead this life process autonomously, instead of being passively led by it, marked the difference between free and unfree societies. In the notion of the "whole" Horkheimer thus possessed a rational yardstick with which to criticize capitalism as well as the

---

105. See, for instance, Horkheimer's essays "On the Problem of Truth" (1935) and "Montaigne and the Function of Skepticism" (1938), both in *Between Philosophy and Social Science: Selected Early Writings*, trans. G. Frederick Hunter et al. (Cambridge, MA: MIT Press, 1993), on pp. 177–215 and 265–311, respectively. On Horkheimer's materialist interpretation of the history of philosophy, see Abromeit, *Max Horkheimer*, chaps. 3 and 6.

106. Horkheimer to Adorno, January 11, 1937, in Adorno, *Briefwechsel, Bd. I: 1927–1937*, 268.

107. Georg Wilhelm Friedrich Hegel, *Phenomenology of Spirit*, trans. A. V. Miller (Oxford: Oxford University Press, 1977), 11.

empirical sciences for their efforts to make sense of it with insufficient means.[108]

In their exchange in New York some years later, Adorno rejected the notion of the "whole" as idealist, anticipating his inversion of Hegel's dictum in *Minima Moralia*: "the whole is the false."[109] In its place, Adorno proposed that truth meant "the negation of everything that is false." Horkheimer, however, suspected that this vague definition could not tell a false state of affairs from a correct one. In fact, he claimed, it pushed Adorno into the vicinity of irrationalists like Klages, who in the name of "immediate life" equated rational thought with life-denying disruption.[110] This disagreement testifies to Adorno's readiness to concede far more to the vitalist critique of reason than Horkheimer was willing to do. Adorno's suspicion of all claims to conceptual closure, no matter how materialistically rendered, can be explained by the extent to which he approved Klages's indictment of logocentrism. No doubt, Adorno's nascent negative dialectics, as emphasized earlier, owed a great deal to the critical Marxism of Lukács and Horkheimer. Yet, I believe that it was from Klages that he obtained—first implicitly via Benjamin and then explicitly in his own struggle with *The Spirit as Adversary of the Soul*—a suspicion of grand idealist concepts such as "totality" and the "whole."[111]

---

108. On Horkheimer's conception of dialectics, see Abromeit, *Max Horkheimer*, chap. 8. See also Karl Marx and Friedrich Engels, *The German Ideology*, in *Collected Works*, vol. 5 (London: Lawrence and Wishart, 1976).

109. Adorno, *Minima Moralia*, 50.

110. See the exchange between Adorno and Horkheimer in New York in April 1939, "Diskussionen über die Differenz zwischen Positivismus und materialistischer Dialektik," in Max Horkheimer, *Gesammelte Schriften, Bd. 12: Nachgelassene Schriften 1931–1949*, ed. Gunzelin Schmid Noerr (Frankfurt: Fischer, 1987), 490–91.

111. Horkheimer's suspicions of Adorno's proximity to Klages may have been strengthened by the fact, as Brian O'Connor notes, that nowhere in his Oxford study did Adorno qualify his "liquidation of idealism" by dismissing as "childish," as he would in *Negative Dialectics*, a view that "would deny the validity of formal logic and mathematics and treat them as ephemeral because they have come to be." See Adorno, *Negative Dialectics*, 40; O'Connor, *Adorno's Negative Dialectic*, 136. We can surmise that without this explicit statement in Adorno's Oxford study, Horkheimer could not help but wonder whether Adorno's insistence on the mediatedness even of logical concepts did not mean a relapse to *Lebensphilosophie*. For implied in Adorno's position seemed to be the implausible assertion that formal logic was a

To answer, then, our question about Adorno's understanding of "the mythical," we can draw the following conclusions. During his first years of exile in Oxford, Adorno had obtained a grasp of the epistemological side of "the mythical" and thereby paved the way for his later masterpiece, *Negative Dialectics*, and its notion of mimetic reason. What Adorno still had not sufficiently understood, however, was the historical origin of the mythical at the dawn of Greek antiquity. This he would manage to articulate only later in *Dialectic of Enlightenment*, into which his and Horkheimer's 1930s project on dialectical logic would evolve with the darkening of the world political horizon at the end of the decade. Before turning to *Dialectic of Enlightenment* and the culmination of Adorno's Klages project in its philosophy of history, however, we should first follow Adorno in his move from Oxford to New York in 1938, for it was on the East Coast of the United States that another major stalwart of interwar *Zivilisationskritik*, Oswald Spengler, began to preoccupy his mind.

---

societal phenomenon, not only in the sense that certain historical circumstances had facilitated humanity's becoming aware of logical truths—as Sohn-Rethel argued with respect to the genesis of pre-Socratic doctrines—or in the sense that modern positivism had "colonized" the more hermeneutic human sciences, but in the questioning of the very validity of formal logic. It was one thing, Horkheimer thought, to view concepts as "imageless images," as sediments of contingent historical experience, and thus to throw light on the conditions of their "genesis." It was entirely another, however, to claim that they were only that and thereby deny their "validity."

2

"CAESARISM"

Spengler's Master Class in Democracy's Self-Destruction

The Weimar Republic is often said to have lacked republicans. But surely this is an overstatement. Leading intellectuals of the time, such as the Kantian philosopher Ernst Cassirer, actively voiced their support for Germany's first democratic experiment. Yet in hindsight, critics have pointed out that Cassirer and his like were unsuccessful because in their trust in reason and progress they were unprepared to face harsh postwar realities and mounting antidemocratic sentiment fed by new radical voices. Commenting on Cassirer's storied 1929 Davos debate with the iconoclastic existentialist Martin Heidegger, Leo Strauss underlined the contrast between Cassirer, an erudite but noncharismatic representative of academic philosophy, and Heidegger, whose novel ontological scrutiny of the human condition "gave adequate expression to the prevailing unrest and dissatisfaction."[1]

---

1. Leo Strauss, "Kurt Riezler," in *What Is Political Philosophy? and Other Studies* (Glencoe, IL: The Free Press, 1959), 246.

Similarly, commemorating the seventieth birthday of the cultural philosopher Oswald Spengler in 1950, Theodor W. Adorno claimed that among his Weimar-era critics Spengler "found hardly an adversary who was his equal."[2]

In the aftermath of World War I, Spengler's *Decline of the West* (published in two volumes in 1918 and 1922) was on everyone's lips in Germany, and to a lesser extent abroad as well. "Never had a thick philosophical work," one contemporary witness observed, occupied the minds of "all reading circles, learned and uneducated, serious and snobbish."[3] Germans, saddened by the catastrophe of military defeat and revolution, felt relieved to learn that their misfortune could be rationalized as an episode in a far more universal doom that even the victorious Allies could not escape. Reception among academic circles, in contrast, was almost without exception condemning. An avalanche of commentaries and reviews, several hundred in total, took exception to Spengler's self-assured proclamations. Whether it was about questions of detail related to his highly speculative cultural history, or "cultural morphology," or, as was more often the case, about his bleak verdict on the inescapable spiritual exhaustion of Western civilization, critics of all ages and across the political spectrum dismissed Spengler as an unwelcome quack. Despite this, in the early 1920s Spengler had undoubtedly become, in the manner of Schopenhauer and Nietzsche in the previous century, "the philosopher of the hour."[4]

Considering this early reckoning with Spengler after World War II and the Holocaust, Adorno argued that "the German mind collapsed when confronted with an opponent who seemed to have inherited all the historical force of its own past."[5] Adorno's scoff was particularly

---

2. Theodor W. Adorno, "Spengler after the Decline," in *Prisms*, trans. Samuel Weber and Shierry Weber (Cambridge, MA: MIT Press, 1981), 54. For the German original, see "Spengler nach dem Untergang: Zu Oswald Spenglers 70. Geburtstag," *Der Monat* 2, no. 20 (1950): 115–28.
3. W. Wolfradt in Manfred Schröter, *Der Streit um Spengler: Kritik seiner Kritiker* (Munich: C. H. Beck, 1922), 7n. Quoted in H. Stuart Hughes, *Oswald Spengler: A Critical Estimate* (New Brunswick, NJ: Transaction Publishers, 1992), 89.
4. Hughes, *Oswald Spengler*, 89–91.
5. Adorno, "Spengler after the Decline," 54.

targeted at the prestigious philosophical journal *Logos*, which in 1920 had gathered an illustrious group of Germany's foremost classicists and historians to demolish the first volume of *The Decline of the West*. These commentators, alarmed by the fact that Spengler's "historical prophecy" was undermining trust in the future of Germany and Europe, waved Spengler off as a hack. "Nowhere did" Spengler's morose vision, they asserted, "stand up to a conscientious assessment."[6] Adorno would have none of what he judged the "pedantic punctiliousness" and "rhetoric of conformist optimism" of these condescending attacks. For Adorno and Strauss, both Jewish exiles from Nazi Germany, Weimar academics' inability to genuinely face, rather than arrogantly dismiss, the challenge of charismatic critics of reason had consequences far surpassing the university. "Led politically by Hitler and intellectually by Heidegger," Strauss concluded, "Germany entered the Third Reich." The weakness of Spengler's critics, Adorno mourned, echoed "the political impotence of the Weimar Republic faced with Hitler."[7]

One wonders why Adorno, who in 1949 had returned to Germany after fifteen years of exile, chose to cast the *Logos* authors in such a negative light. Surely he agreed on the need to criticize Spengler's book, which had made authoritative and influential claims about the past, and which, moreover, had not only described the zeitgeist of the 1920s but played into the hands of the antirepublican and antisocialist forces of Weimar Germany. Adorno's train of thought seems to have gone as follows. While the Weimar academia may have proven wrong Spengler's claims about this or that question of historical detail, in its unshaken confidence in the health of Western civilization—that is, in its "assurance that things aren't really all that bad"—it had missed some unnerving tendencies in modern Western society. Spengler's academic adversaries had made a grave error in refusing to ponder whether behind his fanciful theory of the rise and fall of cultures there lay genuine insights, insights that they had paid scant attention to and that failed to resonate

---

6. "Spenglerheft," *Logos. Internationale Zeitschrift für Philosophie der Kultur* 9, no. 2 (1920–1921): 133–34.
7. Strauss, "Kurt Riezler," 241; Adorno, "Spengler after the Decline," 54.

among the wider reading public as soon as the immediate postwar misery gave way to the merrier "Golden Twenties."[8]

By these insights Adorno meant Spengler's observations, discussed under the term "Caesarism" in the largely neglected second volume of *The Decline of the West*, on post–World War I Europe: the bureaucratization of the party system, the emergence of a new personality type susceptible to propaganda, and the rise of a manipulative mass media. For Spengler, the age of "Caesarism" was one of urban metropolis, shallow materialism, and ruthless thrust for power: an inevitable late stage that every "culture" had to face as it reached the old age of "civilization" (and which the Classical world had experienced in Hellenism and the Roman Empire). For Adorno, always a far more historically oriented thinker, Spengler's ruminations on Caesarism were valuable not as validation of his pompous philosophy of history but as keys to more specific issues of interwar Europe: political, psychological, and cultural "tendencies inherent in democracy which threaten to turn it into dictatorship."[9]

Adorno's essay on Spengler's work, accompanied by a shorter piece from 1955 and scattered remarks here and there,[10] conveys a highly ambivalent stance toward Spengler, a vacillation between harsh denouncement and unexpected praise. Adorno was adamant that the fact of the Holocaust alone made self-complacent dismissals of Spengler's warnings highly dubious. Fueling Adorno's qualified appreciation of Spengler was his wish to prevent West Germany under Konrad Adenauer—when, as often noted, the country was prone to brush aside, rather than work through, the Nazi past—from repeating the mistakes of the Weimar Republic. Adorno did not, however, simply equate the young Bonn republic with its ill-fated predecessor. Speaking against Spengler in the 1950s were the economic miracle and general recovery of the social fabric.[11] Indeed, Adorno refused the label of Spenglerian, insisting in his famous 1959 criticism of

---

8. Adorno, "Spengler after the Decline," 53–54.
9. Adorno, "Spengler after the Decline," 55.
10. Theodor W. Adorno, "Was Spengler Right?", *Encounter* 26, no. 1 (1966): 25–29. For the German original, see "Wird Spengler recht behalten?", *Frankfurter Hefte* 10, no. 12 (1955): 841–46.
11. Adorno, "Was Spengler Right?", 25.

Adenauerian history politics that one should "not mistake [his] fragmentary and often rhapsodic remarks for Spenglerism."[12]

The hazard of erroneously identifying Adorno with Spengler, or making him a passive mouthpiece of the latter, is indeed something that should be avoided at all costs. Hence, before going into Adorno's examination of Spengler's notion of Caesarism, let us at the very outset bring forth all those aspects Adorno objected to, indeed despised, in *The Decline of the West*. This also serves as a brief recapitulation of the core themes of Spengler's bestseller, for what Adorno rejected were just those arrogant historical and metaphysical declarations that in 1918 had made Spengler's book a part of the popular imagination almost overnight.

Adorno denounced Spengler's "cultural morphology," or his comparative history of cultures, as utter nonsense. Spengler maintained that what he called the "great cultures"—Babylonian, Egyptian, Classical, Chinese, Indian, Mesoamerican, Arabian, and Western—each lasted around one thousand years and underwent a similar pattern of development. The pattern consisted of childhood, youth, maturity—brisk and vibrant stages animated by the "soul"—and lastly of old age—a weak, uncreative stage of the "intellect." This organic cycle knew no exceptions. This meant that the "Faustian" West—born in Central Europe c. 900 CE, blossoming in Gothic cathedrals, flourishing in Reformation, Renaissance, and Baroque, displaying autumn colors in the Enlightenment, and freezing into civilizational winter in the tedious isms of the nineteenth century—would by the turn of the millennium undergo a slow but unavoidable decline.[13] For Adorno, a staunch proponent of the secular teachings of Marx and Freud, Spengler's neo-Romantic concept of history was unfounded determinism that verged on astrological superstition at its worst.[14]

---

12. Theodor W. Adorno, "The Meaning of Working Through the Past," in *Critical Models: Interventions and Catchwords*, trans. Henry W. Pickford (New York: Columbia University Press, 2005), 99. On early German attempts to face the Nazi years, see Norbert Frei, *Adenauer's Germany and the Nazi Past: The Politics of Amnesty and Integration*, trans. Joel Golb (New York: Columbia University Press, 2002).

13. Oswald Spengler, *The Decline of the West*, vol. 1, *Form and Actuality*, trans. Charles Francis Atkinson (New York: Knopf, 1994), 3–50.

14. Adorno, "Spengler after the Decline," 68, 70.

Equally untenable was Spengler's related idea of collective cultural "souls"—those allegedly unique dispositions to reality that supposedly dictated every expression of a given culture from its politics and economy to its forms of art and thought. Among the most memorable illustrations of Spengler's thesis were his conceptions of the "Apollonian" culture of Greco-Roman antiquity and of the "Faustian" West. The former, Spengler claimed, had a unique sense for the here and now, for the limited and harmonious, as was shown by the serenity of its temples and statues. Characteristic of the latter, in contrast, was a restless striving for infinity and distance, evident in its medieval cathedrals, mathematical prowess, and technology.[15] Contrary to Spengler's view of cultures as such self-enclosed monads, however, Adorno emphasized their openness by pointing out that the "Faustian" technology of the West had become a part of the way of life globally, even in the allegedly most resistant countries such as Russia.[16]

Finally, despite Adorno's visible dislike of the *Logos* authors' depreciation of *The Decline of the West*, he shared their aversion to the book's "sweeping administrative gesture." Spengler frequently prided himself on standing above the Whiggish nineteenth-century view of European history as progress. But at the same time as Spengler escaped one grand narrative that did violence to the richness of historical reality, he succumbed to another. His doctrine of successive sequences of cultural development squeezed the air out of concrete history with its reduction of "all phenomena down to the formula 'that's all happened before.'" No matter how insufficient the *Logos* authors' positivist adoration of facts as a scientific approach was, Adorno avowed that it held its own when set against Spengler's "tyranny of categories." By the latter, Adorno lamented, Spengler wished "to calculate the unknown in history as far as possible. But it is precisely the unknown in mankind," Adorno underlined, "that cannot be calculated. History is not an equation, an analytic judgment."[17]

---

15. Spengler, *The Decline of the West*, vol. 1, 172–88.
16. Adorno, "Spengler after the Decline," 67–70; "Was Spengler Right?", 28.
17. Adorno, "Spengler after the Decline," 61, 66.

Spengler's conceptual tyranny, Adorno went on, was "closely related to the political tyranny about which Spengler is so enthusiastic."[18] In the Weimar Republic, Spengler campaigned in writing for an authoritarian political solution that would do away with the decadent republic. While Spengler turned a cold shoulder to Nazi invitations to join them, he gave voice to the conservative revolutionary movement and its antiliberal and anti-Marxist aspirations in works such as "Preußentum und Sozialismus" (*Prussianism and Socialism*, 1920), *Neubau des Deutschen Reiches* (New construction of the German Reich, 1924), and *Jahre der Entscheidung* (*The Hour of Decision*, 1933). Like many other radical conservatives in the interwar period, for Spengler the promised land lay not in the rural past of the ancien régime but in the steel-hard future of industrial civilization. As he had already stated in *The Decline of the West*, "I can only hope that men of the new generation may be moved by this book to devote themselves to technics instead of lyrics, the sea instead of the paintbrush, and politics instead of epistemology. Better they could not do."[19] Spengler's future was a rather barren territory with not much to offer. And how could it if Spengler was correct and the Faustian "machine culture" designated the unpreventable old age of Western civilization? Nevertheless, Spengler claimed to see something dignified in all this. It resided in resolutely following the dictates of one's own culture, its soul. "The honorable end is the one thing that can *not* be taken from man."[20] Adorno had nothing but contempt for Spengler's proto-fascist admiration of strong political authority and sacrifice of individual liberties. It is not an overstatement to say that he found the entire idea of cultural morphology a symptom of the interwar zeitgeist characterized by cynical power politics, fatalistic celebration of the will to power, and anti-Enlightenment reaction. "Spengler and his like,"

---

18. Adorno, "Spengler after the Decline," 61.
19. Spengler, *The Decline of the West*, vol. 1, 41. On Spengler's political writings, see Hughes, *Oswald Spengler*, chap. 7.
20. Oswald Spengler, *Man and Technics: A Contribution to a Philosophy of Life*, trans. Charles Francis Atkinson (London: Allen & Unwin, 1932), 104; see also 73, 90, 103.

Adorno concluded, "are not so much prophets of the course the *Weltgeist* will take as its diligent promoters."[21]

Far from identification, then, we have in Adorno's ambivalent remarks on Spengler another instance of his effort, as he stated a year later in *Minima Moralia*, to put "all the reactionary arguments against Western culture in the service of progressive enlightenment."[22] As in the case of Ludwig Klages, very little scholarly attention has been paid to Adorno's "immanent" critique of Spengler, his dialectical attempt to repurpose Spengler's notion of Caesarism for emancipatory ends. In this chapter, I seek to shed light on this attempt and trace it in Adorno's best-known works, *The Authoritarian Personality* (1950) and *Dialectic of Enlightenment* (1947).

I will begin with an exploration of Adorno's post–World War II attraction to Spengler's idea of Caesarism, a topic that George Friedman is the only one to have discussed in any detail.[23] Adorno, I will argue, held Spengler's idea, despite the baggage it carried from past cyclical theories, to be a master class in democracy's self-destruction. Adorno's wish to give Spengler's insights their due, however, predates the first years of West Germany by almost a decade. The original, largely overlooked, version of Adorno's Spengler essay dates from his New York years in 1938–1941, when he took notice of unexpected affinities between Spengler's analysis of Caesarism and the theory of "state capitalism" advanced by the Frankfurt School economist Friedrich Pollock. I will turn to this original version of Adorno's essay in the second section, in which I examine Spengler's and Pollock's parallel remarks on modern history coming to a perplexing standstill. After this, I move on to *The Authoritarian Personality* and *Dialectic of Enlightenment* and argue that one can detect traces of Adorno's

---

21. Adorno, "Spengler after the Decline," 66.
22. Theodor W. Adorno, *Minima Moralia: Reflections from Damaged Life*, trans. E. F. N. Jephcott (London: Verso, 2000), 192.
23. George Friedman, *The Political Philosophy of the Frankfurt School* (Ithaca, NY: Cornell University Press, 1981), 79–86.

repurposing of Spengler in his own later critiques of authoritarianism and culture industry.

Decline of the Weimar Republic

The key term of the second volume (1922) of Spengler's *Decline of the West*, "Caesarism," was coined in mid-nineteenth-century France, when the defeats of the revolutions of 1789 and 1848 were interpreted as analogous to the collapse of the Roman Republic by Julius Caesar. Together with other central concepts of nineteenth-century political thought, "Bonapartism" and "Napoleonism," Caesarism conveyed the perplexity contemporaries faced with a new type of authoritarian rule, which owed its existence to the revolutions yet sought to keep modern mass democracy in check with means more repressive than anything seen during the ancien régime. Were the two Napoleonic regimes, it was asked, idiosyncrasies of French national history, as the terms Bonapartism and Napoleonism implied? Or did they exemplify a more universal phenomenon, either democracy's generic tendency to succumb to despotism or deep-seated structural problems of modern industrial society? In both cases, Caesarism was a suitable term because it could either symbolize the immutable sequence of types of government or remind one of the longevity of Rome's Imperial Period. To what extent, it was also wondered, did the Napoleons attest to the permanent immaturity of the "masses" and the need for strong leaders capable of restoring social order in the wake of revolutionary chaos?[24]

The terms Napoleonism, Bonapartism, and Caesarism, and the worries they expressed, resurfaced in the 1920s as political commentators such as Carl Schmitt and Antonio Gramsci reworked them to come to grips with bolshevism in Russia and fascism in Europe. Used widely as interpretive tools until the end of World War II, in

---

24. On the roots of the term "Caesarism" in nineteenth-century European political thought, see Markus J. Prutsch, *Caesarism in the Post-Revolutionary Age: Crisis, Populace and Leadership* (London: Bloomsbury, 2020).

the 1950s these terms fell out of favor as anachronistic and were replaced by "totalitarianism," which seemed to better capture the unprecedented brutality of national socialism and Stalinism.[25]

Spengler inherited from this discourse on Caesarism and Napoleonism its suspicion of democracy and the "masses" as well as its alarmist tone. In his metaphysical usage, however, these terms lost their historical specificity, redescribed as they were as "morphological" substages of civilization in his culture-civilization scheme. In the West, Spengler argued, the end of vibrant culture and the advent of depraved civilization happened with "Napoleonism," an era ruled by money, abstract intellect, and democracy. With World War I, this development reached its second stage in "the *transition from Napoleonism to Caesarism*," or to "the age of gigantic conflicts," in which power-seeking individuals surrendered the market and democratic values to their egoistic goals.[26] In Spengler's hands, as Markus J. Prutsch notes, the concept of Caesarism thus lost much of its "analytical value" and became "one of the elements of his work that found least eager reception." Nevertheless, he adds, as Spengler's reflections on Germany and Europe in the aftermath of the Great War demonstrate, he had his "finger on the pulse of the time."[27]

Adorno certainly thought so in his essay "Spengler after the Decline." He did not, however, discuss the historical background or contemporary uses of the term Caesarism. Indeed, it seems that Adorno had far less interest in the term itself than in those political, psychological, and cultural phenomena of the 1920s that Spengler examined under it.

Of Spengler's observations on postwar Europe, Adorno drew attention first to his claim that democracy had been "well on the decline" since World War I. Considering the collapse of four empires in 1918 and the establishment of numerous new republics from the

---

25. On interwar discourse on Caesarism, see Peter Baehr, *Caesarism, Charisma and Fate: Historical Sources and Modern Resonances in the Work of Max Weber* (London: Routledge, 2008).
26. Oswald Spengler, *The Decline of the* West, vol. 2, *Perspectives of World-History*, trans. Charles Francis Atkinson (New York: Knopf, 1994), 404–7, 416, 505–6.
27. Prutsch, *Caesarism in the Post-Revolutionary Age*, 190.

Baltic to Iberia, this view invites skepticism. Spengler highlighted, however, the profound transformation the parliamentary system had undergone in the twentieth century. Modern political parties, employing thousands of people, were more interested in guarding the special interests of their members than in debating over the common good in an open dialogue. They had become bureaucratic machines far removed from the nineteenth-century ideal of a deliberative public sphere. This structural problem of the European party system, what Spengler called the "Caesarism of the organizations," was reflected in the 1919 Weimar Constitution, which left itself vulnerable to undemocratic forces. Alluding to the infamous Article 48, which allowed the Reich president to govern by emergency decree without consent of the parliament—and which Hitler would use in the spring of 1933 to crush the republic—Spengler claimed that a major problem in the constitution is "visible already. A few quite small alterations and it confers unrestricted power upon individuals."[28]

Adorno found Spengler's reflections on the bureaucratization of parties "radically confirmed in National Socialism—parties became followings." Spengler echoed cyclical political theorists of the past such as Niccolò Machiavelli and the Stoics. With his unsparing scrutiny of party logic, however, Spengler was superior to his predecessors in that he had actually, as Adorno wrote, "experienced the dialectic of history, though he never names it." In other words, while Spengler never sympathized with democracy, he saw "the mechanisms which allow the party system to turn into dictatorship."[29]

Facilitating the demise of the parliamentary system and the subsequent rise of political authoritarianism were psychological changes in the populace. In the nineteenth century, Spengler noted, people had eagerly fought for "the great truths of Democracy" and "rights without which life seemed not worth the living." In the present, however, when these rights have become reality, "the grandchildren cannot be moved, even by punishment, to make use of them." Behind political apathy Spengler found atomization of urban metropolises. "The splendid mass-cities," he remarked, "harbour lamentable poverty and

---

28. Spengler, *The Decline of the West*, vol. 2, 452, 457n2.
29. Adorno, "Spengler after the Decline," 59.

degraded habits, and the attics and mansards, the cellars and back courts are breeding a new type of raw man."[30]

In Adorno's estimation, Spengler had grasped the linkage "between atomization and the regressive type of man which revealed itself fully only with the onslaught of totalitarianism." By this regressive type, Adorno referred to people who "experience themselves solely as objects of opaque processes and, torn between sudden shock and sudden forgetfulness, are no longer capable of a sense of temporal continuity."[31]

Although Spengler was poorly informed of the economic causes behind the emergence of this urban "second nomad," Adorno thought that he was acutely aware of the role played in its emergence by the new "centralized media of public communication."[32] Spengler lamented the replacement by newspapers of "the book-world, with its profusion of standpoints that compelled thought to select and criticize." Today, he bewailed, "the people reads the *one* paper, 'its' paper, which forces itself through the front doors by millions daily" and "spellbinds the intellect from morning to night." Depicting what he dubbed the "Caesars of the world-press," Spengler claimed that "no tamer has his animals more under his power. Unleash the people as reader-mass and it will storm through the streets and hurl itself upon the target indicated, terrifying and breaking windows."[33]

With a reference to the so-called Night of the Broken Glass (*Kristallnacht*), antisemitic pogrom in Germany in October 1938, Adorno claimed that "Spengler predicted Goebbels." What Spengler discerned in "the modest press magnates" of the World War I era found "their mature form in the techniques of manipulated pogroms and 'spontaneous' popular demonstrations."[34] Further illuminating the decay of critical thinking was Spengler's farsighted inspection of modern mass culture. Urban metropolitans had little understanding of "genuine play" or "pleasure," whereas sports, gambling, and other

---

30. Spengler, *The Decline of the West*, vol. 2, 432, 102.
31. Adorno, "Spengler after the Decline," 55.
32. Adorno, "Spengler after the Decline," 56.
33. Spengler, *The Decline of the West*, vol. 2, 461–62.
34. Adorno, "Spengler after the Decline," 57.

"conscious and practiced fooling" functioned as much-needed distractions from exhausting working life.[35] Adorno credited Spengler with predicting "the static state of culture," which "compels the incessant and deadly repetition of what has already been accepted," while simultaneously "standardized art for the masses, with its petrified formulas, excludes history."[36]

"To Adorno," George Friedman argues, "the catalogue of Spengler's insights was astounding."[37] One would be hard-pressed to dispute this claim. Even a preliminary comparison (to be followed by more detailed ones later) shows that Spengler's remarks on Caesarism find their parallels in Adorno's own works. In *Dialectic of Enlightenment*, Adorno, together with Max Horkheimer, sought to capture the constellation of economic, political, and cultural forces that had molded the public sphere, the greatest achievement of bourgeois revolutions, into a commodified "culture industry," or "enlightenment as mass deception."[38] Again, in *The Authoritarian Personality*, Adorno, together with his coauthors, argued for the existence in the United States of an authoritarian potential that in less favorable societal conditions could be set alight by its homegrown fascist demagogues.[39] Finally, decay of democratic spirit was not an alien concern for Adorno, who held "the growing concentration of the economy, the executive and the bureaucracy" as a major obstacle to individual autonomy. Because of these structural problems, even formally democratic institutions of the post–1945 period struggled to keep alive an inner desire for freedom, threatened by political indifference and the expanding allures of consumerism.[40]

Adorno's guarded fascination with Spengler's observations on Caesarism becomes understandable when we look at the historical

---

35. Spengler, *The Decline of the West*, vol. 2, 103.
36. Adorno, "Spengler after the Decline," 58.
37. Friedman, *The Political Philosophy of the Frankfurt School*, 79.
38. Max Horkheimer and Theodor W. Adorno, *Dialectic of Enlightenment: Philosophical Fragments*, trans. Edmund Jephcott (Stanford, CA: Stanford University Press, 2002), 94–136.
39. Theodor W. Adorno et al., *The Authoritarian Personality* (London: Verso, 2019).
40. Theodor W. Adorno, *History and Freedom: Lectures 1964–1965*, ed. Rolf Tiedemann, trans. Rodney Livingstone (Cambridge: Polity Press, 2008), 5–7.

situation in Germany at the time of his return (after considerable hesitation) in 1949.[41] Foremost on Adorno's mind was persuading his German compatriots to adopt a more critical attitude toward the Nazi past. When Adorno returned to Frankfurt after fifteen years of exile in England and United States, an honest reckoning with the Third Reich had hardly begun. In 1945–1946, leading Nazi figures responsible for the extermination of the Jews were prosecuted in the Nuremberg trials by the International Military Tribunal. The initiative, however, came from the Allies, whereas Germany's own efforts at "denazification," at bringing various kinds of "fellow travelers" to justice, was suspended soon after its initiation during the first years of the Federal Republic of Germany. As a result, the Nazi past and the question of collective responsibility were swept under the rug and ordinary Germans acquitted from any complicity in the atrocities of Hitler's regime. As Adorno observed in his Spengler essay, "The mention of Auschwitz already provokes bored resentment. Nobody is concerned with the past anymore."[42] Behind this collective amnesia were seismic shifts in international politics, as the antifascism of the postwar years gave way to the anticommunism of the 1950s and the nascent Cold War.[43]

This was the political and cultural climate that Adorno encountered in West Germany upon his return. In the same year that "Spengler after the Decline" appeared, the Institute for Social Research, which had just been reestablished in Frankfurt am Main, conducted an empirical study using methods applied in its major 1940s project in the United States, "Studies in Prejudice." The purpose of the new study, called the *Gruppenexperiment*, was "to assess the attitudes of young Germans to the Nazi dictatorship and the occupation, to guilt and democracy."[44] The conclusion of the study was disheartening. A "non-public opinion" prevailed in Germany, the

---

41. On Adorno's return, see Detlev Claussen, *Theodor W. Adorno: One Last Genius*, trans. Rodney Livingstone (Cambridge, MA: Harvard University Press, 2008), chap. 6.
42. Adorno, "Spengler after the Decline," 58.
43. Frei, *Adenauer's Germany and the Nazi Past*.
44. Volker Weiß, Afterword to Theodor W. Adorno, *Aspects of the New Right-Wing Extremism*, trans. Wieland Hoban (Cambridge: Polity Press, 2020), 47.

authors reported, the content of which "can deviate very considerably from the content of the public opinion, but whose formulations circulate alongside those of the public opinion like monetary units of a second currency."[45] As Volker Weiß remarks, the official "convention of civilizatory-democratic chastening was scarcely capable of keeping the latency of fascist elements under control. Any weakness in the higher authority and the appropriate stimuli were enough to let it come rapidly to the surface again." Furthermore, the study indicated that Nazism did not need "any party to survive, and that a party can quickly be formed by falling back on such 'nonpublic' resentments."[46]

Adorno's opinion at the time was that the young Bonn republic, Germany's second experiment in democracy, did not face any imminent threat of collapsing as Weimar did. There was no denying that many things had gotten better. But major problems remained, most notably the concentration of societal power and the Germans' inability and unwillingness to scrutinize the path that had led to Hitler. As Adorno famously expressed his concerns, echoing the *Gruppenexperiment*, "the survival of National Socialism *within* democracy" was a more urgent threat than "the survival of fascist tendencies *against* democracy" (i.e., marginal neo-Nazi organizations).[47] The essay "Spengler after the Decline" counts among the first of Adorno's numerous public interventions in the postwar era to dismantle this threat, the most famous being the lectures "The Meaning of Working Through the Past" (1959) and "Education after Auschwitz" (1966) as well as the only recently published "Aspects of the New Right-Wing Extremism" (1967).[48]

---

45. Friedrich Pollock, ed. *Frankfurter Beiträge zur Soziologie*, vol. 2, *Gruppenexperiment: Ein Studienbericht* (Frankfurt: Campus, 1955), xi. Translation from Weiß, Afterword, 47–48.

46. Weiß, Afterword, 48.

47. Adorno, "The Meaning of Working Through the Past," 90. Emphasis in the original. See also Adorno, "Was Spengler Right?", 26.

48. Adorno, "The Meaning of Working Through the Past," 89–103, and "Education after Auschwitz," 191–204, in *Critical Models: Interventions and Catchwords*, trans. Henry W. Pickford (New York: Columbia University Press, 2005). See also Adorno, *Aspects of the New Right-Wing Extremism*, trans. Wieland Hoban (Cambridge: Polity Press, 2020).

Adorno's appreciation of Spengler's work was, then, understandable after the horrors of total war and the Holocaust. Spengler was helpful, first, as a symptom of the times. In Spengler's "gigantic and destructive soothsaying," Adorno argued, "the petty bourgeois celebrates his intellectual triumph," while the theory of cultural morphology "serves the same purpose for Spengler as graphology did for Klages": both contribute to forsaking the Enlightenment's goal of "conscious self-determination."[49] Yet notwithstanding Spengler's vitalist fatalism, economic dilettantism, and chilling indifference to suffering—that is, all the countless aspects that made his thought a sign of the interwar zeitgeist poisoned by right-wing *Zivilisationskritik*—Adorno thought that *The Decline of the West* had touched on something essential in an age rushing to become one of "extremes," of Europe turning into a "dark continent."[50]

Indeed, Spengler's work was valuable not merely as an informative symptom of the age but also because of its (like Klages's) genuine insights. By waiving Spengler off as a vulgar charlatan, Adorno maintained, his Weimar-era adversaries, from liberals to Marxists, had missed the forest for the trees. By no means did Adorno mean that Spengler would have understood the real socio-economic roots of the discontents of the times, or properly theorized their interconnections. Nevertheless, Adorno saw important kernels of truth in Spengler's observations on Caesarism. No matter how problematic, they forced one to think, as Isaiah Berlin once described his own encounters with unflinching opponents of the Enlightenment (such as Joseph de Maistre).[51] Adorno's ambiguous stance toward Spengler is well captured in the following passage:

> Spengler is one of the theoreticians of extreme reaction whose critique of liberalism proved itself superior in many respects to the progressive one. It would be worthwhile to investigate the reasons for this. It is

---

49. Adorno, "Spengler after the Decline," 66.
50. See Eric Hobsbawm, *The Age of Extremes: The Short Twentieth Century, 1914–1991* (London: Abacus, 1994); Mark Mazower, *Dark Continent: Europe's Twentieth Century* (New York: Penguin, 1998).
51. Isaiah Berlin, "Isaiah Berlin: In Conversation with Steven Lukes," *Salmagundi* 120 (Fall 1998): 90.

the differences in the relationship to ideology which are decisive. To the adherents of dialectical materialism liberal ideology seemed for the most part a false promise. Their spokesmen questioned not the ideas of humanity, freedom, and justice but rather the claim of bourgeois society to have realized those ideas. Ideologies were appearances for them, but the appearance of truth nevertheless. As a result, if not the existent itself at least its "objective tendencies" were endowed with a conciliatory gloss. Talk of the increase of antagonisms and the admission of a real possibility of a regression to barbarism were not taken seriously enough for anyone to recognize ideologies as something worse than apologetic disguises, as the objective absurdity that aids the society of liberal competition to turn into a system of direct oppression.[52]

In the wake of World War I, Spengler had paid attention to the early marks of a path that would lead to this new "system of direct oppression." This was possible, Adorno reasoned, because Spengler resolutely rejected the optimistic conception of history as progress, a conception cherished by those who thought history was on its way toward something like a "realm of freedom." Liberals in Weimar Germany believed in the victory of the parliamentary system. Marxists thought that capitalism would give way to socialism out of a historical necessity. Neither camp, not even the Marxist side with its emphasis on capitalism's crisis tendencies, was truly alert to the possibility that a new kind of barbarism, fascism or Nazism, was looming on the horizon. As much as Adorno cherished the enlightened ideals of liberals and Marxists, he applauded Spengler for offering lessons on why the interwar world had been moving away from rather than toward these ideals. "Spengler's harshness with his contemporaries," Adorno concluded, "might almost have constituted a shock which might have helped to save them."[53]

---

52. Adorno, "Spengler after the Decline," 65.
53. Adorno, "Was Spengler Right?", 29. At other moments, Adorno gave voice to the suspicion raised in the 1950s by theorists of totalitarianism that the key terms of nineteenth-century political theory, such as Caesarism, were helplessly outdated: "Nowhere in the Spenglerian schema," Adorno wrote in 1955, "is there the conception of a highly-organized and thoroughly centralized society as we have come to observe it under totalitarianism. It is something new in history. Never have men been so ruthlessly subjected to political power. In relation to this the Spenglerian prophecies, dark and realistic as they sometimes appear, have something naive and good-natured about them, something of the raised forefinger of a German school-teacher

How much novelty did Adorno accord to Spengler's notion of Caesarism and his reflections on democracy and liberalism? This question arises from the passage just quoted, as well as from the curious fact that, as already mentioned, nowhere in his essay does Adorno discuss the historical nineteenth-century origins of the concept of Caesarism or debates over it in the 1920s. Adorno does, however, mention Spengler's possible indebtedness to two notable early twentieth-century observers of modern politics. Spengler's description of the degeneration of liberal democracy, Adorno surmised, was "presumably inspired" by Robert Michels's *Political Parties: A Sociological Study of the Oligarchical Tendencies of Modern Democracy* (1911). According to Michels's thesis of the "iron law of oligarchy," all political parties, whether on the right or on the left, tended to shun their democratic roots and turn into bureaucratic machines. Regarding Spengler's depiction of the modern urban metropolis and its atomized inhabitants, Adorno remarked that "Werner Sombart developed very similar thoughts in his pamphlet" *Why Is There No Socialism in the United States?* (1906), which maintained that the reason for the nonexistence of a successful US labor party was to be found in the country's advanced capitalist character.[54] We will return to the question of Adorno's estimation of Spengler's originality in the next section, where we examine the original 1941 version of his essay.

Though I draw attention to Adorno's praises of Spengler's perspicacity and recognize the parallels between their positions, we should not forget that Adorno's reception of Spengler was ultimately that of a critical Marxist. Notwithstanding Adorno's misgivings about working-class parties in the interwar era (and later), he always underscored, in striking contrast to Spengler, the central role of capitalism

---

telling his class, '*Schon die alten Römer . . .*' (even in the days of ancient Rome . . .)." Ibid., 26.

54. Adorno, "Spengler after the Decline," 55, 59. See also Adorno, "Was Spengler Right?", 26. Robert Michels, *Political Parties: A Sociological Study of the Oligarchical Tendencies of Modern Democracy*, trans. Eden Paul and Cedar Paul (New York: The Free Press, 1962); Werner Sombart, *Why Is There No Socialism in the United States?* trans. Patricia M. Hocking and C. T. Husbands (London: Macmillan, 1976).

in the troubles of modern liberal democracy. As we saw earlier, Adorno maintained that as a critic of democracy Spengler was better than his cyclical predecessors (like Machiavelli) in that he had recognized "the dialectic of history"—that is, the inner logic by which political parties abandon their democratic features and endanger the parliamentary system. And yet Spengler's morphological approach also suffered from a fateful vagueness. Adorno's allegiance to Marxist social criticism made him allergic to Spengler's quasi-ontological notion of democracy's purportedly inborn failings. In place of such false abstractions, Adorno, as a Marxist, demanded concrete examination of historical eras in their uniqueness. (This was the case even as he, as seen in Chapter 1, was more inclined to see greater continuities between ancient and modern phases of Western history than Max Horkheimer, at least until the 1940s.[55])

Neither should our concentration on Adorno's interest in Spengler make us neglect his profound debts to Freud. Adorno's familiarization with psychoanalysis occurred in the late 1920s and early 1930s when he witnessed the birth of the Freudian-Marxist paradigm of the Institute for Social Research under the auspices of Horkheimer and Erich Fromm.[56] Indeed, there is little doubt that it was to a considerable extent Freud's suspicion of the prospects of peaceful coexistence—voiced in such postwar works as *Massenpsychologie und Ich-Analyse* (*Group Psychology and the Analysis of the Ego*, 1922) and *Das Unbehagen in der Kultur* (*Civilization and Its Discontents*, 1930)—that nourished Adorno's sensitivity to the darker elements of modernity and his skepticism toward Marxist optimism.

To summarize Adorno's opinion of Spengler in 1950, he would have considered it a disgrace that there ever was a serious debate whether history consisted in Spengler's self-enclosed, plant-like

---

55. On this difference between Adorno and Horkheimer, see John Abromeit, *Max Horkheimer and the Foundations of the Frankfurt School* (Cambridge: Cambridge University Press, 2011), 382–93.

56. Susan Buck-Morss, *The Origin of Negative Dialectics: Theodor W. Adorno, Walter Benjamin, and the Frankfurt Institute* (New York: The Free Press, 1977), 179. For more on Adorno's reception of psychoanalysis, see Wolfgang Bock, *Dialektische Psychologie. Adornos Rezeption der Psychoanalyse* (Wiesbaden, Germany: Springer, 2018).

cultures. Approvingly quoting James T. Shotwell's early rebuttal of *The Decline of the West,* Adorno emphasized that historical civilizations "have been inherently lacking in equilibrium" not because of some morphological necessities but "because they have built upon the injustice of exploitation." No grounds existed for the claim "that modern civilization must inevitably repeat this cataclysmic rhythm."[57] In other words, there were far more plausible explanations than Spengler's neo-Romantic speculations both for the demise of the classical Greco-Roman world and for the problems of modern Europe. Yet, at the same time, Adorno wished to give Spengler's suspicion of historical progress its due. Writing in the newly founded West Germany, Adorno wanted to avoid the mistakes of the progressives of the Weimar era, whose well-meaning celebrations of reason, culture, and justice had not been enough to counter societal barbarism. "Spengler could laugh in the face of such blissful confidence," Adorno stressed. "Rather, it is the barbaric element in culture itself which must be recognized."[58]

Adorno's qualified appreciation of Spengler was not, however, a product of the postwar years. The original version of his Spengler essay was composed as early as 1941, a fact often overlooked in previous commentaries. The initial stimulus to his essay did not come from postwar worries over Germany's reconstruction but from his time in New York, when the Frankfurt School strove to comprehend capitalism's recent authoritarian turn.

Rethinking Spengler in New York

In February 1938, Adorno left Oxford and joined the Institute for Social Research in New York, where it had relocated from Frankfurt in 1934. During his years in New York in 1938–1941, Adorno lectured on Spengler at least twice at Columbia University.[59] Based

---

57. Adorno, "Spengler after the Decline," 71; James T. Shotwell, "Spengler," in *The Faith of an Historian and Other Essays* (New York: Walker, 1964), 228–29.

58. Adorno, "Spengler after the Decline," 71.

59. In an editorial note, Rolf Tiedemann relates that Adorno gave the first of these lectures in 1938; see *Gesammelte Schriften, Bd. 10.2: Kulturkritik und Gesell-*

on these lectures, an essay entitled "Spengler Today" appeared in 1941 in the last volume of the institute's journal, *Zeitschrift für Soziaforschung* (which from 1938 on bore the English title *Studies in Philosophy and Social Science*).

Commenting on an early draft of Adorno's essay, Horkheimer demanded that it "*naturally* has to be in the next issue, it fits perfectly to the theme."[60] The theme was "state capitalism," introduced by Friedrich Pollock, the economy expert of Horkheimer's circle. Pollock maintained that in the wake of the 1929 stock market crash capitalism had undergone a profound transformation. Nazi Germany, the Soviet Union, and the New Deal USA had all surrendered economic competition to state administration, thereby eliminating the market as the dynamic regulator of social relationships. This transformation, Pollock argued, was a culmination of a longer historical shift, in which the nineteenth-century "liberal capitalist" competition of private entrepreneurs gave way at the turn of the century to "monopoly capitalism" of large corporations, conglomerates, and joint-stock companies. This centralization reached its zenith in the fusion of economic and political power in the "state capitalism" of the 1930s.[61]

The somewhat ironic outcome of Pollock's thesis was that an economist surrendered economy as an independent realm to politics. A lot was at stake, especially concerning the German situation. Pollock's thesis meant the awkward realization that, contrary to what more orthodox Marxists believed, Nazi Germany was not

---

schaft, ed. Rolf Tiedemann (Frankfurt: Suhrkamp, 1977), 839. The second lecture took place on May 2, 1941; Adorno to Horkheimer, May 3, 1941, in *Briefe und Briefwechsel—Bd. 4: Theodor W. Adorno—Max Horkheimer, Briefwechsel 1927–1969, Bd. II: 1938–1944*, ed. Christoph Gödde and Henri Lonitz (Frankfurt: Suhrkamp, 2004), 109. See also Adorno to Maria and Oscar Wiesengrund, March 28, 1944, in *Briefe und Briefwechsel—Bd. 5: Briefe an die Eltern, 1939–1951*, ed. Christoph Gödde and Henri Lonitz (Frankfurt: Suhrkamp, 2003), 253–54.

60. Horkheimer to Adorno, June 23, 1941, in *Briefwechsel, Bd. II: 1938–1944*, 155.

61. Pollock had studied this latest transformation of capitalism throughout the 1930s. His best-known takes on the topic, however, are two articles from 1941: "State Capitalism: Its Possibilities and Limitations," *Studies in Philosophy and Social Science* 9, no. 2 (1941): 200–225; "Is National Socialism a New Order?", *Studies in Philosophy and Social Science* 9, no. 3 (1941): 440–55.

threatened from within by any insurmountable economic antagonism. To be sure, economic inequalities and systemic problems had in no way been overcome. Yet the "authoritarian state"—the Nazi party, bureaucracy, military, and big industry—could deal with them in various ways, from investments to open terror. And as great as the differences between European totalitarianisms and the democratic United States were, individual initiative in the latter too mattered less and less under the pressure of systemic forces. In a well-known debate at the institute, Horkheimer and Adorno sided with Pollock, while others, such as Franz L. Neumann, the author of *Behemoth: The Structure and Practice of National Socialism* (1942), one of the first widely read analyses of the Nazi regime, and Otto Kirchheimer, another defender of a more differentiated image of Nazi Germany, did not.[62]

As Hubertus Buchstein notes, both Neumann and Kirchheimer, always peripheral figures in Horkheimer's circle, doubted the claim that dominant power groups in Germany formed a unified clique with a coherent set of objectives (or that one could simply lump Nazi Germany, the Soviet Union, and the United States under one framework). Neumann and Kirchheimer proposed instead that these groups formed fierce rivalries and fought one another in order to achieve dominance over the others. The political realm, Kirchheimer argued in "Changes in the Structure of Political Compromise" (1941), although seriously curtailed in a totalitarian country, was still an arena of power struggles whose results were anything but forgone conclusions. And Neumann insisted that even the capitalist market, all but eliminated in Pollock's theory, had not lost all of its previous dynamism. What Pollock, Horkheimer, and Adorno saw as an all-powerful Leviathan with no intrinsic contradictions, Neumann and Kirchheimer judged as a fragile arrangement dependent on more and more aggressive and imperialistic foreign policy. Should

---

62. On Pollock's thesis, see Manfred Gangl, "The Controversy over Friedrich Pollock's State Capitalism," *History of the Human Sciences* 29, no. 2 (2016): 23–41; Martin Jay, *The Dialectical Imagination: A History of the Frankfurt School and the Institute of Social Research, 1923–1950* (Boston, MA: Little, Brown and Co., 1973), 143–66; Rolf Wiggershaus, *The Frankfurt School: Its History, Theories, and Political Significance*, trans. Michael Robertson (Cambridge: Polity Press, 1994), 280–91.

Germany be forced on the defensive in the world war, they thought, political instability would very likely ensue.[63]

The diagnosis of state capitalism, in the form Adorno and Horkheimer adopted and further developed it, is often seen as influenced by Max Weber's portrait of "the apparently ever-moving but, in reality, static iron cage of modernity," in which the calculative rationality of capitalism suffocates the different value spheres of politics, law, science, and art.[64] The resemblance between Weber's diagnosis and the Frankfurt School's theory of state capitalism—in which "the enthronement of the means as the end," as Adorno and Horkheimer wrote a few years later, had come to approximate "overt madness"—is indeed striking.[65] There are, however, grounds to bring Spengler into the picture as well. Adorno said in 1964 that Weber was preoccupied with the same phenomenon as Spengler with his "perspectives on solidification in Caesarist late times." Both Weber and Spengler offered trenchant analyses of post–World War I Europe. Adorno applauded Weber for having predicted the victory of bureaucracy over democracy in Soviet Russia and elsewhere praised Spengler's observations on ominous tendencies at work behind the sunny republican facade of Weimar Germany.[66]

In Adorno's "Spengler Today" (1941), we find an interesting observation (omitted from the 1950 version) on the theories of Spengler and Pollock. Characteristic of the era of Caesarism, Adorno noted, was its ahistorical character "in a most sinister sense." Referencing Pollock's article "State Capitalism: Its Possibilities and

---

63. Hubertus Buchstein, "Otto Kirchheimer and the Frankfurt School: Failed Collaborations in the Search for a Critical Theory of Politics," *New German Critique* 47, no. 2 (2020): 94–95, 101.

64. Jay M. Bernstein, "Negative Dialectic as Fate: Adorno and Hegel," in *The Cambridge Companion to Adorno*, ed. Tom Huhn (Cambridge: Cambridge University Press, 2004), 21. See also Jürgen Habermas, *The Theory of Communicative Action*, vol. 1, *Reason and the Rationalization of Society*, trans. Thomas McCarthy (Boston, MA: Beacon Press, 1984), 366–99; Dana Villa, "Weber and The Frankfurt School," in *The Routledge Companion to the Frankfurt School*, ed. Peter E. Gordon et al. (New York: Routledge, 2019), 266–68.

65. Horkheimer and Adorno, *Dialectic of Enlightenment*, 43.

66. Theodor W. Adorno, *Nachgelassene Schriften. Abteilung 4: Vorlesungen, Bd. 12: Philosophische Elemente einer Theorie der Gesellschaft*, ed. Tobias ten Brink and Marc Phillip Nogueira (Frankfurt: Suhrkamp, 2008), 18–22.

Limitations" (1941), he continued that Spengler's "paradoxical prognosis is clearly paralleled by the tendency of [the] present economy to eliminate the market and the dynamics of competition" and replace them with "static conditions" in which "the life of those who do the work is maintained planfully from above."[67] In Adorno's account, both Pollock and Spengler registered the perplexing fact that history had in fact vanished. Certainly, there was no shortage of world-historical events in the early twentieth century. But the striking feature of this era was that individuals did not make history. They were increasingly not subjects of their fate, but objects of supra-individual forces. Contrary to the Enlightenment's dream of self-determination, individuals were not in charge of societal development, but more like cogs in the machine. This development reached its zenith under the totalitarian regimes of the 1930s, but its seeds had been sown earlier. Whereas Pollock's analysis of the replacement of private entrepreneurs by monopolies and state administration captured the economic dimension of this centralization of power, Spengler had already observed, under the title of Caesarism, the psychological, cultural, and political dimensions of this same tendency in the early 1920s.

Adorno saw, then, similarities between Pollock's Marxist and Spengler's radical conservative *Zeitdiagnosen*, or diagnoses of the times. While I think it is beyond question that he found Pollock's economic thesis ultimately weightier than Spengler's considerations, this is a proper moment to see what the empirical evidence says about the timeline of Adorno's interest in Spengler.

When did Adorno learn of Spengler's work? Considering Spengler's Europe-wide, even global, fame after 1918, it could indeed be, as Christian Thies conjectures, that in his youth Adorno read *The Decline of the West* "already before breakfast."[68] However, if we follow Adorno's path of thinking up to his arrival in New York, it

---

67. Theodor W. Adorno, "Spengler Today," *Studies in Philosophy and Social Science* 9, no. 2 (1941), 310.
68. Christian Thies, *Die Krise des Individuums: Zur Kritik der Moderne bei Adorno und Gehlen* (Reinbek, Germany: Rowohlt, 1997), 32. Giving credence to Thies's conjecture is the fact that Adorno's own copies of the two volumes of Spengler's book are from 1920 and 1922. See the catalogue of Adorno's personal library

seems doubtful that Spengler's ruminations on Caesarism would have left a notable imprint on his intellectual development before 1938. With the exception of Adorno's review of Spengler's short booklet *Der Mensch und die Technik* (*Man and Technics*, 1931)[69]—which shall figure prominently in chapter 3 where we analyze the impetus Spengler's anthropological doctrines gave to *Dialectic of Enlightenment*—Adorno's rare Weimar-era remarks on Spengler's ideas suggest that he saw in them a mere mystification of economic injustices.[70]

Of course, the following hypothetical scenario is possible. Adorno conceded in *Minima Moralia* that while he initially had not expected Hitler's regime to last long (the average length of Weimar governments was eight months) already in the 1920s he had dark premonitions of things to come. "The outbreak of the Third Reich did, it is true, surprise my political judgment, but not my unconscious fear," he noted.[71] We could speculate that *The Decline of the West* was one source (along with terrible experiences of being bullied at school by "five patriots," early harbingers of "the German awakening") behind Adorno's unease amid the seemingly happy "Golden Twenties," and that Pollock's "state capitalism" thesis later offered Adorno a more compelling economic explanation for his fears. But this speculation is just that. It seems more plausible that Spengler, or at least his theory of Caesarism, only began to preoccupy Adorno in New York in the late 1930s.

Indeed, Adorno later described "Spengler Today" as an outgrowth of debates in New York with other émigré intellectuals, among them the theologian Paul Tillich (Adorno's ex-supervisor and colleague in Frankfurt), and such American colleagues as the theologian Reinhold

---

(items 403 and 404), published by the *Akademie der Künste* in Berlin: https://www.adk.de/de/archiv/bibliothek/pdf/Nachlassbibliothek-Theodor-W.-Adorno.pdf.

69. Theodor W. Adorno, review of *Der Mensch und die Technik. Beitrag zu einer Philosophie des Lebens,* by Oswald Spengler, *Zeitschrift für Sozialforschung* 1, nos. 1–2 (1932): 149–51.

70. See, for instance, Theodor W. Adorno, *Der Begriff des Unbewussten in der transzendentalen Seelenlehre,* in *Gesammelte Schriften, Bd. 1: Philosophische Frühschriften,* ed. Rolf Tiedemann (Frankfurt: Suhrkamp, 1973), 319–20.

71. Adorno, *Minima Moralia*, 192.

Niebuhr. What all these discussants shared was a soft spot, despite their progressive political leanings, for Spengler's pessimist prognosis regarding the West. As already seen, in his reproach of the *Logos* authors Adorno claimed that the calcified Weimar academia had no capacity to live up to the challenge posed by Spengler, a thinker who, Adorno went as far as declaring, "seemed to have inherited all the historical force" of Germany's intellectual past. Significantly, the New York discussions with Tillich, Niebuhr, and others, Adorno later recalled, "counted among those American experiences in which the German tradition was continued in the most unbroken fashion." The implication of this recollection was that, in Adorno's estimation, these discussions were the ones that truly sustained the critical and emancipatory impulses of classical German philosophy. That is, they operated at high enough level to come to terms with a critic of Spengler's caliber. It was, then, these New York surroundings, "for me a source of greatest stimulation," that on the eve of and during World War II gave Adorno the impetus to engage in a rethinking of Spengler's worth.[72]

Let us return to our comparison of Spengler's and Pollock's theories. Even if Adorno had studied Spengler's theory of Caesarism in the 1920s, many years before he familiarized himself with Pollock's Marxist train of thought about capitalism's authoritarian curve, it still ought to be emphasized that in "Spengler Today" his reflections on Caesarism were decisively filtered by Pollock's state capitalism thesis. The psychological, cultural, and political phenomena described by Spengler remained obscure, Adorno was adamant, so long as they were not viewed as moments in a larger historical change in which the transformation of capitalism from its liberal phase to its more authoritarian iterations held the primary place.

However, when Adorno looked back at the immediate post–World War I years, the time when Spengler had penned his remarks

---

72. Adorno's contribution to "Erinnerungen an Paul Tillich," in *Werk und Wirken Paul Tillichs: Ein Gedenkbuch* (Stuttgart: Evangelisches Verlagswerk, 1967), 35. On Spengler's impact on Tillich and Niebuhr, see John P. Clayton, *The Concept of Correlation: Paul Tillich and the Possibility of a Mediating Theology* (Berlin: De Gruyter, 1980), 143; Ronald H. Stone, *Professor Reinhold Niebuhr: A Mentor to the Twentieth Century* (Louisville, KY: Westminster/John Knox, 1992), 41.

on Caesarism, he thought that Spengler's observations and predictions surpassed the ones offered by the Left at the time. Spengler was one of those "theoreticians of extreme reaction," Adorno contended, who already in the early 1920s, before the rise of Nazism, had paid attention to liberalism's vulnerabilities. Of course, Adorno acknowledged Marxists' awareness of capitalism's "societal antagonisms." He lamented, however, that their warnings about historical regression had not been taken seriously, not even by Marxists themselves, whose faith in history's progression muted their fears of its "potential relapse into barbarism."[73] Adorno did not specify who he was targeting here. Perhaps he had in mind the Social Democrats, whose notion of automatic historical progress Walter Benjamin had derided in 1940 in his "On the Concept of History."[74] But Adorno could equally have directed his complaints at the entire Marxist tradition, beginning with Marx and Engels who, despite stressing capitalism's inescapable crisis tendencies, expected socialism's eventual victory.

What is curious about Adorno's remarks on Spengler's acuity is their silence on concurrent Marxist debates on fascism and Nazism. "Spengler Today" gives the impression that there was practically no Marxist theorizing about the problems of Caesarism in the early 1920s. Adorno says nothing, for example, about Clara Zetkin's warnings in 1923 about the Europe-wide threat of fascism after Mussolini's March on Rome in 1922. Nor does he comment on August Thalheimer's 1928 investigation of Italian Fascism as twentieth-century "Bonapartism," which, like Zetkin's earlier warning, underlined the attraction of certain sections of the working class to fascist ideology.[75] It is unlikely that Adorno was unaware of these discussions. Yet perhaps the reason he left them out was that for the great majority of Marxists the movements of Mussolini and Hitler posed

---

73. Adorno, "Spengler Today," 318.
74. Walter Benjamin, "On the Concept of History," trans. Harry Zohn, in vol. 4 of *Selected Writings*, ed. Howard Eiland and Michael W. Jennings (Cambridge, MA: The Belknap Press of Harvard University Press, 2003), 392.
75. On Zetkin and Thalheimer, see William David Jones, *The Lost Debate: German Socialist Intellectuals and Totalitarianism* (Urbana: University of Illinois Press, 1999), 24–27, 43–45.

no problem in the long run, as they were expressions, according to Marxist-Leninist orthodoxy, of capitalism in its final death throes, soon to be replaced by communism. The only exception Adorno mentions (in 1941 though no longer in 1950) is Georg Lukács. Together with a few other unnamed "dialecticians of the Hegelian tradition" (likely including Karl Korsch, the author of *Marxism and Philosophy* from 1923), Lukács was the only Marxist who had challenged the dogma of the proletariat. Alluding to Lukács's *History and Class Consciousness* (1923), Adorno wrote that Lukács had questioned whether the existing working class, the "psychologically mutilated" victims of capitalist oppression, was up to its task as the agent of the revolution.[76]

In this context it also bears mentioning that in "Spengler Today," unlike in the 1950 version of the essay, Adorno makes no mention of Robert Michels's "iron law of oligarchy" or Werner Sombart's *Why Is There No Socialism in the United States?* as likely influences on Spengler's criticism of liberalism. Taken together with Adorno's silence on Marxist discussions of Caesarism in the 1920s, it may well be that in 1941 he still saw Spengler as a more original thinker than he did a decade later.

The considerable stature that Adorno accorded to Spengler as a sharp-eyed observer of Germany and Europe in the early postwar years brings us to another intriguing aspect of his essay: his guarded sympathy for Spengler's anti-positivism. What Spengler called his "physiognomic tact" aimed to present historical "objects and relations illustratively instead of offering an army of ranked concepts."[77] For Spengler physiognomic observation, a rare capacity of a few gifted seers, was about "instinctively seeing through the movement of events," a virtue that "the born statesman and the true historian" had in common.[78] We saw earlier that Adorno detested Spengler's "tyranny of categories" and the way Spengler's morphological determinism ultimately made his physiognomic approach as blind as

---

76. Adorno, "Spengler Today," 318.
77. Spengler, *The Decline of the West*, vol. 1, xiv.
78. Oswald Spengler, "Pessimismus," in *Reden und Aufsätze*, ed. Hildegard Kornhardt (Munich: C. H. Beck, 1937), 67.

traditional metaphysical categorizations and positivist worship of empirical facts. "Instead of plunging into the expressive character of the phenomena," Adorno complained, Spengler "swiftly sells under shrill advertising slogans the phenomena he has uncharitably raked together."[79]

Adorno's criticism should not, however, prevent us from acknowledging his appreciation of the *intention* he saw behind Spengler's denunciation of received thought patterns. The phrase "expressive character of the phenomena" in the passage above is illuminating. Adorno had introduced it in his 1931 inaugural address "The Actuality of Philosophy" as that side of objects that any "actual" philosophy, or cultural criticism worthy of the name, should adhere to. These were the essential features of a given object, those aspects of it that were unique to it rather than universal attributes of all objects falling into its class. But this was precisely the feature that traditional idealism, with its classifying conceptual maneuvers, had been blind to. Spengler, Adorno maintained, was right in criticizing idealism and looking for new avenues for thought. Significantly, in an early draft of his 1941 essay (titled "Spengler and the Present Situation"), the above-cited passage reads: Spengler "boasts about the physiognomic character of his method, but stronger than his physiognomic glance, *that is, his faculty of plunging into the expressive character of the phenomenon*, is his will to sell the phenomena he has uncharitably raked together under shrill advertising slogans."[80]

Despite Spengler's ultimate failure, Adorno implied that Spengler too was after those decisive aspects of the historical situation that remained inaccessible both for old idealist abstractions and for modern positivism. Or, as H. Stuart Hughes writes, "Spengler belonged to the handful of German writers since Nietzsche who had tried to understand the contemporary scene in all its depth and complexity." Because established academic scholars (such as the *Logos*

---

79. Adorno, "Spengler Today," 315.
80. Theodor W. Adorno, "Spengler and the Present Situation" (c. end of April 1941), unpublished manuscript, 16–17. Theodor W. Adorno Archive, Ts. 23427–54, Institute for Social Research, Goethe University Frankfurt. My emphasis.

authors) either abstained from such attempts or viewed modernity through a too rosy lens, it was left to eccentric outsiders like Spengler "to catch the essential quality of the present in flashes of inspired understanding."[81]

What this restrained admiration of Spengler's discernment means, I believe, is that Adorno counted him among those early twentieth-century thinkers, such as Edmund Husserl and Henri Bergson, who underscored a need for something like "micrology," a form of thought that aimed at the bigger picture through careful immersion in details rather than through conceptual abstractions.[82] As seen in chapter 1, even though Adorno in these lecture remarks from 1966, uttered shortly before the appearance of *Negative Dialectics*, explicitly dismissed Ludwig Klages as a neo-Romantic charlatan, elsewhere he expressed more approving comments on Klages's critique of Western "logocentrism." The same, I think, is the case with Spengler. Although Adorno did not mention Spengler in these remarks and often hurled derogatory remarks at him, he respected Spengler's striving for the essential. As he conceded in a letter to Heinz Hartmann from 1966, Spengler, despite his countless flaws, had "in many instances demonstrated a downright astonishing physiognomic power."[83]

Do expressions such as this mean that Spengler influenced Adorno with his observations on the Weimar Republic's undemocratic tendencies? George Friedman thinks so. He writes about Spengler's "direct influence" on Adorno and the early Frankfurt School as a whole and claims that the critical theorists "incorporated Spengler's criticism into their own."[84] However, we need to be more specific than this. To begin with, Friedman focuses on the 1950 version of Adorno's essay and omits the 1941 version. And he does not offer answers to the question of when Adorno became interested in Spengler. My answer is that we may speculate about the possible impact

---

81. Hughes, *Oswald Spengler*, 93.
82. Theodor W. Adorno, *Lectures on Negative Dialectics: Fragments of a Lecture Course 1965/1966*, ed. Rolf Tiedemann, trans. Rodney Livingstone (Cambridge: Polity Press, 2008), 70.
83. Adorno to Heinz Hartmann, April 1966, Theodor W. Adorno Archive 552/9, Institute for Social Research, Goethe University Frankfurt.
84. Friedman, *The Political Philosophy of the Frankfurt School*, 85, 80.

Spengler's observations on Caesarism had on the young Adorno in the 1920s, but this remains speculation. The empirical evidence at our disposal strongly suggests that Adorno only became interested in Spengler's observations after 1938 in New York.

What are we to make, then, of Adorno's preoccupation with Spengler in New York? Rather than an expression of Spengler's influence on Adorno, as Friedmann frames their intellectual relationship, in my view "Spengler Today" should be seen as Adorno's ex post facto recognition of the acuity of Spengler's comments on democracy after World War I as well as of certain notable parallels between their otherwise very different forms of social criticism.

At the same time, however, it would be hasty to conclude that there is nothing more to be found in Adorno's relation to Spengler than this ex post facto recognition. For we still have not touched on the question of whether Adorno's New York reflections on Spengler indicate that the latter stimulated his subsequent path of thinking. This is an important question. Adorno's years on the East Coast were the incubation period for *Dialectic of Enlightenment*, which Adorno and Horkheimer began to write in the fall of 1941 in California; in chapter 3 we will tackle the question of what kind of push Spengler's bleak philosophy of history may have given to their thesis of the entanglement of myth and reason. Here, however, we should stay with the notion of Caesarism. We should inquire whether the "astonishing physiognomic power" that Spengler had directed at modern Western society inspired Adorno's later reflections in the 1940s on authoritarianism and culture in his most famous works: *The Authoritarian Personality* and *Dialectic of Enlightenment*.

That Spengler inspired these works is suggested by the following lines on "masses" and culture in "Spengler Today," which followed Adorno's appraisal of Spengler as one of the thinkers of "extreme reaction" whose scrutiny of liberalism showed itself "superior in many respects to that which came from the left wing."

> Concepts such as those of the masses or of culture were largely exempt from dialectical criticism. No one cared much about how they were involved within the total process of our society. There was no realization that the masses in the specific sense of the term are not merely the majority

of exploited toilers but that their characteristics as "masses" are themselves due to the present phase of class society. Nor was there acknowledgment of the extent to which culture is changing into a regulative system of class domination.[85]

As we turn to *The Authoritarian Personality* and the "culture industry" chapter of *Dialectic of Enlightenment,* we are searching for, it bears repeating, signs not so much of Spengler's influence on Adorno as of the stimuli Spengler may have given to him. I believe that George Friedman simplifies the issue by approaching the Adorno-Spengler connection as a question of influence (or no influence). To reframe this relationship as one of stimuli, or inspiration, leaves room for the crucial qualification that Adorno, even though he was impressed by Spengler's ideas, did not simply mimic them but sought, through active reinterpretation, to redirect them (in the spirit of his later maxim to put "all the reactionary arguments against Western culture in the service of progressive enlightenment"[86]).

Spengler and *The Authoritarian Personality*

The Authoritarian Personality (1950) was a social-psychological milestone, though controversial one, that Adorno coauthored with Else Frenkel-Brunswik, Daniel J. Levinson, and R. Nevitt Sanford in California in the latter half of the 1940s. Written immediately after the collapse of European Fascism, and only a few years before McCarthyism, driving the study was the consideration whether the United States was immune to the lure of fascism that had just destroyed Europe. Part of the larger Studies in Prejudice project, led by Max Horkheimer and funded by the American Jewish Committee, *The Authoritarian Personality* did not seek to measure factual support for fascism. Instead, it aimed to identify what the authors called "the *potentially fascistic* individual." This was a personality type that was exceptionally "susceptible to anti-democratic propaganda," one

---

85. Adorno, "Spengler Today," 318–19.
86. Adorno, *Minima Moralia,* 192.

that "would readily accept fascism if it should become a strong or respectable social movement."[87] The authoritarian individual of the twentieth century, Horkheimer wrote in his preface to the book, was not "the bigot of the older style" but a new "'anthropological' species we call the authoritarian type of man," characteristic of which was a fusion of utmost rationalism and utter irrationalism. Such a person was marked by contradictions: "enlightened and superstitious, proud to be an individualist and in constant fear of not being like all the others, jealous of his independence and inclined to submit blindly to power and authority."[88]

Where did this notion of a specifically modern type of authoritarian come from? One readily thinks of Freud, to whom *The Authoritarian Personality* indeed owed a lot. Adorno's thought, as well as the early Frankfurt School as a whole, would be unthinkable without Freud's libido theory and its emphasis on human beings' natural condition as key to understanding their history. Freud offered a psychoanalytical account of the emergence of human subjectivity from nature and bemoaned how this civilizing process had hardened humans' affective capacities to such a degree that they struggled to enjoy its fruits. As for post–World War I Europe, in works such as *Civilization and Its Discontents* Freud questioned, as Adorno wrote, "the liberalistic illusion that the progress of civilization would automatically bring about an increase of tolerance

---

87. Adorno et al., *The Authoritarian Personality*, 1. Emphasis in the original. Characteristics that made a person a potential follower of a fascist movement were the following: "*Conventionalism.* Rigid adherence to conventional, middle-class values," "*Authoritarian submission.* Submissive, uncritical attitude toward idealized moral authorities of the ingroup," "*Authoritarian aggression.* Tendency to be on the lookout for, and to condemn, reject, and punish people who violate conventional values," "*Anti-intraception.* Opposition to the subjective, the imaginative, the tender-minded," "*Superstition and stereotypy.* The belief in mystical determinants of the individual's fate; the disposition to think in rigid categories," "*Power and 'toughness.'* [. . .] identification with power figures [and] exaggerated assertion of strength and toughness," "*Destructiveness and cynicism.* Generalized hostility, vilification of the human," "*Projectivity.* The disposition to believe that wild and dangerous things go on in the world; the projection outwards of unconscious emotional impulses," and "*Sex.* Exaggerated concern with sexual 'goings-on.'" Ibid., 228. Emphasis in the original.

88. Max Horkheimer, Preface to *The Authoritarian Personality*, lxxi.

and a lessening of violence against out-groups."[89] One could with some reservations view the Frankfurt School's first-ever collective effort, a 1929 study directed by Horkheimer and Erich Fromm, as a protoversion of *The Authoritarian Personality*. Equipped with the Freudian conceptual arsenal, the study sought to find out how the German middle and working classes would react if national socialism, the success of which was marginal before the Nazi Party's major electoral victory in 1930, managed to increase its popularity. To the dismay of the study's Marxist authors, authoritarian character traits turned out to be alarmingly high even among leftist voters, implying that opposition to Hitler was not as solid as the Left's relatively strong electoral numbers indicated.[90]

Nevertheless, the idea at the center of *The Authoritarian Personality* of a specifically modern type of authoritarian did not derive only, or even primarily, from Freud. As undeniable as Freud's presence in Adorno's thought is, Adorno never entirely identified with Freud. Racist prejudice, or psychological phenomena in general, could not in Adorno's view be investigated independently from larger societal developments. Indeed, contrary to the official message of *The Authoritarian Personality*, Adorno, in his remarks (not published until 2019) on the study from 1948, stressed that the twentieth century, with its increasing concentration of societal power, had in fact made Freud's teachings about the individual obsolete; a conclusion that, perhaps not incidentally, Adorno had expressed for the first time at the turn of the 1940s in New York when Spengler was on his mind.[91] Freud had modeled his psychoanalytic

---

89. Theodor W. Adorno, "Freudian Theory and the Pattern of Fascist Propaganda," in *The Essential Frankfurt School Reader*, ed. Andrew Arato and Eike Gebhardt (New York: Continuum, 1988), 129. See also Adorno, "Education after Auschwitz," 191–92.

90. For the 1929 study (originally titled *Arbeiter und Angestellte am Vorabend des Dritten Reiches*), see Erich Fromm, *The Working Class in Weimar Germany: A Psychological and Sociological Study*, trans. Barbara Weinberger (Warwickshire, UK: Berg Publishers, 1984). See also Helmut Dubiel, *Theory and Politics: Studies in the Development of Critical Theory*, trans. Benjamin Gregg (Cambridge, MA: MIT Press, 1985), 11–15.

91. Theodor W. Adorno, "Remarks on *The Authoritarian Personality*," in *The Authoritarian Personality*, xlii. See also Adorno's remarks on the "new anthropol-

view of the mature individual, capable of self-direction and self-reflection, on the nineteenth-century liberal ideal, and to an extent reality, of the autonomous individual, engendered by the Enlightenment and requirements of the liberal market economy. This bourgeois era, however, had collapsed under the weight of monopoly capitalism, and fascism—which Adorno's colleague Leo Löwenthal dubbed "psychoanalysis in reverse"—had ultimately undermined the very foundations of the critical individual.[92]

Thus, it is in vain, I believe, that we search only in Freud for the inspiration for the idea of "the authoritarian personality." Peter E. Gordon has recently made an interesting point about *The Authoritarian Personality*. He suggests that Adorno anticipated some of the book's analyses of social conformism and the decline of the individual in his essay "On Kierkegaard's Doctrine of Love" (1940). Whereas in his 1933 book on Kierkegaard Adorno had taken existentialism to task for its failure to engage in social criticism, he now praised Kierkegaard as a critic of a society that produces authoritarianism. Kierkegaard was sensitive, Adorno argued, to "a tendency in today's mass society which, during his time, must have been very latent: the substitution of spontaneous thinking by 'reflectory' adaptation taking place in connection with modern forms of mass information." No matter how conservative and anti-humanist Kierkegaard's unsparing indictment of nineteenth-century society was, Adorno claimed, he had "an inkling of the mutilation of men by the very mechanisms of domination which actually change men into a mass."[93]

Significantly from the perspective of the Spengler question, the Kierkegaard essay, as Adorno later recalled, was an outgrowth of the same New York discussions with Tillich, Niebuhr, and others

---

ogy" from 1941, "Notizen zur neuen Anthropologie," in *Briefwechsel, Bd. II: 1938–1944*, 453–71.

92. On Löwenthal's remark, see Martin Jay, "Introduction to a Festschrift for Leo Löwenthal on His Eightieth Birthday," in *Permanent Exiles: Essays on the Intellectual Migration from Germany to America* (New York: Columbia University Press, 1986), 101.

93. Peter E. Gordon, *Adorno and Existence* (Cambridge, MA: Harvard University Press, 2016), 32; Theodor W. Adorno, "On Kierkegaard's Doctrine of Love," *Studies in Philosophy and Social Science* 8, no. 3 (1939–1940), 413–29.

that inspired him to write "Spengler Today." The New York years, Gordon notes, pushed Adorno to modify his view of Kierkegaard as an arch-existentialist captivated by effusive introspection and recognize his merits as a social critic. It seems evident to me, however, that not only Kierkegaard but also, to a large extent, Spengler nurtured Adorno's assumption of the decline of the individual. Spengler's portrayal in *The Decline of the West* of modern atomized city dwellers, liable to relieve their insecurities by identifying with authoritarian leaders, provided a more accurate image of the twentieth century than the anachronistic liberal one that Freud still held on to. With his notion of Caesarism, Spengler paid close attention to political and cultural factors facilitating the decline of the individual. Although the exact dialectic interconnecting these factors, as emphasized earlier, escaped him, their outcome, the rootless metropolitan "mass," was at the heart of his analysis.

Adorno always insisted that ego-weakness was not limited to people living under totalitarian regimes. Shortly after the appearance of *The Authoritarian Personality*, he reported to Thomas Mann from Germany how Spengler's "new cave dweller" was a fitting characterization not only of Germans of the Nazi era, but often also those of the postwar period: "people who are damaged with respect to the ego, to autonomy, to spontaneity."[94] And in 1964, while discussing Spengler and Freud, Adorno praised David Riesman's 1950 idea of the conformist "other-directed" character, "the social character whose actions are guided by outside influences," as an apt diagnosis of widespread ego-weakness in the United States.[95] To be sure, Adorno applauded Freud for the attention he gave, particularly in *Civilization and Its Discontents*, to the qualitatively new pressures of modern industrial society, while he simultaneously took Spengler to task for his ahistorical cultural morphology and its false abstractions.[96] Yet, as

---

94. Adorno to Mann, June 3, 1950, in *Theodor W. Adorno/Thomas Mann: Correspondence 1943–1955*, ed. Christoph Gödde and Thomas Sprecher, trans. Nicholas Walker (Cambridge: Polity Press, 2006), 46.

95. Adorno, *History and Freedom*, 6–7; David Riesman, *The Lonely Crowd: A Study of the Changing American Character* (New Haven, CT: Yale University Press, 2001), 19–24.

96. Adorno, "Was Spengler Right?", 28.

we have seen, in 1941 Adorno praised Spengler's more historically sensitive analysis of Caesarism for its similar insights against Spengler's own self-understanding as a "morphologist" of ontological invariants.

We can say, then, that Adorno, as indicated by his 1948 qualifications on *The Authoritarian Personality*, to a certain extent shared Spengler's (and Kierkegaard's) misgivings of the immaturity of the "masses." Of course, Adorno took great care not to eternalize what was essentially a historical state of affairs. He rebuked Spengler for his conservative prejudice, according to which people would remain a mass and could never become independent subjects (and thereby anticipated his polemics in the 1960s against Arnold Gehlen's conservative philosophical anthropology).[97] This Machiavellian assumption, Adorno complained, whose "sympathy lies with those who rule," pushed Spengler's diagnostic gifts into an elitist "contempt for men."[98] Adorno turned Spengler's portrait of an atomized urban populace against its author by stressing that it was just those contingent political and cultural factors that Spengler himself had heeded—together with economic ones that he had missed—that were to blame for the emergence of the modern unthinking and undemocratic "masses," not some unchangeable human condition.

Spengler and "Culture Industry"

Besides the exploitative and alienating capitalist economy itself, the chief factor guilty of this spiritual "massification" of the lower classes was modern popular culture, a phenomenon, Adorno bemoaned, that had been neglected by the Left. Spengler, in contrast, had recognized "the frame of mind gripping the masses outside the actual process of production, matters usually referred to under the head of 'leisure time'". Spengler had anticipated, Adorno underscored, the ways in which critical thinking could be paralyzed by

---

97. On the later disputes between Adorno and Gehlen, see Thies, *Die Krise des Individuums*.
98. Adorno, "Spengler Today," 313–14.

"centralized means of public communication," such as newspaper and radio, as well as by stupefying pastime activities like jazz and sports. Rather than helping people gain awareness of societal forces dictating their lives, these means kept them in thrall of what Adorno called "sudden shock and sudden oblivion" and made them incapable of forming "any continuous sense of time."[99]

George Friedman and Michael Pauen have observed, correctly in my view, that there are evident parallels between Spengler's diagnosis of the decline of critical thinking in the era of modern mass medias and the chapter "Culture Industry: Enlightenment as Mass Deception" in *Dialectic of Enlightenment*.[100] It would be incorrect, however, to interpret Spengler as the most important impetus behind Adorno and Horkheimer's bleak view of the "culture industry." As Thomas Y. Levin has argued, until c. 1935 Adorno had been considerably more open-minded toward new forms of popular culture and media technologies such as radio. Thereafter, however, his stance grew more skeptical. This new outlook surfaced in his debates with Walter Benjamin over the critical potential of cinema and popular music to challenge the social status quo. Representative of this bleaker judgment are Adorno's essays "Über Jazz" ("On Jazz," 1936) and "Über den Fetischcharakter in der Musik und die Regression des Hörens" ("On the Fetish-Character in Music and the Regression of Listening," 1938). It received its most sustained expression, however, in *Dialectic of Enlightenment*.[101]

It seems highly unlikely, then, or at least very difficult to prove given the lack of evidence, that Adorno's skeptical turn resulted from reading Spengler. Adorno's skepticism was already present in the

---

99. Adorno, "Spengler Today," 307–8.
100. Friedman, *The Political Philosophy of the Frankfurt School*, 80, 82; Michel Pauen, *Dithyrambiker des Untergangs. Gnostizismus in Ästhetik und Philosophie der Moderne* (Berlin: Akademie Verlag, 1994), 358–60.
101. Thomas Y. Levin, "For the Record: Adorno on Music in the Age of Its Technological Reproducibility," *October* 55 (Winter 1990): 23–47. See also Miriam Bratu Hansen, *Cinema and Experience: Siegfried Kracauer, Walter Benjamin, and Theodor W. Adorno* (Berkeley: University of California Press, 2011), 208.

mid-1930s, whereas his attraction to Spengler's Caesarism, as noted several times already, begun in earnest only in 1938.[102]

Given Adorno's praise of Spengler in 1941, at a time when he and Horkheimer began to sketch *Dialectic of Enlightenment*, what role should we accord Spengler in the development of the conception of the "culture industry"—a term Adorno and Horkheimer preferred over "mass culture" to convey its instrumental, manipulative, and nonspontaneous character? Although Spengler cannot be said to have ignited Adorno's darker criticism of the culture industry, I would argue that he gave Adorno confirmation in his disagreement with Benjamin. The aspect of *Dialectic of Enlightenment*'s culture industry chapter where a trace of Adorno's interest in Spengler is most readily visible, I believe, is in its bleak conviction that the mass-produced, standardized products of modern popular culture simply imprint themselves on supposedly helpless consumers who allegedly have little to no capacity to resist their conformist message. In the 1960s, however, Adorno came to repudiate this assessment as too cynical.

---

102. What about Ludwig Klages, whom Adorno included in the group of "theoreticians of extreme reaction" who had offered trenchant criticisms of modern life and culture? Michael Grossheim argues that Klages anticipated the Frankfurt School's theory of the culture industry with his claim that urban metropolitans had become "slaves of the frenzy of distraction." Accompanied by a growing automatization of new realms of life, this culture of diversion led to mechanization of life. "The more the mechanization advances," Klages complained, "the more it outdoes the personality." Adorno echoed this verdict in *Minima Moralia* (written in the mid-1940s) by asserting that "technology is making gestures precise and brutal, and with them men. It expels from movements all hesitation, deliberation, [and] civility. It subjects them to the implacable, as it were ahistorical demands of objects." As seen in chapter 1, Adorno's interest in Klages had already begun in the early 1930s—several years before he adopted a more pessimistic view of modern popular culture, which was around 1935, according to Levin. This fact would allow the interpretation that Klages had stimulated Adorno's pessimistic view and thereby the culture industry chapter of *Dialectic of Enlightenment*. Michael Grossheim, "'Die namenlose Dummheit, die das Resultat des Fortschritts ist.'—Lebensphilosophische und dialektische Kritik der Moderne," *Logos. Zeitschrift für systematische Philosophie* 3, no. 2 (1996), 120–21; Ludwig Klages, "Mensch und Erde," in *Sämtliche Werke, Bd. 3*, ed. Ernst Frauchiger et al. (Bonn: Bouvier Verlag, 1974), 623; Ludwig Klages, "Die Grundlagen der Charakterkunde," in *Sämtliche Werke, Bd. 4*, ed. Ernst Frauchiger et al. (Bonn: Bouvier Verlag, 1976), 408; Adorno, *Minima Moralia*, 40.

More attentive to the undeniable differences between the lot of culture (both its production and reception) under fascist and democratic conditions, he distanced himself somewhat from *Dialectic of Enlightenment*'s grim judgment, as Martin Jay notes.[103]

But what made Adorno susceptible to this judgment in the first place? Although he was already moving in this direction by the mid-1930s, Adorno had some key experiences during his New York exile that go a long way toward answering this question. First, there were his discussions with Paul Tillich, Reinhold Niebuhr, and others about Spengler and the fate of the Western world, in which questions of culture and its decline, we can surmise, figured prominently. Second, there was Adorno's ill-fated participation in 1938 in Princeton University's Radio Research Project led by Austrian émigré Paul Lazarsfeld. Adorno departed from the project's methodological assumptions, which he feared reflected "democratic bias" and failed to acknowledge the liquidation of the individual and larger cultural decay.[104] Third, on October 9–10 of the same year, the Nazis, directed by Propaganda Minister Joseph Goebbels, orchestrated the infamous Kristallnacht pogrom in Germany, the violence of which surpassed the regime's previous antisemitic actions.

Spengler foresaw Goebbels, Adorno stated in "Spengler Today."[105] It is, I think, this burst of violent antisemitism that more than anything explains Adorno's willingness to take seriously Spengler's ponderings on culture as a tool of domination rather than enlightenment. Masqueraded in the Nazi propaganda as a spontaneous popular uprising, this horrendous event had direct consequences for Adorno's parents. His father was arrested and the family's wine business was destroyed, after which Adorno's parents decided to flee Germany.[106]

---

103. Theodor W. Adorno, "Free Time," in *Critical Models: Interventions and Catchwords*, trans. Henry W. Pickford (New York: Columbia University Press, 2005), 175; Martin Jay, *Adorno* (Cambridge, MA: Harvard University Press, 1984), 128.
104. David Jenemann, *Adorno in America* (Minneapolis: University of Minnesota Press, 2007), chaps. 1 and 2.
105. Adorno, "Spengler Today," 309.
106. Adorno to Benjamin, February 1, 1939, in Theodor W. Adorno, *The Complete Correspondence, 1928–1940: Theodor W. Adorno and Walter Benjamin*, ed. Henri Lonitz, trans. Nicholas Walker (Cambridge, MA: Harvard University Press,

This dreadful experience very likely made Adorno think still more critically about the ways modern mass medias could be used to manipulate people for authoritarian purposes. This was not, however, only the problem of totalitarian countries like Germany, Adorno maintained. Even in nontotalitarian ones, such as the Unites States, the culture industry functioned to stupefy thinking and infantilize people, as he warned in a 1945 lecture in New York after Germany was defeated.[107]

All these factors from the year 1938 or immediately thereafter give us grounds to conclude that echoes of Spengler's unsparing reflections on culture in the age of mass medias can be found in the bleakest version of Adorno's culture industry thesis that the chapter in *Dialectic of Enlightenment* represented, but which he came to reconsider in the 1960s.

What about high culture, often celebrated as the enlightening antipode to dull popular culture? If modern cultural production could be harnessed for political authoritarianism, or if it at the very least weakened critical thinking, what counterforces were there? In this struggle against barbarism, Adorno claimed in "Spengler Today," one should not romanticize traditional forms of European high culture, whose weaknesses Spengler (and the arrogant treatment he had received from its established guardians in the 1920s) had laid bare. Indeed, Adorno appreciated Spengler not only as a staunch critic of popular culture but also with respect to its highbrow antipode, both in science and art. Adorno had never held academic philosophy or the *Geisteswissenschaften* (humanities) in particularly high regard, unable as they were to address the truly urgent questions related to the magnitude of the crisis of European modernity. Adorno's distrust was only deepened by the Weimar academe's unshaken trust in "the healthiness of culture" and its complacent efforts to wave off Spengler's *Decline of the West* as nonsense. Traditional bourgeois high art fared little

---

1999), 298–99; Stefan Müller-Doohm, *Adorno: A Biography*, trans. Rodney Livingstone (Cambridge: Polity Press, 2009), 261.
    107. Theodor W. Adorno, "What National Socialism Has Done to the Arts," in *Essays on Music: Selected, with Introduction, Commentary, and Notes*, ed. Richard Leppert, trans. Susan H. Gillespie (Berkeley: University of California Press, 2002), 373–90.

better. Having been sucked into the culture industry, Adorno bemoaned, it had turned into a static relic that offered escapism rather than insight. However, notwithstanding Spengler's legitimate criticism of affirmative "official culture," Adorno argued, he had mistakenly thrown "its non-conformist opposite"—the artistic avant-garde—into the same pile of rubbish. Spengler had erroneously ignored those "forces set free by decay"—expressionists like the poet Georg Trakl—who demur "obedience to this life, its culture, its rawness and sublimity." Or, as Adorno concluded his Spengler essay (throwing yet another jab at what to him was the complacent establishment): "That which stands against the decline of the west is not the surviving culture but the Utopia that is silently embodied in the image of decline."[108]

"A Real Preparatory Work for Our Things"

"There is no document of culture which is not at the same time a document of barbarism."[109] This sentence from Walter Benjamin's so-called theses on the philosophy of history, written shortly before his suicide in 1940 and published posthumously as "Über den Begriff der Geschichte" ("On the Concept of History"), reads like a crystallization of the message of *Dialectic of Enlightenment*. Indeed, on receiving a copy of Benjamin's theses from Hannah Arendt in June 1941, Adorno reported in an oft-cited letter to Horkheimer that "none of Benjamin's works shows him closer to our own intentions. More than anything it is about the idea of history as a permanent catastrophe, the critique of progress and domination of nature, and the stance towards culture."[110] When Adorno some months later mentioned to Horkheimer the future title of *Dialectic of Enlightenment* for the first time, he referred to it as "the dialectic of enlightenment or the dialectic of culture and barbarism."[111] Was this title, however, inspired only by Benjamin's "theses," as the

---

108. Adorno, "Spengler Today," 316, 325.
109. Benjamin, "On the Concept of History," 392.
110. Adorno to Horkheimer, June 12, 1941, in Adorno, *Briefwechsel, Bd. II: 1938–1944*, 144.
111. Adorno to Horkheimer, November 10, 1941, 286.

accepted wisdom has it? I believe that some of the credit should go to Spengler. In less well-known lines of Adorno's letter to Horkheimer about Benjamin's "theses," he continued, "Here there is a coincidence that has moved me a lot." Benjamin's passage on "culture as barbarism stands *verbatim* in the last paragraph of Spengler [Adorno's essay]." Adorno had composed "Spengler Today" in April 1941, independently of Benjamin's text: "We both knew nothing about each other's formulations."[112]

"Masterpiece" was how Horkheimer described an early draft of Adorno's Spengler essay in a letter to him from June 23, 1941. Despite the preciseness of its treatment of details, Horkheimer praised it for adhering to what was essential in *The Decline of the West*. Moreover, he emphasized that the essay highlighted themes especially important in the contemporary period that were in need of further reflection, such as the idea of an "ahistorical character of the present," a provocative and paradoxical idea in an era filled with events of world-historical magnitude—Hitler's invasion of Soviet Union, Operation Barbarossa, had begun the previous day.[113] Horkheimer's words should not come as a surprise. By 1941, Horkheimer, who also frequented the aforementioned New York discussions with Tillich, Niebuhr, and others, had begun to feel more at home amid such sweeping civilizational ruminations. The debate over state capitalism, as it is often noted, marked a pessimistic turn in his thought. In addition to Friedrich Pollock's economic theory of capitalism's authoritarian development, this turn was also influenced by depressing political events, most notably the 1939 pact between Hitler and Stalin, as well as Horkheimer's growing contact with Adorno.

Of course, for Horkheimer a wider philosophical perspective on societal phenomena had always been essential. Thus, if Pollock saw state capitalism as the culmination of a decades-long economic trend, Horkheimer's "classical" critical theory of the 1930s viewed it through the lens of an "anthropology of the bourgeois era," a sort of Hegelian-Marxist-Freudian account of developmental tendencies of capitalism from c. 1500 to the present and the historically specific

---

112. Adorno to Horkheimer, June 12, 1941, 144–45.
113. Horkheimer to Adorno, June 23, 1941, 153–54.

character structures generated by this economic order.[114] By 1941, however, Horkheimer's scope had expanded from centuries to millennia, as evidenced by his bleak essay "The End of Reason," in which his earlier cautious differentiations between various historical periods, thinkers of the same period, and present political systems had given way to a more ruthless, one could say Adornoian, critique of Western reason and society. Echoing Adorno's monolithic view on Western philosophy's repressive qualities, Horkheimer stated bluntly that "the new order of fascism is reason revealing itself as unreason." This transformation in Horkheimer's outlook was certainly not straightforward, and his lifelong admiration of Arthur Schopenhauer and the latter's pessimistic mindset remain challenges for biographers seeking to divide Horkheimer's path into distinct phases.[115]

Anyhow, with regard to Spengler there was an apparent change in Horkheimer's attitude around 1940. Before adopting his new somber stance, he had found little to his liking in Spengler's theories. Even if Horkheimer had acknowledged that *The Decline of the West* had its merits in discrediting idealist conceptions of progress, he had not minced words in criticizing Spengler's irrational reduction of history to blind nature.[116] And whereas in 1941 Adorno applauded the acuity of Spengler's notion of the new "raw man," or the urban city dweller, Horkheimer had criticized this notion as a derogatory slander on the working class.[117] But Horkheimer's praise of Adorno's

---

114. Abromeit, *Max Horkheimer*, chap. 7. See, for instance, Horkheimer's essays "Egoism and Freedom Movements: On the Anthropology of the Bourgeois Era," in *Between Philosophy and Social Science: Selected Early Writings*, trans. G. Frederick Hunter et al. (Cambridge, MA: MIT Press, 1993), 49–110; "Authority and the Family," trans. Matthew J. O'Connell, in *Critical Theory: Selected Essays* (New York: Continuum, 1972), 47–128.

115. Max Horkheimer, "The End of Reason," *Studies in Philosophy and Social Science* 9, no. 3 (1941): 387. On Horkheimer's pessimistic turn, see Abromeit, *Max Horkheimer*, 394–424.

116. See Horkheimer's two pieces from 1928 and 1933: "Zur Emanzipation der Philosophie von der Wissenschaft," in *Gesammelte Schriften, Bd. 10: Nachgelassene Schriften 1914–1931*, ed. Alfred Schmidt (Frankfurt: Fischer, 1990), 295, and review of *Jahre der Entscheidung I Teil: Deutschland und die weltgeschichtliche Entwicklung*, by Oswald Spengler, *Zeitschrift für Sozialforschung* 2, no. 3 (1933): 421–24.

117. See Horkheimer's 1934 essay "The Rationalism Debate in Contemporary Philosophy," in *Between Philosophy and Social Science: Selected Early Writings*,

Spengler essay shows that by 1941 he had come to appreciate Spengler a lot more. Whereas Adorno had judged Spengler as a dilettante in economic matters, in Horkheimer's opinion Spengler had real insights here as well, particularly pertaining to the shift from liberal to monopoly capitalism.[118] This change in his friend's thought did not go unnoticed by Adorno, who only a few years prior, as seen in chapter 1, had struggled in vain to convince Horkheimer that his sweeping critique of Western reason was valid. "I am especially happy," Adorno replied, "that you really liked the Spengler [essay]. You cannot imagine what our agreement in these things means to me."[119]

In this chapter, we have examined Adorno's qualified appreciation of Spengler's sensitivity to the entanglement of barbarism and culture and explored Adorno's attempts to harness Spengler's analysis of Caesarism in his own studies on authoritarianism and the culture industry. Considering that both Adorno and Horkheimer showed respect for Spengler in 1941, only months before they began working on *Dialectic of Enlightenment*, it is not far-fetched if we next weigh the possibility that Spengler, among other figures, stimulated their major collaborative effort on the philosophy of history. This question is especially pertinent, because Adorno expressed to Horkheimer his hope that his Spengler essay would mean "a real preparatory work for our things."[120]

---

trans. G. Frederick Hunter et al. (Cambridge, MA: MIT Press, 1993), 229.
    118. Horkheimer to Adorno, June 23, 1941, in Adorno, *Briefwechsel, Bd. II: 1938–1944*, 153–54.
    119. Adorno to Horkheimer, July 2, 1941, 159. In the 1950s and 1960s, Horkheimer would become even more welcoming of aspects of Spengler's cultural criticism. Although, like Adorno, he never found Spengler's cultural morphology compelling, he lamented that "despite his false theories Spengler is right: the Western world is declining. For it has no content anymore. In place of God or a utopia, one is being offered a fattened ox, a symbol of the raised standard of living." Horkheimer also judged Spengler's notion of "modern caveman" an apt depiction of humankind in the postwar era. Max Horkheimer, "Eine neue Politik der Linken," *Gesammelte Schriften, Bd. 14: Nachgelassene Schriften 1949–1972: Notizen*, ed. Gunzelin Schmid Noerr (Frankfurt: Fischer, 1988), 365; "Begriff der Bildung," in *Gesammelte Schriften, Bd. 8: Vorträge und Aufzeichnungen 1949–1973*, ed. Gunzelin Schmid Noerr (Frankfurt: Fischer, 1985), 413.
    120. Adorno to Horkheimer, May 3, 1941, in Adorno, *Briefwechsel, Bd. II: 1938–1944*, 109.

3

"Demystification of Antiquity"

Dialectic of Enlightenment

In 1944, Theodor W. Adorno and Max Horkheimer circulated a small edition of mimeographed copies of their *Philosophical Fragments*, a work officially published three years later as *Dialectic of Enlightenment*. In this darkest of books, written in California where the two émigrés had relocated in 1941, Adorno and Horkheimer attempted to grasp why, after two and a half millennia of Western civilization, "the wholly enlightened earth is radiant with triumphant calamity": of Nazism, Stalinism, and the Western culture industry. Their answer was surprising. The roots of the present catastrophe, Adorno and Horkheimer claimed, were as old as Western civilization itself. Motivating their immersion in ancient Greek mythology, especially Homer's *Odyssey*, was not a fascination with mythic tales themselves, but a certain one-sided form of thought they saw underlying these youngest "documents of bourgeois Western civilization." What made a recourse to these documents imperative, they argued, was the disheartening observation that this one-sidedness was something that later stages of Western civilization had not been able to overcome. Hence their two legendary postulates: "myth is already enlightenment" and "enlightenment reverts to mythology."[1]

Dialectic of Enlightenment, as is often noted, departs from the Institute for Social Research's earlier Marxist emphasis on capitalism as the key explanatory factor behind the catastrophes of the first half of the twentieth century. Unlike in the Frankfurt School's classic works of the 1930s, in this book economic domination appears only as one form of oppression among others. Some of this change of emphasis ensued from the authors' wish to avoid being labeled as communists in postwar Germany. Yet substantial theoretical factors contributed to it as well. As Adorno and Horkheimer began to sense that economic factors could explain neither the civilizational collapse of the 1940s nor the longer trajectory of Western history, they began to search for alternative explanations. The crucial background of this shift was their final disillusionment with the Soviet Union and its horrendously failed attempt to set up a rationally organized society. The tightening grip of Stalin's totalitarianism, on display in the notorious show trials of the late 1930s as well as in the Hitler-Stalin pact of 1939, implied that perhaps one should not blame the malady of reason on capitalism, but on reason itself.[2] "Why the shadow had fallen" on modern Europe, Martin Jay asks in reference to the dilemma taken up by Adorno and Horkheimer, "was not, however, explicitly spelled out." Rather than offering a clear answer to the question of the causes of the present "calamity," *Dialectic of Enlightenment* remained undecided whether

---

1. Max Horkheimer and Theodor W. Adorno, *Dialectic of Enlightenment: Philosophical Fragments*, trans. Edmund Jephcott (Stanford, CA: Stanford University Press, 2002), 1, xviii.

2. On the place of *Dialectic of Enlightenment* in the history of the Frankfurt School, see Gunzelin Schmid Noerr and Eva-Maria Ziege, Introduction to *Zur Kritik der regressiven Vernunft: Beiträge zur "Dialektik der Aufklärung"* (Wiesbaden, Germany: Springer, 2019), 5–10; Willem van Reijen and Jan Bransen, "The Disappearance of Class History in 'Dialectic of Enlightenment': A Commentary on the Textual Variants (1947 and 1944)," in Horkheimer and Adorno, *Dialectic of Enlightenment*, 248–52.

"the celestial body that had passed before the rational sun" was economic or anthropological.³

In standard interpretations of *Dialectic of Enlightenment*, the diminished Marxist stress on "social being" and a new focus on "consciousness" is explained by the authors' indebtedness to Walter Benjamin, Sigmund Freud, and Max Weber. Benjamin's weighty influence on Adorno and, by extension, on *Dialectic of Enlightenment*, is well recorded. Adorno's first book, *Kierkegaard* (1933), which offered a protoversion of his and Horkheimer's later idea of the entwinement of myth and reason, was stimulated by Benjamin's 1920s work, such as the early drafts of his grandiose, never-completed lifework on the nineteenth-century commercial arcades of Paris.⁴ Anticipating *Dialectic of Enlightenment*'s key postulates about myth and enlightenment, Benjamin's axiom in his *Arcades Project*, or *Das Passagen-Werk*, was: "No historical category without its natural substance, no natural category without its historical filtration."⁵ Benjamin's last work, "On the Concept of History" (1940), which presented a somber judgment of culture's entanglement with barbarism, is also often cited as a vital impetus for Adorno and Horkheimer's ruminations on myth and enlightenment.⁶

As for Freud, the Frankfurt School critical theory, as was noted in the previous chapter, would be unthinkable without his libido theory and his emphasis on human nature as a key to making sense of

---

3. Martin Jay, *Reason after Its Eclipse: On Late Critical Theory* (Madison: University of Wisconsin Press, 2016), 104.
4. Benjamin was prophetic in his 1934 review of Adorno's *Kierkegaard* when he suggested that "the author's subsequent writings may someday emerge from it." Walter Benjamin, "Kierkegaard: The End of Philosophical Idealism," in vol. 2/2 of *Selected Writings*, trans. Rodney Livingstone and Others, ed. Howard Eiland et al. (Cambridge, MA: The Belknap Press of Harvard University Press, 1999), 705.
5. Walter Benjamin, *The Arcades Project*, trans. Howard Eiland and Kevin McLaughlin (Cambridge, MA: Harvard University Press, 2002), 864.
6. Susan Buck-Morss, *The Origin of Negative Dialectics: Theodor W. Adorno, Walter Benjamin, and the Frankfurt Institute* (New York: The Free Press, 1977), 59, 168–75; Robert Hullot-Kentor, "Critique of the Organic: Kierkegaard and the Construction of the Aesthetic," in *Things beyond Resemblance: Collected Essays on Theodor W. Adorno* (New York: Columbia University Press, 2006), 78, 83–84; Richard Wolin, *Walter Benjamin: An Aesthetic of Redemption* (Berkeley: University of California Press, 1994), 265–72.

history. Freud's idea of "the return of the repressed" is frequently cited as an important model for Adorno and Horkheimer's narrative of enlightenment's self-destruction. "Beneath the known history of Europe," they write, evidently with Freud in mind, "there runs a subterranean one." This neglected history is comprised of "the fate of the human instincts and passions repressed and distorted by civilization. From the vantage point of the fascist present, in which the hidden is coming to light, the manifest history is also revealing its connection to that dark side."[7] Freud's presence is particularly palpable in a section of *Dialectic of Enlightenment* titled "Elements of Anti-Semitism: Limits of Enlightenment," which probes the psychological dynamics behind the long history of European antisemitism.

With respect to Weber, the theory of "state capitalism" underlying *Dialectic of Enlightenment*, as seen in chapter 2, is repeatedly perceived as building on Weber's bleak portrayal of the "iron cage" of modern industrial society. Furthermore, besides the phenomenon to be explained, the modern bureaucratic nightmare, Weber is often named as an inspiration for Adorno and Horkheimer's explanatory efforts. In Jürgen Habermas's oft-cited estimation, both Weber and *Dialectic of Enlightenment* saw the societal crisis of twentieth-century Europe as an almost inevitable result of Western reason as such. Weber saw behind the iron cage the "disenchantment of the world" (*Entzauberung der Welt*), a process of intellectualization that in the post-Reformation era freed science, morality, and art from the straitjacket of religious and metaphysical dogmas while at the same time letting loose calculative economic rationality. Read through the lens of the "reification" theory of Weber's Marxist student Georg Lukács, Habermas argues, Weber's theory became Adorno and Horkheimer's notion of instrumental reason.[8] The opening page of *Dialectic of Enlightenment*'s lead chapter "The Concept of Enlightenment," although it does not explicitly name

---

7. Horkheimer and Adorno, *Dialectic of Enlightenment*, 192.
8. Jürgen Habermas, *The Theory of Communicative Action*, vol. 1, *Reason and the Rationalization of Society*, trans. Thomas McCarthy (Boston, MA: Beacon Press, 1984), 366–99; Max Weber, "Science as a Vocation," in *From Max Weber: Essays in Sociology*, trans. and ed. H. H. Gerth and C. Wright Mills (New York: Oxford University Press, 1958), 139, 155.

Weber, contains an allusion to him: "Enlightenment's program was the disenchantment of the world."⁹

There is nothing wrong with these readings of *Dialectic of Enlightenment*. They are all entirely reasonable. However, an intriguing minor current of research has turned elsewhere in search of the book's anti-Marxian impetus. Axel Honneth was the first to propose that this impetus may have derived from the locus classicus of the interwar philosophy of life, *The Spirit as Adversary of the Soul* (1929–1932) by Ludwig Klages. *Dialectic of Enlightenment* contains only a brief dialogue with Klages. Nevertheless, Honneth drew attention to the affinity between Adorno and Horkheimer's view of "prehistorical compulsion to instrumental self-assertion" and Klages's anthropological notion of human nature as a battleground of antagonistic principles of "life" and "spirit." Equally noteworthy, Honneth contended, was the parallel between Adorno and Horkheimer's conviction that an excessively instrumental relation to nature is ultimately self-defeating and Klages's incessant warnings that reason (or "spirit") disrupts the harmony between life and the cosmic forces of nature.¹⁰ In Honneth's footsteps, Albrecht Wellmer underlined Klages's role in *Dialectic of Enlightenment*'s diagnosis, according to which, in Wellmer's words, "the repression of inner nature with its anarchical lust for happiness is the price paid for the formation of a unified self, which was itself necessary for the sake of *self-preservation* and the control of external nature."¹¹ More recently, Stefan Breuer has explained *Dialectic of Enlightenment*'s aforementioned undecidedness by suggesting that Adorno "remained fixated with Klages on the critique of the identity principle and was ultimately unable to make up his mind" whether this principle was based on anthropology or economy.¹²

---

9. Horkheimer and Adorno, *Dialectic of Enlightenment*, 1.
10. Axel Honneth, "Anthropologische Berührungspunkte zwischen der Lebensphilosophischen Kulturkritik und der 'Dialektik der Aufklärung,'" in *21. Deutscher Soziologentag 1982. Beiträge der Sektions- und hoc-Gruppen*, ed. Friedrich Heckmann and Peter Winter (Opladen, Germany: Westdeutscher Verlag, 1983), 791.
11. Albrecht Wellmer, *The Persistence of Modernity: Essays on Aesthetics, Ethics and Postmodernism*, trans. David Midgley (Cambridge: Polity Press, 1991), 3. Emphasis in the original.
12. Stefan Breuer, *Kritische Theorie: Schlüsselbegriffe, Kontroversen, Grenzen* (Tübingen: Mohr Siebeck, 2016), 252.

"Demystification of Antiquity" 121

I believe that the interpretative path carved by Honneth and others[13] has been unfairly neglected in the reception history of *Dialectic of Enlightenment*.[14] Plausible as the standard readings, underscoring the role of Benjamin, Freud, and Weber, are, they all come with caveats.

Initially Freud's work was a central object of criticism for Adorno and Horkheimer. By sticking to the liberal nineteenth-century ideal of the mature individual capable of steering her life autonomously, Freud failed, they argued, to give proper consideration to powerful societal tendencies that in the twentieth century were threatening to make, and in fact already had, this ideal anachronistic.[15] Again, Freud's theory of the origins of civilization succumbed to an anachronism of another kind by mistakenly "dissolving" ancient myths "within the immanent sphere of consciousness."[16] In other words, by erroneously approaching mythic thought with epistemic and psychological categories of nineteenth-century European modernity, Freud constructed a sort of reassuring teleology from myth to

---

13. See also Georg Stauth, "Critical Theory and Pre-Fascist Social Thought," *History of European Ideas* 18, no. 5 (1994): 719–22; Michael Grossheim, "'Die namenlose Dummheit, die das Resultat des Fortschritts ist.'—Lebensphilosophische und dialektische Kritik der Moderne," *Logos. Zeitschrift für systematische Philosophie* 3, no. 2 (1996): 121–30; Wolin, *Walter Benjamin*, xxx.

14. Tellingly, Rolf Tiedemann, the editor of Adorno's collected works, does not include Klages or Spengler in his list of possible influences on the book's central conception of myth and reason. This is curious, to say the least, because some pages later Tiedemann recognizes that Adorno "did not shy away" from making use of their ideas for his own ends. Rolf Tiedemann, "'Gegenwärtige Vorwelt': Zu Adornos Begriff des Mythischen (I)," in *Frankfurter Adorno Blätter*, vol. 5, ed. Rolf Tiedemann (Munich: edition text + kritik, 1992), 24; see also 17–22.

15. See the discussions between Adorno and Horkheimer in January 1939: "Diskussionen über die Differenz zwischen Positivismus und materialistischer Dialektik," in Max Horkheimer, *Gesammelte Schriften, Bd. 12: Nachgelassene Schriften 1931–1949*, ed. Gunzelin Schmid Noerr (Frankfurt: Fischer, 1987), 436–66. See also Adorno's draft on the "new anthropology" from 1941: "Notizen zur neuen Anthropologie," in *Briefe und Briefwechsel—Bd. 4: Theodor W. Adorno—Max Horkheimer, Briefwechsel 1927–1969, Bd. II: 1938–1944*, ed. Christoph Gödde und Henri Lonitz (Frankfurt: Suhrkamp, 2004), 453–71.

16. Adorno to Benjamin, September 22, 1937, in *The Complete Correspondence, 1928–1940: Theodor W. Adorno and Walter Benjamin*, ed. Henri Lonitz, trans. Nicholas Walker (Cambridge, MA: Harvard University Press, 1999), 212.

reason.[17] In addition, their quote regarding the dark, "subterranean" nature of European history from *Dialectic of Enlightenment*, allegedly only an insight of Freud's, was followed by praise of Klages as one of the thinkers (along with Friedrich Nietzsche and Stefan George) who had "recognized the nameless stupidity which is the result of progress."[18]

One should also pay heed to the possibility that *Dialectic of Enlightenment*'s remark on the "disenchantment of the world," frequently taken as a self-evident allusion to Weber, could refer to Klages as well. In his book *Vom kosmogonischen Eros* (1922), Klages had inquired into reason's ultimate purpose. "It has indeed been said many times," Klages noted, that reason "counts" and "measures." Yet what does this mean for life? "Simply this—disenchantment (*Entzauberung*)!" A few lines later he explicitly used the expression "disenchantment of the world" (*Entzauberung der Welt*).[19] It is somewhat curious that although Adorno and Horkheimer only once refer to Weber, in a footnote, his ideas are said to have offered "the foundation and basic conceptual structure of much, if not all, of their work."[20] Apart from Horkheimer's brief discussion of Weber's sociology in *Eclipse of Reason* (1947), however, there is no evidence of a sustained engagement with Weber.[21] This need not mean, to state the obvious, that Weber's ideas were not important for Horkheimer and Adorno. But it points to the need to consider other, largely overlooked figures such as Klages, whose polemic against "logocentrism," as chapter 1 showed, demonstrably occupied Adorno's thinking throughout the 1930s.[22]

---

17. Horkheimer and Adorno, *Dialectic of Enlightenment*, 6–7. See also the 1952 discussion between Adorno and the classical scholar Karl Kerenyi: "Mythologie und Aufklärung: Ein Rundfunkgespräch," in *Frankfurter Adorno Blätter*, vol. 5, 98–99.
18. Horkheimer and Adorno, *Dialectic of Enlightenment*, 194.
19. Ludwig Klages, *Vom kosmogonischen Eros*, in *Sämtliche Werke, Bd. 3*, ed. Ernst Frauchiger et al. (Bonn: Bouvier Verlag, 1974), 481–82.
20. Dana Villa, "Weber and The Frankfurt School," in *The Routledge Companion to the Frankfurt School*, ed. Peter E. Gordon et al. (New York: Routledge, 2019), 268.
21. Max Horkheimer, *Eclipse of Reason* (New York: Continuum, 2004), 5, 52, 55–56.
22. We saw in chapter 1 that Adorno was likely already familiar with Klages's *Vom kosmogonischen Eros* in 1922, because, as Nitzan Lebovic notes, Siegfried

Furthermore, the readings of Honneth and others, which date chiefly from the 1980s and 1990s, can be backed with subsequently published or previously underappreciated sources. One of these is Adorno's letter to Siegfried Kracauer, his erstwhile mentor, from 1933. Referencing the review essay of Klages's *Spirit as Adversary of the Soul* that he was working on, Adorno reported that he was engaged in it, "most of all, to come to grips with the mythical."[23] Another notable source is Adorno's letter to Horkheimer three years later, in which he emphasized the need to demarcate a progressive "critique of hypostatized reason" from Klages's complete "abandonment of reason."[24] As I argued in chapter 1, Adorno began his "Klages project" after the appearance of the final volume of *The Spirit as Adversary of the Soul* in 1932 and continued it in his Oxford manuscript on epistemology. In the present chapter, I wish to read *Dialectic of Enlightenment* as the culmination of this Klages project. Whereas Adorno's Oxford manuscript addressed the problem of "the mythical" from an epistemological perspective, *Dialectic of Enlightenment* approaches it from the angle of philosophy of history. The book, I believe, completes Adorno's effort to "come to grips with the mythical" that he had pursued in a dialogue with Klages's book since last years of the Weimar Republic.

Another neglected provocateur whose ideas we have empirical grounds to believe pushed Adorno and Horkheimer to consider reason's intrinsic defects is Oswald Spengler. *Dialectic of Enlightenment* does not mention Spengler. Yet George Friedman and Michael Pauen have urged us to pay heed to the book's debt to Spengler's *Decline of*

Kracauer had published passages of the book in the *Frankfurter Zeitung*, whose feuilleton section he oversaw. See *Frankfurter Zeitung*, June 14, 1922, feuilleton section, 1–2; Nitzan Lebovic, *The Philosophy of Life and Death: Ludwig Klages and the Rise of a Nazi Biopolitics* (New York: Palgrave Macmillan, 2013), 85.

23. Adorno to Kracauer, March 14, 1933, in *Theodor W. Adorno/Siegfried Kracauer: Correspondence, 1923–1966*, ed. Wolfgang Schopf, trans. Susan Reynolds and Michael Winkler (Cambridge: Polity Press, 2020), 207.

24. Adorno to Horkheimer, December 15, 1936, in *Briefe und Briefwechsel—Bd. 4: Theodor W. Adorno—Max Horkheimer, Briefwechsel 1927–1969, Bd. I: 1927–1937*, ed. Christoph Gödde and Henri Lonitz (Frankfurt: Suhrkamp, 2004), 263.

*the West.*²⁵ Indeed, in his essay "Spengler Today" from 1941, the same year that the work on *Dialectic of Enlightenment* began, Adorno praised Spengler's sensitivity to "the dual character of enlightenment." Moreover, in his essay, as seen in chapter 2, Adorno criticized Spengler's early critics for avoiding the deeper challenge posed by *The Decline of the West*. Rather than complacently playing putatively healthy culture against barbarism, Spengler's highbrow adversaries would have done better to recognize "the element of barbarism inherent in culture itself."²⁶ This recognition was something that had impressed Adorno not only in the thinking of Walter Benjamin but also in that of Spengler.²⁷ On this basis, it is not surprising that Adorno suggested to Horkheimer that his Spengler essay could serve as "a real preparatory work for our things."²⁸

The present chapter aims to deepen our understanding of Klages's and Spengler's presence in *Dialectic of Enlightenment*, especially in its opening chapter, "The Concept of Enlightenment," and the excursus, "Odysseus or Myth and Enlightenment."²⁹ Concerning

---

25. George Friedman, *The Political Philosophy of the Frankfurt School* (Ithaca, NY: Cornell University Press, 1981), 83–84; Michel Pauen, *Dithyrambiker des Untergangs. Gnostizismus in Ästhetik und Philosophie der Moderne* (Berlin: Akademie Verlag, 1994), 358.

26. Theodor W. Adorno, "Spengler Today," *Studies in Philosophy and Social Science* 9, no. 2 (1941), 309, 325.

27. Adorno to Horkheimer, June 12, 1941, in Adorno, *Briefwechsel, Bd. II: 1938–1944*, 144–45; Adorno, "Spengler Today," 324.

28. Adorno to Horkheimer, May 3, 1941, in Adorno, *Briefwechsel, Bd. II: 1938–1944*, 109.

29. As for the question of authorship, *Dialectic of Enlightenment*, as Adorno and Horkheimer frequently underlined, was a collaborative work. However, which of the two authors left a stronger imprint on its individual chapters has been a point of some contention. It seems apparent that Adorno was principally responsible for the excursus on Homer's *Odyssey*; his early draft of the excursus is a strong proof of this. The lead chapter, "The Concept of Enlightenment," has, in contrast, been attributed to Horkheimer, most notably by Jürgen Habermas. I am, however, of Robert Hullot-Kentor's view that Adorno's strong presence is palpable in this chapter as well, because stylistically it follows Adorno's unique paratactic style. See Robert Hullot-Kentor, "Back to Adorno," in *Things beyond Resemblance: Collected Essays on Theodor W. Adorno* (New York: Columbia University Press, 2006), 25–27; Jürgen Habermas, "Remarks on the Development of Max Horkheimer's Work," trans. Kenneth Baynes and John McCole, in *On Max Horkheimer: New Perspectives*, ed. Seyla Benhabib et al. (Cambridge, MA: MIT Press, 1993), 57.

Klages, I argue that his romanticized conception of so-called Pelasgians, the half-mythical indigenous people of the ancient Aegean, served as a considerable stimulus to Adorno and Horkheimer's reading of the *Odyssey* and their postulates about the entwinement of myth and reason. As for Spengler, I will focus on his short 1931 book *Man and Technics* (reviewed by Adorno in 1932) and suggest that its anthropological account of the domination of nature served as another underappreciated stimulus for Adorno and Horkheimer to develop anthropological arguments of their own. However, before exploring these main themes of the chapter, I would like to pause for a few moments to examine some long-overlooked aspects of *Dialectic of Enlightenment* crucial for my interpretation: first, the book's critical assessment of the tradition of German philhellenism, or love of Greek culture, and, second, its prehistory in Adorno's academic encounters in Oxford in the mid-1930s.

Adorno and German Philhellenism

Since the days of Johann Joachim Winckelmann, Friedrich August Wolf, and Wilhelm von Humboldt, romantically inclined German humanists of the *Goethezeit* (the period of 1770–1830, covering the literary activity of Johann Wolfgang von Goethe) had set against utilitarianism and the fragmentation of their own age an idealized image of ancient Greece. The wholeness that Jean-Jacques Rousseau expected to find in nature these philhellenes sought in the beauty, harmony, and serenity of classical Athens (490–323 BCE), for them the ultimate standard of human excellence. What started off as a cultural rebellion of a handful of outsiders, however, had by the mid-nineteenth century turned into sterile academicism in the service of Prussian, and subsequently German, nation-building. As German philhellenes were accused of abandoning their lofty pedagogical ideals for sober positivism, the ideal itself was reshaped at the margins of the movement. In *Die Geburt der Tragödie* (*The Birth of Tragedy*, 1872), Friedrich Nietzsche interpreted the "Apollonian" Athens as inferior to the raw "Dionysian" forces of Homer's archaic era (c. 750–490 BCE), while in *Das Mutterrecht* (*The Mother Right*,

1861) Johann Jakob Bachofen projected behind the Periclean patriarchy an older matriarchal order of "Pelasgians," the fabled pre-Greek inhabitants of the Aegean. Fighting the stagnation of German philhellenism, yet in keeping with its original revitalizing impulse, the two maverick classicists thus located the ideal antiquity earlier in history, looked askance at as barbarian both by the classical Hellenes and their modern German admirers.[30]

This fascination with "irrational" stages of ancient history, spurned as anathema by academic classical studies, received greater attention at the turn of the twentieth century in the emerging disciplines of anthropology and comparative mythology. Encouraging this turn to the preclassical period was also a wider German interest in myth after World War I, in the wake of which philosophers such as Ernst Cassirer and Martin Heidegger, and psychologists, from Sigmund Freud to Carl Gustav Jung, labored to revise the prevalent overly sanguine notion of the human as *animal rationale*.[31] The so-called Bachofen renaissance of the 1920s reflected this widespread yearning to reach back to the primordial roots of human life (whatever one thought those to be) and to challenge, even unlearn, some taken-for-granted wisdoms of cultural modernity: rationalism, progress, individualism, liberalism, materialism, and so forth. Chiefly responsible for this enthusiasm for Bachofen, a long-forgotten Swiss scholar of Greco-Roman burial sites, were two Munich-based bohemian circles: the *George-Kreis* led by the lyrical poet Stefan George and the *Kosmischer Rund* (Cosmics) steered by the eccentric *Lebensphilosoph* Ludwig Klages. What attracted these groups to Bachofen was his view that myths of classical antiquity were not epitomes of some perfect standard, revered by the early German philhellenes of the *Goethezeit*. Neither were they mere reflections of prosaic social

---

30. Suzanne L. Marchand, *Down from Olympus: Archaeology and Philhellenism in Germany, 1750–1970* (Princeton, NJ: Princeton University Press, 1996), chap 1; Peter Davies, *Myth, Matriarchy and Modernity: Johann Jakob Bachofen in German Culture 1860–1945* (Berlin: De Gruyter, 2010), chap. 1.

31. Fritz Graf, *Greek Mythology: An Introduction*, trans. Thomas Marier (Baltimore, MD: Johns Hopkins University Press, 1993), chap. 2; Steven M. Wasserstrom, *Religion after Religion: Gershom Scholem, Mircea Eliade, and Henry Corbin at Eranos* (Princeton, NJ: Princeton University Press, 1999), chap. 7.

reality, soberly investigated by the later positivist philology led by Ulrich von Wilamowitz-Moellendorff, the grand old man of the guild and a rival of Nietzsche. For Bachofen, they were instead "symbols." What did they symbolize? According to Bachofen, Joseph Mali notes, classical myths "expressed and explained a far more primitive stage in human history, that of archaic religiosity and of mythology, in which men encoded their most seminal confrontations with primordial natural and social realities." These symbols—or archaic images (*Urbilder*) as Klages came to call them—were still accessible to the moderns if they managed to free themselves of their rationalist excesses.[32]

Dialectic of Enlightenment, it seems apparent to me, is a chapter in the history of German philhellenism. The book enters a dialogue with "cultural fascists," later epigones of Nietzsche and Bachofen, who in their animosity toward liberal individualism perceive even in Homer's *Odyssey* (commonly believed to date from c. 750 BCE) a "democratic element," belittle it as a "product of seafarers and traders," and denounce it "for its overly rational discourse." In so doing, however, these "fashionable irrationalists," Adorno and Horkheimer note, have also laid bare something crucial about "bourgeois Western civilization." They have shown that links between "reason, liberality, and middle-class qualities do indeed extend incomparably further back than is assumed by historians who date the concept of the burgher from the end of medieval feudalism." Going against the conventional wisdom of European history (which Horkheimer too had underwritten only a few years prior) this "neo-Romantic reaction equates world history with enlightenment." With its polemics against Homer, however, it unintentionally pays him and the civilization it despises "involuntary homage." Latter-day irrationalists are "forced to acknowledge," Adorno and Horkheimer note with pleasure, "enlightened thinking even in the remotest past."[33]

---

32. Joseph Mali, "The Reconciliation with Myth: Benjamin's Homage to Bachofen," *Journal of the History of Ideas* 60, no. 1 (1999): 179; Lebovic, *The Philosophy of Life and Death*, chap. 3.
33. Horkheimer and Adorno, *Dialectic of Enlightenment*, 36–37, 40, xviii.

The twentieth-century followers of Nietzsche and Bachofen, Adorno and Horkheimer remind their readers, were rather selective in borrowing from their masters. Nietzsche viewed Homer, and the demythologization process he inaugurated, with mixed feelings. He saw "in enlightenment both the universal movement of sovereign mind, whose supreme exponent he believed himself to be, and a 'nihilistic', life-denying power." Only the latter aspect, however, was noticed by his later copycats on the radical Right. An exemplary figure was the essayist and cultural historian Rudolf Borchardt (1877–1945), whom *Dialectic of Enlightenment* briefly comments on. Whereas Nietzsche had defended Homer, Borchardt disliked the fallible and anthropomorphic features of Homer's Olympian gods. Against them, he set the lyric poet Pindar (518–438 BCE) and the philosopher poet Xenophanes (560–478 BCE), allegedly two late guardians of primordial popular religion and genuinely mythical Greece.[34] Adorno and Horkheimer, however, argue that Borchardt ignored the fact that "the primal powers he extols themselves represent a stage of enlightenment," as evinced by Pindar's use of irony and Xenophanes's pursuits in ontological inquiry.[35]

Dialectic of Enlightenment sought to challenge neo-Romantic interpretations of antiquity such as Borchardt's. In tune with these interpretations, it views Odysseus as "the prototype of the bourgeois individual" who outwits the powers of nature represented by the mythical figures he encounters on his return home from the Trojan War.[36] But instead of lamenting this demythologization process, as the neo-Romantic archaists did, *Dialectic of Enlightenment* welcomed it. As even a casual reader of the book immediately observes, however, for Adorno and Horkheimer demythologization does not mark unambiguous progress. Indeed, the reading of Homer they advance is at odds not only with protofascist interpretations such as Borchardt's, but also with latter-day philhellenes of a more liberal

---

34. Rudolf Borchardt, *Pindarische Gedichte* (Munich: Deschler, 1929/1930), 106–7, 109, 116.
35. Horkheimer and Adorno, *Dialectic of Enlightenment*, 36–37; Theodor W. Adorno, "Geschichtsphilosophischer Exkurs zur *Odyssee*: Frühe Fassung von *Odysseus oder Mythos und Aufklärung*," in *Frankfurter Adorno Blätter*, vol. 5, 43–44.
36. Horkheimer and Adorno, *Dialectic of Enlightenment*, 35.

"Demystification of Antiquity"   129

bent, who, as Adorno wrote in the early draft of the Odysseus excursus, clung naively to the rational legacy of classical Athens and wished "to know as little about pre-history as about Nietzsche."[37]

It is worth noting that Adorno and Horkheimer's dialogue with the tradition of German philhellenism, however, predated their work in California by several years. It may be impossible to determine its starting point with certainty. We have a good hint, however, in Adorno's demand in 1936 "to uncover the foul magic that is being done today with antiquity."[38] With this statement, Adorno was probably thinking of the prestige Stefan George's neohumanist ideals had enjoyed in German classical studies since the early 1920s. George's rejection of academic antiquarianism, Martin A. Ruehl remarks, had a substantial influence on a number of notable classicists (such as Werner Jaeger and Karl Reinhardt) who in the interwar era "transformed the discipline of *Altertumswissenschaft*" through "their reinvention of 'the classical' as an educational ideal."[39]

I am of the opinion, however, that we should hear in Adorno's statement (as he restated it some months later) that "a demystification of antiquity is absolutely indispensable"[40] an echo of his own "Klages project." The project, as he described it to Siegfried Kracauer in 1933, was about gaining a better understanding of "the mythical." There should, I think, be little doubt that it was in *Dialectic of Enlightenment* that Adorno finally managed to put on paper his thoughts on Klages's relevance, which had troubled him for over a decade (in his Oxford manuscript from the mid-1930 his confrontation with Klages had been implicit). Although the book's dialogue with Klages is brief, it frequently relies on conceptual dualisms

---

37. Adorno, "Geschichtsphilosophischer Exkurs zur *Odyssee*," 38.

38. Adorno to Horkheimer, June 25, 1936, in Adorno, *Briefwechsel, Bd. I: 1927–1937*, 166.

39. Martin A. Ruehl, "Aesthetic Fundamentalism in Weimar Poetry: Stefan George and His Circle, 1918–1933," in *Weimar Thought: A Contested Legacy*, ed. Peter E. Gordon and John P. McCormick (Princeton, NJ: Princeton University Press, 2013), 242. See also Uvo Hölscher, "Strömungen der deutschen Graezistik in den zwanziger Jahren," in *Altertumswissenschaft in den 20er Jahren: Neue Fragen und Impulse*, ed. Hellmut Flashar (Stuttgart: Franz Steiner Verlag, 1995), 65–85.

40. Adorno to Horkheimer, November 28, 1936, in Adorno, *Briefwechsel, Bd. I: 1927–1937*, 235.

familiar from *The Spirit as Adversary of the Soul*: image and word, soul and reason, and chthonic and logocentric.[41]

Significantly, in the early draft of the Odysseus excursus, Adorno named, next to Borchardt, not only Klages but also Spengler as those reactionary thinkers who "have shown more insight" than their invocation of "primordial powers" would allow one to assume.[42] Spengler's diagnosis of the Caesarist tendencies of the Weimar Republic, as observed in chapter 2, only began to intrigue Adorno after his arrival in New York in 1938 and especially after the antisemitic pogroms in Germany later that year. Spengler's anthropological reflections, however, were familiar to him earlier. In 1932, Adorno wrote a review of Spengler's booklet *Man and Technics* for the *Zeitschrift für Sozialforschung*. This short review, although approving of Spengler's anthropological approach, did not further elaborate on the topic. In his 1941 Spengler essay, however, Adorno implied that *Man and Technics*, which "was not allowed to be in the same class as the smart philosophical anthropologies of the same time," was unfairly overlooked.[43] Moreover, as already observed, Adorno hoped that his Spengler essay would form a "real preparatory work" for his collaborative efforts with Horkheimer.[44] There is, then, a wealth of evidence to support the

---

41. Lars Bjurman and Carl-Henning Wijkmark, Editorial remarks on *Dialectic of Enlightenment*'s Swedish translation *Upplysningens dialektik: Filosofiska fragment* (Gothenburg, Sweden: Daidalos, 1981), 287.

42. Adorno, "Geschichtsphilosophischer Exkurs zur *Odyssee*," 40.

43. Adorno, "Spengler Today," 305. Adorno likely had in mind Max Scheler's *The Human Place in the Cosmos* (1928), Martin Heidegger's *Being and Time* (1927), Ernst Cassirer's *Mythic Thought* (1925), and Nicolai Hartmann's *The Problem of Spiritual Being* (1931).

44. Certainly, other works were also considered, such as Adorno's *Philosophy of New Music* (the first part of which dates from 1940–1941) and Horkheimer's essay "The End of Reason" (1941). Nor should we forget the 1942 debate at the Institute for Social Research on Nietzsche as another signpost of the early Frankfurt School's (especially Horkheimer's) path from Marxist ideology critique to a more sweeping critique of all of Western civilization. The core theme in these works and in the Nietzsche debate, however, was the same as in Adorno's Spengler essay: domination of outer and inner nature as the definitive feature of Western history. See Horkheimer to Adorno, August 28, 1941, in Adorno, *Briefwechsel, Bd. II: 1938–1944*, 212–18; John Abromeit, *Max Horkheimer and the Foundations of the Frankfurt School* (Cambridge: Cambridge University Press, 2011), 394–95. On the Nietzsche

argument that Spengler's and Klages's teachings served as a powerful spur for Adorno and Horkheimer's conception of *Dialectic of Enlightenment*.

By the early twentieth century, the tradition of German philhellenism had assumed an increasingly reactionary outlook far removed from its cosmopolitan beginnings in the *Goethezeit*. We have seen that the interpretations of Homer and Greek prehistory by the *völkisch* epigones of Nietzsche and Bachofen served as important background for Adorno and Horkheimer's questioning of the origins of Western civilization. These origins, however, were not only discussed in Germany. To fulfill our story of the prehistory of *Dialectic of Enlightenment*, we need to look at Adorno first years in exile at Oxford University, "at the time possibly the most prestigious university" in classical studies.[45]

Oxford Encounters

Adorno's effort to understand antiquity and "the mythical" began in Frankfurt, before his emigration to Oxford. His two remarks from 1936, however, suggest that he took major steps forward in England. We saw in chapter 1 that Adorno learned from his fellow émigré Alfred Sohn-Rethel about the societal underpinnings of pre-Socratic philosophy. Besides this Marxist maverick, Adorno absorbed a great deal from renowned academic experts at Oxford. One of them was Gilbert Murray (1866–1957), the Regius Professor of Greek and one of the most prominent authorities on ancient Greece. In the early Odysseus draft, Adorno wrote, with an endorsing reference to Murray, that the insight into modern aspects of Homeric epics, trumpeted in Germany by the latter-day epigones of Nietzsche and Bachofen, was "no privilege of repressive neo-Romantic

---

debate, see "Special Section on Frankfurt School and Nietzsche," *Constellations: An International Journal of Critical and Democratic Theory* 8, no. 1 (2001): 127–47.

45. Andreas Kramer and Evelyn Wilcock, "'A Preserve for Professional Philosophers': Adornos Husserl-Dissertation 1934–37 und ihr Oxforder Kontext," *Deutsche Vierteljahrsschrift für Literaturwissenschaft und Geistesgeschichte* 73 (October 1999), 121.

archaism." Adorno quoted from Murray's *Five Stages of Greek Religion*: "The things that have misled us moderns in our efforts towards understanding the primitive stage in Greek religion have been first the widespread and almost ineradicable error of treating Homer as primitive."[46]

Yet perhaps the most fruitful of Adorno's Oxford encounters was with Murray's disciple Cecil Maurice Bowra (1898–1971), from 1938 onward the Warden of Wadham College. Adorno considered Bowra a perfect contributor to his campaign against the neo-Romantic falsification of the roots of Western civilization. What made Bowra a credible ally in Adorno's eyes was not only his status as an esteemed academic authority on Greek poetry. Equally important was his high standing among the George Circle (both Klages and Borchardt were former members). Bowra had translated George's works into English, and on top of this he was personally acquainted with some of the members of the circle, such as Ernst Kantorowicz. Although Bowra came from a similar culturally conservative milieu, and to a great degree shared their neo-Romantic aesthetic preferences, he was no naïve spokesperson for their elitist mission for cultural regeneration. Bowra possessed, as his colleague Isaiah Berlin later recalled, "Byronic irony about the very Romantic values that were closest to his heart."[47] This irony made him an "ideal" partner for Adorno.[48]

In 1937, Bowra wrote an article to the Institute for Social Research's journal in which he charted the societal background of ancient Greek poetry. He cast a critical eye on popular notions of "Greek civilization as the product of a national spirit" (*Volkseele*) and of Greek art "as a national art" (*Volkskunst*). What this meant, and what must have delighted, even influenced Adorno—he and

---

46. Adorno, "Geschichtsphilosophischer Exkurs zur *Odyssee*," 41n9; Gilbert Murray, *Five Stages of Greek Religion* (New York: Columbia University Press, 1925), 24.

47. Isaiah Berlin, "Memorial Address in St Mary's," in *Maurice Bowra: A Celebration*, ed. Hugh Lloyd-Jones (London: Duckworth, 1974), 17.

48. Adorno to Horkheimer, November 28, 1936, in Adorno, *Briefwechsel, Bd. I: 1927–1937*, 236.

Horkheimer first suggested Odysseus as their chief protagonist only in the early 1940s[49] —was Bowra's conviction that Homeric epics were not a popular art form that had arisen from "popular spirit," or from the so-called common people. Instead, the tales of the Trojan War and Odysseus's homecoming were based on an unmistakably aristocratic tradition of oral recitation, which made them a cultural artifact relevant only for a small segment of Greek society. Further evidence against the view of the *Iliad* and the *Odyssey* as manifestations of elementary popular religion, Bowra argued, was their exceptional literary quality. They were structured around a clear "architectural plan" and showed substantial "knowledge of human nature." The language of the Homeric epics, "extraordinarily flexible and rich throughout," Bowra went on, could "never have been a spoken vernacular." Finally, although the *Iliad* and the *Odyssey* built on "a traditional theme," they altered it "by what can only be called an ethical outlook alien to the original story."[50] In *Dialectic of Enlightenment*, Adorno and Horkheimer echo Bowra's arguments. The *Odyssey*, they write, "shows clear links to myth: the adventures are drawn from popular tradition. But as the Homeric spirit takes over and 'organizes' the myths, it comes into contradiction with them." Signs of this demythologization, they stress, "are still visible at the joints where editors have stitched the epic together."[51]

Another person worth mentioning in the context of Adorno's Oxford years is the philosopher Ernst Cassirer (1874–1945), a major figure in early twentieth-century European thought and another German Jewish émigré with whom Adorno established contact in England. While their personal discussion revolved around Adorno's wish for help from the famous senior scholar to secure himself a

---

49. On the adoption of Odysseus as their central figure, see Anson Rabinbach, *In the Shadow of Catastrophe: German Intellectuals between Apocalypse and Enlightenment* (Berkeley: University of California Press, 1997), 181–86.

50. Cecil Maurice Bowra, "Sociological Remarks on Greek Poetry," *Zeitschrift für Sozialforschung* 6, no. 2 (1937): 382–88. On Bowra's life and work, see Leslie Mitchell, *Maurice Bowra: A Life* (Oxford: Oxford University Press, 2009).

51. Horkheimer and Adorno, *Dialectic of Enlightenment*, 35.

position at Oxford,[52] the reason Cassirer deserves our attention is that Gérard Raulet has raised him to the status of a chief stimulator of *Dialectic of Enlightenment*. Raulet suggests that the book's non-Marxist, anthropological questioning got its "bearings" from Cassirer's *Mythical Thought* (1925), the second volume of his tripartite *Philosophie der symbolischen Formen* (*The Philosophy of Symbolic Forms*, 1923–1929). According to Raulet, Adorno and Horkheimer's thesis concerning the continuity of mythical and rational thinking was an "almost literal application" of Cassirer's ideas. Rather than antithetical dispositions, one "barbaric" and the other "civilized," myth and reason, for Cassirer, shared much more than was commonly realized. Both were efforts at what he called "symbolization," at making sense of the world. To appreciate this continuity between *Mythos* and *Logos*, one had to understand myth not primarily "as a complex of belief and narrative" but as a "spiritual form," and moreover as one that "remains effective in the deep structures of thought" even in modernity.[53]

Raulet's is an intriguing interpretation. *Dialectic of Enlightenment*'s complete silence on Cassirer, however, taken together with Adorno's derogatory remarks elsewhere, where he stated Cassirer was "a conformist idiot" and "totally gaga," do not seem to support it.[54] Other evidence against it includes the marked differences between their admittedly similar notions of myth and reason. In a 1937 letter to Benjamin, Adorno apparently alluded to Cassirer when he insisted that one should not reduce the importance of myth "through an appeal to 'symbolism,'" a verdict that echoed Benjamin's earlier suspicion of Cassirer's "attempt to present mythical

---

52. Kramer and Wilcock, "'A Preserve for Professional Philosophers,'" 121–22.

53. Gérard Raulet, "Secularization, Myth, Anti-Semitism: Adorno and Horkheimer's *Dialectic of Enlightenment* and Cassirer's *Philosophy of Symbolic Forms*," trans. Ladislaus Löb, in *The Early Frankfurt School and Religion*, ed. M. Kohlenbach et al. (London: Palgrave, 2004), 173–74, 182; Ernst Cassirer, *The Philosophy of Symbolic Forms*, vol. 2, *Mythical Thought*, trans. Ralph Manheim (New Haven, CT: Yale University Press, 1955).

54. Adorno to Horkheimer, November 2, 1934, and May 13, 1935, in Adorno, *Briefwechsel, Bd. I: 1927–1937*, 25, 68.

thought in concepts."⁵⁵ Moreover, as Edward Skidelsky stresses, the neo-Kantian Cassirer, unlike Adorno and Horkheimer, never viewed reason as inherently mythical, even as he occasionally bemoaned its ossification into an abstract instrument. Attesting further to their differences, whereas Cassirer in *The Myth of the State* (1946) saw Nazism as an expression of the endurance of mythic thinking in modern times, Adorno and Horkheimer held reason's own mythical aspects to be a crucial precondition for Nazism's triumph.⁵⁶

Tae-Yeoun Keum has recently offered an insightful clarification of the parallels and disparities between *The Myth of the State* and *Dialectic of Enlightenment*. Both Cassirer and Adorno and Horkheimer wrote in an era in which the over one-hundred-year-old belief in political and epistemic progress had shipwrecked. The nineteenth century, proud of its maturity and rationality, had congratulated itself for abandoning the old fictional narratives of supernatural heroes and gods, cultural artifacts typical to putatively precritical Greco-Roman antiquity and non-European indigenous cultures. Societal, political, and cultural developments of the early twentieth century West, however, showed that this self-indulgence was premature. To be sure, "literary myths," or a definitive literary genre impervious to logical argumentation, was clearly a thing of the past. However, mythical habits of thought and perception, or "a kind of dense and fraught cognitive" inclination "to approach any given aspect of reality one way," were alive and well even in the modern disenchanted West.⁵⁷

In the interwar era, these mythical habits received their most sinister expression in the Nazi myth of a superior "Aryan" race. A

---

55. Adorno to Benjamin, September 22, 1937, in Adorno, *The Complete Correspondence*, 212; Benjamin to Hugo von Hofmannsthal, December 28, 1925, in Walter Benjamin, *The Correspondence of Walter Benjamin, 1910–1940*, ed. Gershom Scholem and Theodor W. Adorno, trans. Manfred R. Jacobson and Evelyn M. Jacobson (Chicago: University of Chicago Press, 1994), 287.

56. Edward Skidelsky, *Ernst Cassirer: The Last Philosopher of Culture* (Princeton, NJ: Princeton University Press, 2008), 153; Ernst Cassirer, *The Myth of the State* (New Haven, CT: Yale University Press, 1946).

57. Tae-Yeoun Keum, *Plato and the Mythic Tradition in Political Thought* (Cambridge, MA: The Belknap Press of Harvard University Press, 2020), 7.

good deal of *Dialectic of Enlightenment*'s scrutiny of what Adorno in 1933 called "the mythical" is, unsurprisingly, directed at this resurrection of mythic thought patterns in their most brutal, indeed genocidal, form. This observation brings *Dialectic of Enlightenment* into the company of Cassirer's *The Myth of the State* as well as many other contemporary and later analyses of Nazism. But Adorno and Horkheimer's distinctive contribution to the understanding of what Keum calls "deep myths" lies elsewhere, namely in their observation that these myths are also visible in phenomena commonly thought to be furthest removed from superstition and prejudice: scientific reason and technology. What is similar in these otherwise so different relations to the world, *Dialectic of Enlightenment* argues, is a certain tacit form of thought or mentality. As Keum succinctly defines it, it is "a kind of fatalistic orientation toward the world, or the perception that the established order of things is beyond change."[58]

Hence, Adorno and Horkheimer claimed, in tune with Cassirer, that the ancient notion of "fate" was alive in the Nazi demand to surrender to iron laws of racial aggression, in which individual liberties mean nothing. But they went further than Cassirer by contending that this fatalism was equally on display in the "dog eat dog" reality of modern capitalism, which perpetuated the struggle for existence at a time of unprecedented technological progress, when its pacification was no longer unrealistic. Again, in the realm of thought, scientific philosophy (logical positivism of the Vienna Circle and American pragmatism), also exhibits mythical fatalism. As great as its capacity for mathematical abstraction and means-ends calculations is, it withdraws from all considerations of reorganizing modern industrial society in nonantagonistic terms.

Cassirer may well be, with the abovementioned reservations, one source behind *Dialectic of Enlightenment*'s turn to the anthropological investigation of reason. But other sources are plausible too, sources that could have provided equal stimulus to Adorno and Horkheimer's continuity thesis and that viewed reason and modernity through a far darker lens than Cassirer ever did. Moreover, we

---

58. Keum, *Plato and the Mythic Tradition in Political Thought*, 228.

have abundant empirical evidence that stresses the important role of these sources.

In the following sections, I will argue in detail regarding why I think *Dialectic of Enlightenment* ought to be read as a critical rejoinder to Klages and Spengler. This adds a decisive layer to the narrative that I tell in this book about Adorno's preoccupation with the German critique of civilization. In his Oxford study on epistemology, Adorno had (implicitly) countered Klages's anthropological critique of reason with a quasi-Marxist view, informed by Alfred Sohn-Rethel, of history of Western philosophy as a mirror effect of capitalism. In *Dialectic of Enlightenment*, however, Adorno marshals against *Zivilisationskritik*'s anthropological claims not only societal arguments but also anthropological ones of his own. Why this shift in his thought? The inspiration he received from Benjamin and Freud (and Weber and perhaps Cassirer too) was surely important, and I by no means wish to trivialize their contributions. But another factor, I believe, was Adorno's steadily more intensive pondering on the dark anthropological theories of Klages and Spengler. This shift, it should be noted, was a gradual one, as fleeting anthropological lines of thinking start to appear in Adorno's writings at the beginning of the 1930s. Only in *Dialectic of Enlightenment*, however, do they assume a more systematic character, to the extent that one can thus describe these "philosophical fragments."[59]

---

59. Anticipations of Adorno's anthropological account of the origins of instrumental reason are visible in his qualified praise of the French sociologist Roger Caillois's study *La mante religieuse. Recherche sur la nature et la signification du mythe* (The praying mantis: An investigation into the significance of myth, 1937). Adorno wrote to Benjamin in 1937 that he was pleased with Caillois's decision of not "dissolving the myths within the immanent sphere of consciousness"—as Freud was guilty of doing—or "reducing their significance through an appeal to 'symbolism'"—as Cassirer, as seen above, did. What attracted Adorno in Caillois's understanding of myths was that the latter was "really seeking to grasp their actuality." Callois's approach, Adorno added, was "a kind of materialism he shares with Jung, and certainly with Klages." Regrettably, Adorno added, "he shares more than that." Notwithstanding Callois's dubious protofascist reduction of humanity to blind nature, Adorno argued that the task remained for critical theory to try "to shatter the reified separation of spheres like the biological on one side and the socio-historical on the other." Adorno to Benjamin, September 22, 1937, in Adorno, *The Complete Correspondence*, 212. See also Adorno, review of *La mante religieuse. Recherche sur la*

Klages's Pelasgians

Dialectic of Enlightenment's short dialogue with Klages in its Odysseus excursus focuses only on a couple of pages of the latter's gigantic *The Spirit as Adversary of the Soul*—namely on the book's last part, "The Worldview of Pelasgianism," and its concluding section on "the original meaning of sacrifice."[60] Nevertheless, I contend that this short section is intimately connected to Adorno and Horkheimer's key thesis about the entanglement of myth and reason. At the heart of their dialogue with Klages stands the latter's romanticized image of the so-called Pelasgians, the mysterious aboriginal people of ancient Greece, whose "chthonic" worldview Klages juxtaposes to what for him is the fundamentally flawed "logocentrism" of Western civilization.

---

nature et la signification du mythe, by Roger Caillois, *Zeitschrift für Sozialforschung* 7, no. 3 (1938): 410–11. Already in the early 1930s, during the writing of his book on Kierkegaard, Adorno conceded the following in a discussion with his supervisor Paul Tillich and other Frankfurt colleagues: "The demythologization process is not straightforward but dialectical. The mythical cannot simply be utterly destroyed, but must be confronted again and again, and ... the actual productive forces [*Produktivkräfte*] of history indeed ensue from these mythical sources. I would grant this." Theodor W. Adorno's contribution to "Diskussion über die Aufgabe des Protestantismus in der sekularen Zivilisation," in Max Horkheimer, *Gesammelte Schriften, Bd. 11: Nachgelassene Schriften 1914–1931*, ed. Gunzelin Schmid Noerr (Frankfurt: Fischer, 1987), 367. These productive forces, Adorno implied, were not Marx's economic ones but anthropological ones related to the relationship between humanity and nature. Adorno elaborated on this theme in his July 1932 lecture on "natural-history." By nature, Adorno meant "myth," that "what has always been, what as fatefully arranged predetermined being underlies history and appears in history." By history, in contrast, he referred to "the qualitatively new," to "a movement that does not play itself out in mere identity, mere reproduction of what has always been." While Adorno claimed that with these ideas he was involving himself in an immanent critique of Heidegger's *Being and Time*, they may have also been related to his Klages project—begun, as we have seen, a month earlier in June 1932—and his dialectical reformulation of Klages's dualism of "soul" and "spirit." Adorno, "The Idea of Natural-History," trans. Robert Hullot-Kentor, in Hullot-Kentor, *Things beyond Resemblance*, 253.

60. Ludwig Klages, *Der Geist als Widersacher der Seele: Fünftes Buch* [The spirit as adversary of the soul: Book five]. *Sämtliche Werke, Bd. 2*, ed. Ernst Frauchiger et al. (Bonn: Bouvier Verlag, 1966), 1401–15.

"Demystification of Antiquity"   139

Not much is known for certain of the Pelasgians, who got their name from the ancient Greeks. Apparently, they had been living in the Balkan Peninsula and Aegean Islands since the Bronze Age. Even after the triumph of Greek-speaking Hellenic tribes at the end of the Bronze Age, small, dispersed Pelasgian communities, presumably speaking a language of their own, continued to live in the area well into the classical period. Several ancient authors mention the Pelasgians. Homer writes in the *Iliad* that they had participated in the Trojan War on the sides of both the Achaeans and the Trojans, whereas in the *Odyssey* he lists the "proud Pelasgians" among the numerous tribes living in Crete.[61] The Pelasgians also show up in the *Histories* by Herodotus, in Thucydides' *History of the Peloponnesian War*, and in the geographer Pausanias's *Description of Greece*.[62]

In the modern era, it was Johann Jacob Bachofen who had done the most to raise awareness of the Pelasgian culture. Bachofen commended what he saw as the Pelasgians' matriarchal social order, out of which Greek-speaking antiquity purportedly only later arose.[63] Bachofen's teachings found one of their most passionate readers in Ludwig Klages. The latter endorsed the Pelasgians' chthonic paganism, which he thought was free of many ill-fated features of the later Olympian religion of the Hellenes. Unlike logocentrism, visible

---

61. Homer, *The Iliad*, trans. Robert Fagles (New York: Penguin Books, 1991), 2.681–2.684, 2.840–2.843; *The Odyssey*, trans. Robert Fagles (New York: Penguin Books, 1996), 19.201.

62. Herodotus, *The Histories*, trans. Aubrey de Sélincourt (New York: Penguin Books, 2003), 1.56–1.58, 6.137–6.140; Thucydides, *History of the Peloponnesian War*, trans. Rex Warner (New York: Penguin Books, 1974), 1.3.2, 2.16–2.17; Pausanias, *Description of Greece*, vols. 1–5, trans. W. H. S. Jones (Cambridge, MA: Harvard University Press, 1989), 8.14–8.16, 8.41.

63. On current scholarly views of the Pelasgians, or what is today called the question of the "Aegean substratum," see Margalit Finkelberg, *Greeks and Pre-Greeks: Aegean Prehistory and Greek Heroic Tradition* (Cambridge: Cambridge University Press, 2005); Cynthia W. Shelmerdine, ed. *The Cambridge Companion to the Aegean Bronze Age* (Cambridge: Cambridge University Press, 2008). On the question of the credibility of Bachofen's matriarchal theories, see Uwe Wesel, *Der Mythos von Matriarchat: Über Bachofens Mutterrecht und die Stellung von Frauen in frühen Gesellschaften* (Frankfurt: Suhrkamp, 1999); Brigitte Röder et al., *Göttinnendämmerung: Das Matriarchat aus archäologischer Sicht* (Königsfurt, Germany: Krummwisch, 2001).

already in Homeric deities and then increasingly in Judeo-Christian monotheism, the Pelasgian religion, Klages enthused, was uniquely receptive to the presence of *Urbilder*, or primal images.[64] Ritual practices of the Pelasgians, Klages claimed, occurred in a state of "ecstasy that temporally breaks and dissolves the bounds of individuality."[65] The Pelasgians' rituals were still "magical." That is, they surrendered themselves to cosmic forces of nature rather than set themselves apart from these forces in the quasi-rational manner of the later Greeks and especially of the Judeo-Christian tradition. The latter were both marked by anthropomorphism, which Klages judged to be profoundly alien to the Pelasgian worldview.

In a passage cited by Adorno and Horkheimer, Klages summarizes this magical character of Pelasgian rituals: "The general necessity to offer sacrifices affects everyone, because everyone, as has been seen, receives his or her share of life, and all the goods of life they can obtain—the original *suum cuique*—only through the constant exchange of gifts. This, however, is not exchange in the ordinary sense of exchanging goods (although at the very beginning that, too, was consecrated by the idea of sacrifice) but of exchanging fluids or essences by *abandoning one's own soul to the supporting and nurturing life of the world*."[66] The Pelasgians' nonindividuating surrender to the powers of the world, Klages emphasized, contrasted decisively with the later Homeric conception of sacrifice. The Homeric gift, Adorno and Horkheimer noted, "falls midway between exchange and sacrifice." It is already on its way to becoming an instrument used by a clever semirational agent to secure individual self-preservation amid overpowering nature.[67]

---

64. Klages, *Der Geist als Widersacher der Seele: Fünftes Buch*, 1260, 1405–6. It should be noted that as in the case of Nietzsche, in that of Bachofen as well his twentieth-century epigones on the radical right intentionally downplayed certain aspects of his teachings to make them more suitable for their own *völkisch* purposes. Thus, Klages belittled, for example, Bachofen's unwavering allegiance to Christianity. Mali, "The Reconciliation with Myth," 184; Lebovic, *The Philosophy of Life and Death*, 89.

65. Klages, *Der Geist als Widersacher der Seele: Fünftes Buch*, 1405.

66. Klages, *Der Geist als Widersacher der Seele: Fünftes Buch*, 1409; Horkheimer and Adorno, *Dialectic of Enlightenment*, 260n6. My emphasis.

67. Horkheimer and Adorno, *Dialectic of Enlightenment*, 39.

Significantly, however, Klages conceded—and this was a concession that Adorno and Horkheimer seize on—that even the Pelasgian elementary religion was in danger of turning into an anthropomorphic divinization of the "person." This happened with the arrival of a priest-king, who with the help of taboos set himself apart from the rest of the community, which then started worshipping him instead of the deities of nature. What made this development fateful in Klages's eyes was the fact that "the personal I" was the very "site by virtue of which the spirit"—the ever-present enemy of the "soul"—"exists in the world." Only in Homer's Olympian religion and especially in the Christian conception of Jesus Christ did the principle of spirit gain prominence. Klages conceded, however, that the threat of "the divinization of the person" was there "already in Pelasgianism."[68] In *Dialectic of Enlightenment*, Adorno and Horkheimer quote Klages: "It is no longer merely pagan belief but pagan superstition which compels the king of the gods, on ascending his throne, to swear that henceforth he will cause the sun to shine and the field to be covered in fruits."[69]

With this acknowledgment of the anthropomorphic potential of Pelasgian religion, that already this prehistorical cultural practice was prone to replace abandonment to the world with instrumental self-assertion, Klages's theory offers support, against its intention, for *Dialectic of Enlightenment*'s stance that "myth is already enlightenment." Klages maintained that in Pelasgianism the "spirit" was only a marginal, almost hypothetical danger. Adorno and Horkheimer, in contrast, saw it as an inherent dialectical element of the Pelasgian worldview, or any mythic worldview for that matter. They explain this dialectic as follows: "The twofold character of sacrifice—the magic self-abandonment of the individual to the collective (in whatever form) and the self-preservation achieved through the technology of this magic—implies an objective contradiction which necessitates further development of the rational element in sacrifice. Still under the influence of magic, rationality, as the behavior of the

---

68. Klages, *Der Geist als Widersacher der Seele: Fünftes Buch*, 1408, 1411.
69. Horkheimer and Adorno, *Dialectic of Enlightenment*, 260n6; Klages, *Der Geist als Widersacher der Seele: Fünftes Buch*, 1408.

performer of the sacrifice, becomes cunning." Why does this happen? It happens because "all sacrificial acts, deliberately planned by humans, deceive the god for whom they are performed: by imposing on him the primacy of human purposes they dissolve away his power."[70] Pelasgianism was no exception to this anthropological rule.

By maintaining that "myth is already enlightenment," Adorno and Horkheimer argued against Rudolf Borchardt that the works of Pindar and Xenophanes, written during the transition from the archaic to classical period in the sixth century BCE, and for Borchardt steeped in mythical dwelling, were in truth shot through with rational motifs. In their criticism of Klages, Adorno and Horkheimer went one step further by arguing that the process of demythologization was already at work in the much older Pelasgian religion of the second millennium BCE. It bears repeating that they did this by following Klages's own lead. Ironically, Klages, "the zealous apologist of myth and sacrifice" and staunch opponent of liberal individualism, helped Adorno and Horkheimer to realize that "myth is already enlightenment."[71]

"The gods," *Dialectic of Enlightenment* elaborates regarding the dialectical character of ritual sacrifice, "are overthrown precisely by the system created to honor them." This element of deceit in sacrificial rituals "is the prototype of Odysseyan cunning, just as many of Odysseus's ruses are wrapped up, as it were, in an offering to natural deities."[72] Decisive for Adorno and Horkheimer's case against Klages is the latter's own concession concerning the nascent secular, or logocentric, features of the Pelasgian religion. Supporting their case is also their observation (informed by classical philology) that this secularization is evident in the oldest scenes of the *Odyssey*. These scenes date roughly from the same late Bronze Age era when the Pelasgians' chthonic religion is supposed to have had its heyday.[73]

---

70. Horkheimer and Adorno, *Dialectic of Enlightenment*, 40, 260n6.
71. Horkheimer and Adorno, *Dialectic of Enlightenment*, 260n6, xviii.
72. Horkheimer and Adorno, *Dialectic of Enlightenment*, 40.
73. Adorno and Horkheimer drew on Adolf Kirchhoff's *Die homerische Odyssee* (1879) and Walter Leaf's *Homer and History* (1915). See Horkheimer and Adorno, *Dialectic of Enlightenment*, 59–60; Adorno, "Geschichtsphilosophischer Exkurs zur *Odyssee*," 41n10.

One such scene is the commentary on the blissful forgetfulness experienced by eaters of lotus flowers, a scene which, Adorno and Horkheimer propose, "might be characterized as a stage in the struggle with the chthonic powers." They argue that this bliss of self-abandonment, which Klages would have appreciated, is "an illusion" comparable to using of narcotics. It means a mere "absence of the awareness of unhappiness." Real happiness would require an end to suffering, something that can only result from "historical work."[74] The tale of Circe, an ambiguous erotic seducer (which, Adorno and Horkheimer remark, "may contain echoes of the chthonic cult of Demeter"), offers another example of the *Odyssey*'s grapple with a mythic power whose "magic" threatens, by way of oblivion, to dissolve the self.[75] Finally, in the Hades scene, Odysseus realizes the illusory nature of the images of those "matriarchal" figures that the emerging Olympian "religion of light" had expelled to "the Underworld." "Only when subjectivity masters itself by recognizing the nullity of images," *Dialectic of Enlightenment* stresses, "does it begin to share the hope which images vainly promise."[76]

That myths are already fused with the logic of self-preservation was the conclusion that Klages desperately wanted to avoid. Nevertheless, as Adorno and Horkheimer underline, Klages "came up against this contradiction and found himself obliged, even within the ideal image of Pelasgianism, to distinguish between genuine and false communication with nature." Crucially for the argument of *Dialectic of Enlightenment*, Klages was "unable to derive from mythical thinking itself any opposing principle to set against the illusion of the magical mastery of nature." The reason was evident: "that very illusion constitutes the essence of myth."[77]

However, besides pushing Adorno and Horkheimer toward the realization that "myth is already enlightenment," I believe Klages also assisted them in developing their second core maxim: that "enlightenment reverts to mythology." The demythologization process

---

74. Horkheimer and Adorno, *Dialectic of Enlightenment*, 49, 50n20.
75. Horkheimer and Adorno, *Dialectic of Enlightenment*, 54–55.
76. Horkheimer and Adorno, *Dialectic of Enlightenment*, 59.
77. Horkheimer and Adorno, *Dialectic of Enlightenment*, 260n6.

inaugurated by the mythic logic described above demonstrated the irrationality of the mythic "principle of sacrifice." Adorno and Horkheimer emphasized, however, that this principle, instead of having disappeared with advancing enlightenment, only shifted its shape. "The identical, enduring self which springs from the conquest of sacrifice," they assert, "is itself the product of a hard, petrified sacrificial ritual in which the human being, by opposing its consciousness to its natural context, celebrates itself." What makes enlightenment mythical? As human beings in the process of controlling outer nature deny their inner nature, "not only the *telos* of the external mastery of nature but also the *telos* of one's own life becomes confused and opaque." When they forget their own natural constitution, "all the purposes for which they keep themselves alive—social progress, the heightening of material and intellectual forces, indeed, consciousness itself—become void." Crucially, this elevation of "the means as the end," which in the twentieth century has assumed "the character of overt madness, is already detectable in the earliest history of subjectivity."[78]

The demythologization process, in which liberation from the shackles of nature turns into domination not only of outer nature but also of one's own natural inclinations, "appears prototypically in the hero who escapes the sacrifice by sacrificing himself." Or as *Dialectic of Enlightenment* summarizes the whole process: "The history of civilization is the history of the introversion of sacrifice—in other words, the history of renunciation."[79] Giving Klages his due, Adorno and Horkheimer concede that "that much is true of the famous story in Nordic mythology according to which Odin was hung from a tree as a sacrifice to himself" (a scene that concludes *The Spirit as Adversary of the Soul*) "and of Klages's thesis that every sacrifice is a sacrifice of the god to the god, as is still apparent in Christology, the monotheistic disguise of myth."[80]

Dialectic of Enlightenment sees the ambivalent character of demythologization on display not only in the history of religion but also in

---

78. Horkheimer and Adorno, *Dialectic of Enlightenment*, 42–43.
79. Horkheimer and Adorno, *Dialectic of Enlightenment*, 43.
80. Horkheimer and Adorno, *Dialectic of Enlightenment*, 42; Klages, *Der Geist als Widersacher der Seele: Fünftes Buch*, 1414–15.

the history of philosophy. It is apparent, first, in the struggle between pre-Socratic *Logos* and Homeric *Mythos* beginning in the seventh century BCE and, subsequently, in the history of Western philosophy as an increasing emptying of reason of its noninstrumental, nonmeasurable, or uncountable features.[81] *Dialectic of Enlightenment*'s view of Western rationality as filled with mythic remnants is stimulated by Klages's critique of what Adorno already in 1931 called "bourgeois ideology," meaning essentially the same thing as what he in *Negative Dialectics* would call "constitutive subjectivity": reduction of the world to subjective thought categories. Klages's view of the continuity of Western philosophy from Parmenides and Heraclitus to modern phenomenology, as seen in chapter 1, left its mark on Adorno's "liquidation of idealism," which he pursued in his Oxford manuscript on Husserl and epistemology in the mid-1930s.

The cognitive demythologization that occurred in religion and philosophy had its equivalent on a societal level in the emerging capitalist economy, which Adorno, following the lead of Alfred Sohn-Rethel, understood as an economic order very much alive already in the ancient Greek past. "Bargaining one's way out of sacrifice by means of self-preserving rationality," we read in *Dialectic of Enlightenment*, "is a form of exchange no less than was sacrifice itself." Homer's Odysseus, "the lone voyager armed with cunning is already *homo oeconomicus*." Or, as Adorno put it in his early draft of the Odysseus excursus: "The old cunning," epitomized by Odysseus in his adventures, "is an early form of bourgeois exchange-value."[82]

What has been said thus far throws into sharp relief, in my estimation, the push that Klages's portrait of prehistorical Pelasgians gave to *Dialectic of Enlightenment*'s thesis about the entwinement of myth and reason. Another point worth emphasizing here, to which we have already alluded in the previous section, is the fact that in order to deal with the challenge posed by Klages's bleak diagnosis of Western civilization, Adorno and Horkheimer marshal against it not only societal, more or less Marxist arguments, but also

---

81. Horkheimer and Adorno, *Dialectic of Enlightenment*, 5, 9.
82. Horkheimer and Adorno, *Dialectic of Enlightenment*, 42, 48; Adorno, "Geschichtsphilosophischer Exkurs zur *Odyssee*," 63.

arguments of a clearly anthropological bent—arguments that do not necessarily fit easily next to one another.

In their more Marxist moments, Adorno and Horkheimer argue that the Homeric myths go back to "the time of territorial dominion and its strongholds, when a warlike race of overlords"—presumably Greek-speaking Hellenes—"imposed itself on the defeated indigenous population"—apparently the Pelasgians. Along with this social revolution "the supreme god among gods came into being with this civil world in which the king, as leader of the arms-bearing nobility, tied the subjugated people to the land while doctors, soothsayers, artisans, and traders took care of circulation." At the helm of the new postnomadic societal order was "a property owner like Odysseus." Echoing the arguments of Sohn-Rethel on the economic roots of the pre-Socratics' philosophies of nature, Adorno and Horkheimer claim that "the self which learned about order and subordination through the subjugation of the world soon equated truth in general with classifying thought."[83]

At other times, however, Adorno and Horkheimer seek to counter Klages's anthropological arguments with anthropological arguments of their own. In doing so, one could say that they try to think with Klages against Klages. Rather than a result of some historically specific societal arrangements, reason, they now suggest, is *inherently* geared toward instrumental ends: "Like the material tool which, as a thing, is held fast as that thing in different situations and thereby separates the world, as something chaotic, multiple, and disparate, from that which is known, single, and identical, so the concept is the *idea-tool* which fits into things at the very point from which one can take hold of them."[84] This notion of conceptual thinking is, as Michael Grossheim plausibly notes, clearly a "Klagesian motif."[85]

Yet, does not this understanding of reason as inherently problematic push *Dialectic of Enlightenment* right into Klages's arms? Axel Honneth suggested in his pioneering interpretation that Adorno and Horkheimer come alarmingly close to Klages's view that

---

83. Horkheimer and Adorno, *Dialectic of Enlightenment*, 9–10.
84. Horkheimer and Adorno, *Dialectic of Enlightenment*, 31. My emphasis.
85. Grossheim, "'Die namelose Dummheit,'" 127.

consciousness somehow disturbs life's normal unfolding. Similarly, Michael Pauen highlights the difficulty Adorno and Horkheimer have in differentiating critical theory from Klages's vitalism.[86] This undesirable proximity to Klages's philosophy of life was exactly the risk that in the late 1930s still aroused Horkheimer's suspicion of Adorno's version of critical theory.[87] By *Dialectic of Enlightenment*, however, Horkheimer had apparently assured himself that such a risk was minimal and that what Adorno had called their "critique of hypostatized reason" stood at a safe distance from Klages's "complete abandonment of reason."[88] Despite their incessant polemics against the "identity principle" in all its cognitive and social manifestations, Adorno and Horkheimer think that they are free from Klages's vitalist assumptions. The mythic world that intoxicates Klages is for them "bloody untruth." Moreover, the demythologization process, they insist, can learn from its mistakes. Rational thought, when self-reflexive, can learn to view concepts, rather than as abstract tools, as something like "imageless images," condensations of historical experience, as Adorno had shown in his epistemological reflections in Oxford (see chapter 1).[89] This transformation required conceptual thought to relate itself to the world not merely through classifying abstraction but through

---

86. Honneth, "Anthropologische Berührungspunkte," 791; Pauen, *Dithyrambiker des Unterhanges*, 368.
87. Horkheimer's contribution to "Diskussionen über die Differenz zwischen Positivismus und materialistischer Dialektik," 490.
88. Adorno to Horkheimer, December 15, 1936, in Adorno, *Briefwechsel, Bd. I: 1927–1937*, 263. Their Frankfurt School followers were less convinced about this distance. Echoes of Horkheimer's earlier suspicion of Adorno's proximity to Klages can be heard not only in Honneth's text but also in Jürgen Habermas's later characterization of *Dialectic of Enlightenment*: "The paradox in which the critique of instrumental reason is entangled, and which stubbornly resists even the most supple dialectic, consists then in this: Horkheimer and Adorno would have to put forward a *theory* of mimesis, which, according to their own ideas, is impossible. Thus they are only being consistent when they do not attempt to explicate 'universal reconciliation' as Hegel had done, as the unity of the identity and nonidentity of spirit and nature, but let it stand as a code, almost in the manner of *Lebensphilosophie*." Habermas, *The Theory of Communicative Action*, vol. 1, 382–83.
89. The expression "imageless images" is from Adorno's later 1963 work *Hegel: Three Studies*, trans. Shierry Weber Nicholsen (Cambridge, MA: The MIT Press, 1993), 123.

"determinate negation—that is, understanding by truth not increasing distance from objects but disclosure of their "social, historical, and human meaning."[90]

In their conclusion to the Odysseus excursus, Adorno and Horkheimer seek to underline *Dialectic of Enlightenment*'s fundamental remoteness from Klages. "It is a yearning for the homeland," they contend, "which sets in motion the adventures by which subjectivity, the prehistory of which is narrated in the *Odyssey*, escapes the primeval world." And yet, "the fact that—despite the fascist lies to the contrary—the concept of homeland is opposed to myth constitutes the innermost paradox of epic." Bespeaking Klages's presence in the Odysseus excursus is its unconditionally anti-Klagesian message: "The Promised Land for Odysseus is not the archaic realm of images." What, and where, then, is home? "Homeland is a state of having escaped," Adorno and Horkheimer write. Quoting the Romantic poet Friedrich Hölderlin, they conclude their *Auseinandersetzung* with Klages and other neo-Romantic "cultural fascists"; it is precisely because of this that the reactionary "criticism that the Homeric legends 'withdraw from the earth' is a warranty of their truth. They 'turn to men.'"[91]

Spengler's Beast of Prey

In chapter 2, we assessed Adorno's enthusiasm during his New York years with Spengler's analysis of Caesarism: those political, cultural, and psychological tendencies that had undermined the Weimar Republic and facilitated the rise of national socialism. Commenting on Adorno's essay "Spengler Today" (1941), Horkheimer had praised its view of the contemporary era as ahistorical "in a most sinister sense." He had gone on to propose that "one should consider in detail whether not history has actually always consisted in

---

90. Horkheimer and Adorno, *Dialectic of Enlightenment*, 6, 18, 20.
91. Horkheimer and Adorno, *Dialectic of Enlightenment*, 59–61; Friedrich Hölderlin, "Autumn," in *Poems and Fragments*, trans. Michael Hamburger (Cambridge: Cambridge University Press, 1980), 595.

being none—except for few moments. Perhaps the concept of history requires disintegrating criticism."[92]

Horkheimer's comment indicates that Spengler, besides illuminating the troubled present with his observations on its Caesarist tendencies, also offered theoretical inspiration for *Dialectic of Enlightenment*'s narrative of self-defeating reason. By this theoretical inspiration Horkheimer certainly did not have in mind Spengler's "cultural morphology," which he, no less than Adorno, considered a neo-Romantic hoax. Rather, what intrigued him was Spengler's anthropological conception of the human species and domination of nature as its inherent feature. This conception already underlay *The Decline of the West*, but Spengler articulated it explicitly only in his 1931 book *Man and Technics*, which Adorno reviewed for the institute's journal the following year. In another illuminating comment on Adorno's 1941 essay, Horkheimer suggested that its critique of Spengler's conception could function as a springboard for their own work: "We can reopen [the theme of] the dialectic of nature from here."[93]

What, then, did Spengler claim about human nature? Unlike Klages, with his idealized image of the Pelasgians living in harmony with nature, Spengler did not believe that humanity had ever been anything else but a beast of prey, "a foe to everyone, killing, *hating*, resolute to conquer or die." With his thoughts and deeds, Spengler argued in *Man and Technics*, this "*inventive carnivore*" had affected the entire globe to such a degree that it seemed appropriate "to call *his* brief history 'world-history.'" Yet this history, in which nature formed merely "a background, an object, and a means," was not one of increasing freedom and justice. According to Spengler, a path led "from the primeval warring of extinct beasts to the processes of modern inventors and engineers" and "from the trick, oldest of all weapons," to modern technology.[94] Are these trains of thought not

---

92. Horkheimer to Adorno, June 23, 1941, in Adorno, *Briefwechsel*, Bd. II: *1938–1944*, 154.
93. Ibid.
94. Oswald Spengler, *Man and Technics: A Contribution to a Philosophy of Life*, trans. Charles Francis Atkinson (London: Allen & Unwin, 1932), 11–12, 35, 41–42. Emphasis in the original.

anticipations of *Dialectic of Enlightenment*'s argument that "myth is already enlightenment?" The first of Spengler's claims brings to mind Adorno's bleak judgment in *Negative Dialectics* of Western history as a path "from the slingshot to the megaton bomb."[95] The second one comes close to *Dialectic of Enlightenment*'s view, examined in the previous section, that "cunning," the early embodiment of which is the story of Odysseus, "originates in the cult." Both of Spengler's claims echo in Adorno and Horkheimer's wariness of philosophies of history arranged "in terms of categories such as freedom and justice."[96]

Furthermore, Spengler looks like a precursor to Adorno and Horkheimer's other maxim: "enlightenment reverts to mythology." For in *Man and Technics* Spengler proclaimed that human beings' domination of nature turns against them. "The thinking, the intellect, the reason," he wrote, sets "itself up against soul and life." To his mighty calculative capacity—Spengler wrote in an argument resembling Klages's—the human being "sacrifices an important element of *his own* life," for this compulsion to pragmatic reasoning "requires a firmer and firmer hold on the life of the soul." While Spengler considered this tragedy to be universal, he thought it reached its climax in modern European "machine culture," which was rapidly moving toward its end. Klages dreamt of a return from civilization to the womb of prehistorical myths. Spengler, in contrast, saw no way out of the iron wheel of history: "We are born into this time and must bravely follow the path to the destined end."[97]

Dialectic of Enlightenment often comes close to Spengler's opinion that there is only one logic in history: "The awakening of the subject is bought with the recognition of power as the principle of all relationships."[98] The enlightenment embodied by Odysseus does not put an end to the zero-sum game of creaturely existence. It merely replaces the previous winner, nature, with a new one, humanity. At the level of thought, the self-harming character of this

---

95. Theodor W. Adorno, *Negative Dialectics*, trans. E. B. Ashton (New York: Continuum, 2007), 320.
96. Horkheimer and Adorno, *Dialectic of Enlightenment*, 40, 184.
97. Spengler, *Man and Technics*, 57–59, 73, 90, 104.
98. Horkheimer and Adorno, *Dialectic of Enlightenment*, 5.

"Demystification of Antiquity"   151

demythologization shows itself in philosophy's compulsion to undermine every substantial, unmeasurable conception of reason (Platonic, Kantian, etc.) as irrational, the end result being modern positivism's reduction of thought to numbers. At the societal level, demythologization leads to modern industrial capitalism, in which the elevation of means over ends resembles "overt madness" and which no longer possesses any rational resources to question the status quo.[99]

How has this fateful occurrence come about? As noted earlier, Adorno and Horkheimer offer divergent accounts for it. On the one hand, they seek to explain it by social-historical means. "The distance of subject from object, the presupposition of abstraction," they argue in a quasi-Marxist manner, "is founded on the distance from things which the ruler attains by means of the ruled." Or, again: "the generality of the ideas developed by discursive logic, power in the sphere of the concept, is built on the foundation of power in reality."[100] With such arguments from social history Adorno and Horkheimer are building on Alfred Sohn-Rethel's statements on pre-Socratic philosophy, which Sohn-Rethel argued was enabled by certain economic developments (such as the introduction of coinage) in seventh-century BCE Greece. "Alfred Sohn-Rethel was the first to point out," Adorno would acknowledge in *Negative Dialectics*, "that hidden in this principle" of logical identity "lies work of an inalienably social nature."[101]

On the other hand, the authors of *Dialectic of Enlightenment* claim in a more anthropological key that the "tendency toward self-destruction has been inherent in rationality from the first, not only in the present phase when it is emerging nakedly." At its origin, they find "the splitting of life into mind and its object."[102] Or as Horkheimer

---
99. Horkheimer and Adorno, *Dialectic of Enlightenment*, 2, 17–23, 43. In *Art and Enlightenment: Aesthetic Theory after Adorno* (Lincoln: University of Nebraska Press, 1991), 73–74, 81, David Roberts offers an interesting analysis of the theme of domination of nature in the context of music by looking for traces of Spengler's morphology of "Faustian" music in Adorno's theory of musical rationalization in his *Philosophy of New Music*, ed. and trans. Robert Hullot-Kentor (Minneapolis: University of Minnesota Press, 2006), the first part of which dates from 1940–1941.
100. Horkheimer and Adorno, *Dialectic of Enlightenment*, 9–10.
101. Adorno, *Negative Dialectics*, 177.
102. Horkheimer and Adorno, *Dialectic of Enlightenment*, xix, 195.

observes in *Eclipse of Reason*, written around the same time as *Dialectic of Enlightenment*: "If one were to speak of a disease affecting reason, this disease should be understood not as having stricken reason at some historical moment, but as being inseparable from the nature of reason in civilization as we have known it so far. The disease of reason is that reason was born from man's urge to dominate nature."[103] Marxism, which idealized "unfettered activity," "uninterrupted procreation," and "chubby insatiability," suffered from this same sickness, as Adorno maintained in *Minima Moralia* (which also dates from the mid-1940s). It was because of Marxism's producerist understanding of "freedom as frantic bustle" that it too was implicated in the present "barbarism."[104]

With these sullen comments on Western reason, Adorno and Horkheimer did not wish to say that they shared Spengler's anthropological premises. Spengler, they maintained, was utterly incapable of conceiving of a qualitatively different future from the Hobbesian *bellum omnium contra omnes* (war of all against all) that he adored with morbid fascination. *Dialectic of Enlightenment* was an effort at genuinely historical thinking. It should be read as an attempt to divorce Spengler's insights from their radical-conservative universe and put them into service of, as Adorno wrote in 1941, "impulses that go beyond the relationships of domination prevailing in history up to now."[105]

What Spengler's *Man and Technics*, subtitled "A Contribution to a Philosophy of Life," was blind to, ironically, was the somatic dimension and material needs as essential to the human condition. The impulse to dominate nature does not originate, *Dialectic of Enlightenment* argues, in some obscure carnivore ethics, as Spengler would have it. Neither are its roots found in the mysterious depths of the Faustian "soul," as Spengler claimed in *The Decline of the West*. Spengler's fanciful theories overlook one simple fact. Reason has its origin in humanity's real and understandable fear of threatening

---

103. Horkheimer, *Eclipse of Reason*, 119.
104. Theodor W. Adorno, *Minima Moralia: Reflections from Damaged Life*, trans. E. F. N. Jephcott (London: Verso, 2000), 156.
105. Adorno, "Spengler Today," 313.

nature.[106] Adorno had sarcastically noted in his 1932 review of *Man and Technics* that for Spengler the human being was "a beast of prey," not because of her biological constitution but because of her "soul." Indeed, for Adorno Spengler was "by no means a materialist."[107] In "Spengler Today," Adorno picked up on this point by arguing that Spengler's seemingly concrete, but in truth overly idealist, conception "disdainfully thrusts aside the nature with which men have to struggle in history." Spengler's doctrines had no room for humanity's "desire to survive." Spengler's neo-Romantic metaphysics of the soul prevented him from understanding that all culture, notwithstanding its entanglement with barbarism, also contained "an element of resistance to blind necessity: the will for self-determination through Reason."[108]

This individuation from nature can, to be sure, lead to a one-sided technological domination of nature. Given that in the mid-1940s Adorno and Horkheimer saw this threat manifested all around them, it is no wonder that occasionally they imply, as Martin Jay remarks, that a more "primordial mimetic relationship between man and nature" was "still preserved in the sympathetic magic of the world of myth."[109] This guarded sympathy toward myths is illustrated in their commentary on Odysseus's outwitting of the Cyclops Polyphemus, a prehistorical "chthonic" figure from the pre-Olympian world. Polyphemus, a son of Poseidon and therefore an enemy of Zeus, "is not simply the villain he appears to be according to the taboos of civilization." He also has, Adorno and Horkheimer observe, "redeeming traits." By gently looking after his sheep, Polyphemus "shows a concern for creaturely life itself." This mimetic relationship between suffering, worldly creatures, they write, appears also in the conclusion to Homer's epic, "when the homecoming Odysseus is recognized by the old dog Argus."[110]

---

106. Horkheimer and Adorno, *Dialectic of Enlightenment*, 25, 32.
107. Theodor W. Adorno, review of *Der Mensch und die Technik. Beitrag zu einer Philosophie des Lebens*, by Oswald Spengler, *Zeitschrift für Sozialforschung* 1, nos. 1–2 (1932), 150.
108. Adorno, "Spengler Today," 322.
109. Jay, *Reason after Its Eclipse*, 102.
110. Horkheimer and Adorno, *Dialectic of Enlightenment*, 52.

Beyond such occasional musings Adorno and Horkheimer show little patience with any appeals for returning to nature. Odysseus, they underscore, is "right not to endure life among the Lotus-eaters," just as he is right in resisting the lure of the Sirens who try to seduce him with their singing.[111] Fascism and Nazism, Horkheimer wrote in *Eclipse of Reason*, promised a "rebellion of nature against civilization." This rebellion appealed to those mutilated by capitalist modernization: the atomized urban city dwellers "Spengler once called the 'new raw man.'" It was, however, "a satanic synthesis of reason and nature—the very opposite of that reconciliation of the two poles that philosophy has always dreamed of."[112]

True reconciliation could only happen by improving enlightenment, not by turning one's back on it. As Albrecht Wellmer describes the conviction of *Dialectic of Enlightenment*, reason can be mimetic, a mode of existence that is "sensually receptive, expressive and communicative" and which calls for "a non-violent unity of the diverse in the reconciliation of relations between all living things."[113] Civilization, Adorno and Horkheimer accentuate, has advanced "not only mastery but also the prospect of its alleviation." Everything depends on thinking becoming self-reflective. Besides classifying formalism, which distances humans from nature and from each other, thinking also "enables the distance which perpetuates injustice to be measured. Through this remembrance of nature within the subject, a remembrance which contains the unrecognized truth of all culture, enlightenment is opposed in principle to power."[114]

Ludwig Klages's *Spirit as Adversary of the Soul* and Oswald Spengler's *Man and Technics* trained Adorno to perceive myths as ambivalent sites of human maturation. That is my conclusion from the preceding interpretation of their significance for *Dialectic of Enlightenment*. No doubt this perception was inspired by other thinkers too, most notably by Walter Benjamin, Sigmund Freud, and Max

---

111. Horkheimer and Adorno, *Dialectic of Enlightenment*, 49.
112. Horkheimer, *Eclipse of Reason*, 83.
113. Wellmer, *The Persistence of Modernity*, 4.
114. Horkheimer and Adorno, *Dialectic of Enlightenment*, 32.

Weber, and perhaps even by Ernst Cassirer. Their contributions, however, have received ample scholarly attention. The story of the surprising marks left on *Dialectic of Enlightenment* by Klages and Spengler, in contrast, has remained largely untold thus far.

Adorno held against Klages's neo-Romantic theory that myths, rather than expressions of pristine harmony between humanity and nature, already expressed a wish for self-determination, a wish to control one's destiny. This wish, an embryonic expression of the Enlightenment's ethical maxim of autonomy, was a pivotal element in the human condition that Spengler's social-Darwinist lens severely distorted as a mere beast of prey. Nevertheless, Klages and Spengler alerted Adorno to the fact that modernity's optimistic faith in its ability to overcome the mythic logic of self-preservation was mistaken too. Whatever Adorno may have taken from Cassirer, he held against him that Western reason had never quite succeeded in mastering—or rather working through—this ambivalent logic inherited from myth.

Adorno's was, then, a struggle on two fronts. Against his fellow enlighteners, Cassirer and Freud, he held that one oversimplified mythic consciousness if one saw it teleologically as a straightforward precursor of rationality. Against his reactionary enemies in the "conservative revolutionary" camp, he maintained that one also falsified mythic thought if one viewed it as a simple adversary of reason. The truth was rather that "the mythical" was harder to grasp than either of these antipodes was willing to admit. Hence the term *Urgeschichte*, or "earliest history of subjectivity" in *Dialectic of Enlightenment*.[115] The book's unsettling message, however, was that this history, rather than a onetime episode in a distant Greek past, was still very much alive in the twentieth century.

---

115. Horkheimer and Adorno, *Dialectic of Enlightenment*, 43.

Epilogue

Legacies of Adorno's Gamble

Wolf Lepenies's 1969 book *Melancholy and Society* boldly situated Theodor W. Adorno's critical social theory in the vicinity of Arnold Gehlen's conservative diagnosis of the times. Nevertheless, Adorno held no objections to the publication of the book, as he informed the Suhrkamp publishing house before its appearance. In fact, Adorno found Lepenies's suggestion noteworthy. This was the case even though, as he expressed to Gehlen, Lepenies's book came with a regrettable "undertone, apparently inevitable these days, that if one does not cover the dark side of reality with a veil of roses one gets accused of resignation."[1]

Resignation was a charge not infrequently leveled at Adorno in the 1960s. Three years before Lepenies's book, in 1966, Adorno had opened his *Negative Dialectics* by stating that the most urgent task

---

1. Adorno to Gehlen, January 15, 1969, Theodor W. Adorno Archive 453/55, Institute for Social Research, Goethe University Frankfurt.

in the present was to try to understand, rather than to change, the bureaucratic nightmare that was advanced industrial society.[2] Consequently, radical leftist students, many of whom had sat in Adorno's classes, saw this as quietism and as a betrayal of his and the Frankfurt School's earlier teachings. The student complaints echoed those made a few years prior by the Marxist critic Georg Lukács, who lamented Adorno's choice to live in what he famously labeled the "Grand Hotel Abyss"—that is, to lead an abundant life dedicated to contemplation rather than revolution.[3]

Although it had not been Adorno's intention, critics like Lepenies identified his skepticism about immediate social change with discouraged theses such as Gehlen's "post-history," which viewed as irreversible modernity's slide into ossified bureaucracy. In a radio talk in February 1969, a month after he had written to Gehlen about Lepenies's book, Adorno rejected the charge of resignation. Turning the tables on the student radicals, he insisted that "thinking, as a mere instrument of activist actions, atrophies like all instrumental reason."[4] And yet, with regard to Lepenies's claim about the affinities between him and Gehlen, Adorno had admitted to Gehlen that "without question the man is on to something important."[5]

In the preceding chapters, I have argued that decades before Adorno's "friendship" with Gehlen, or whatever one chooses to call their unexpectedly cordial relationship in the 1960s, his concern with saving enlightened rationality not only from the Counter-Enlightenment but also from itself was decisively encouraged by interwar *Zivilisationskritik*, or critique of civilization. To be more precise, Adorno, I have tried to demonstrate in this book, managed to articulate the key elements of his own thought by critically redirecting Oswald

---

2. Theodor W. Adorno, *Negative Dialectics*, trans. E. B. Ashton (New York: Continuum, 2007), 3, 6.
3. Georg Lukács, Preface to the *The Theory of the Novel: A Historico-Philosophical Essay on the Forms of Great Epic Literature*, trans. Anna Bostock (London: Merlin Press, 1971), 22.
4. Theodor W. Adorno, "Resignation," in *Critical Models: Interventions and Catchwords*, trans. Henry W. Pickford (New York: Columbia University Press, 2005), 292.
5. Adorno to Gehlen, January 15, 1969.

Spengler's and Ludwig Klages's radical conservative ideas to emancipatory ends.

By focusing on this largely overlooked motif in Adorno's intellectual biography, my purpose has been neither to create a dichotomy between previous scholarship and my own nor to trivialize the better-known ingredients of Adorno's thought: Freudian psychoanalysis, artistic modernism, Jewish theology, and particularly critical Marxism informed by classical German philosophy. Critical Marxism is undoubtedly, as Martin Jay rightly notes, the "brightest star" in the constellation of Adorno's thought,[6] stimulated by various unorthodox Marxists from Walter Benjamin, Siegfried Kracauer, and Georg Lukács to Ernst Bloch, Max Horkheimer, Alfred Sohn-Rethel, and Friedrich Pollock. By reconstructing what I have called Adorno's "gamble" with interwar German *Zivilisationskritik*, my goal has been to create a dialogue with earlier scholars and their brilliant work. Rather than dismissing the well-known other ingredients of Adorno's critical theory as of minor importance, I have examined how they *coexisted* with the radical conservative ideas—or, it bears repeating, Adorno's active repurposing of them—in his thought. I have carefully weighed the respective importance of Spengler and Klages on the one hand and of Marx, Freud, and others on the other in the emergence of key ideas of Adorno's: in chapter 1 "mimetic" reason, in chapter 2 the frailty of democracy, and in chapter 3 the dialectic of enlightenment.

In chapter 1, I argued that Ludwig Klages's critique of Western "logocentrism" in *The Spirit as Adversary of the Soul* (1929–1932), the locus classicus of interwar *Lebensphilosophie,* served as a crucial provocation that pushed Adorno to formulate his idea of mimetic reason, the central component of his later masterpiece, *Negative Dialectics*. This idea, the chapter showed, was already germinating in the final years of the Weimar Republic when Adorno—first implicitly under the influence of Walter Benjamin (who was himself enthralled by Klages) and then explicitly in his own "Klages project"—struggled to deal with the implications of Klages's polemics against the two-thousand-year reign of Western rationalism and its

---

6. Martin Jay, *Adorno* (Cambridge, MA: Harvard University Press, 1984), 15.

colonization of particular objects with life-denying conceptual abstractions. Adorno never managed to put his Klages project on paper. Yet I argued that this project came to saturate his most important philosophical text of the 1930s, an epistemological manuscript he wrote in Oxford exile in 1934–1937.

Adorno's preoccupation with Klages, palpable, though not visible, in the Oxford manuscript, helped us make sense of other more familiar episodes on his intellectual path in the 1930s. The Klages project played a crucial role in Adorno's well-recorded departure from Benjamin, whose infatuation with Klages's antirationalism he came to find troubling. It also served as a significant framework for Adorno's concomitant discovery of Hegel, whose dialectics, when divorced from its totalistic aspirations, he came to value as a better way to safeguard Klages's concern with the particular than the latter's obscure vitalism might. Further, the Klages project coincided with Adorno's renewed dialogue with the Marxist maverick Alfred Sohn-Rethel, whose controversial extension of Marxist categories to Greek antiquity convinced Adorno of the societal roots of logocentrism. The latter was no anthropological constant of the human condition, as Klages would have it, but a mirror effect of nascent capitalist exchange. The facts that Adorno later developed his Oxford manuscript into *Against Epistemology* (1956) and once described the latter as "a ramp leading up to" *Negative Dialectics*[7] led me to conclude that his early preoccupation with Klages was an important element in his finding his own philosophical voice and articulating the idea of mimetic reason.

If Klages stimulated Adorno to come to terms with the complicated legacy of Western philosophy, Spengler stimulated his working through of a more concrete sort, namely of those political, psychological, and cultural tendencies of the Weimar Republic that had paved the way for Hitler. Horrified by the antisemitic *Kristallnacht* pogrom in Germany in 1938, and ambivalent about the democratic form of life in the United States, during his New York exile in

---

7. Adorno to Kracauer, September 28, 1966, in *Theodor W. Adorno/Siegfried Kracauer: Correspondence, 1923–1966*, ed. Wolfgang Schopf, trans. Susan Reynolds and Michael Winkler (Cambridge: Polity Press, 2020), 490.

1938–1941 Adorno took interest in Spengler's analysis of "Caesarism" in *The Decline of the West*. Whereas in the early 1920s liberal and Marxist thinkers (Georg Lukács being the lone exception for Adorno) had allowed their hopeful expectations of the future to blind their judgment of the present, Adorno, in his essay "Spengler Today" (1941), praised Spengler for having predicted the rise of Nazism at a very early stage.

Adorno by no means accepted Spengler's "morphological" analysis of politics, which, like past cyclical theories, viewed democracy's defects in helplessly abstract terms. Rather, he placed Spengler's observations on Caesarism in the service of the concrete historical present, the most decisive aspect of which was the transformation of capitalism from a liberal to centralized and increasingly authoritarian form. This was a shift that Spengler, with his arrogant dismissal of economic matters as mere epiphenomena, had failed to penetrate, but to which the Marxist theorists of the Frankfurt School, most notably Friedrich Pollock, had attached great importance. Adorno's interest in Spengler's notion of Caesarism was filtered by his approval of Pollock's theory of "state capitalism." At the same time, Adorno appreciated Spengler's insights into the bureaucratization of the party system, the emergence of a new personality type vulnerable to propaganda, and the rise of manipulative mass media for illuminating the authoritarian turn of capitalism from other, noneconomic perspectives.

Indicating Spengler's enduring relevance for Adorno after the war was his choice to republish his Spengler essay in 1950. The defeat of Nazism, Adorno maintained, had not freed Germany, or other Western countries, from those same Caesarist tendencies that had aided its rise to power. No doubt Adorno had learned a great deal about psychological authoritarianism from Sigmund Freud and the Freudo-Marxist work of the Institute for Social Research. Yet I argued in chapter 2 that the grimness of Adorno's own understanding of the decline of critical individualism—visible, for instance, in his private remarks on *The Authoritarian Personality* (1950), a social-psychological landmark coauthored with Else Frenkel-Brunswik, Daniel J. Levinson, and R. Nevitt Sanford—carried traces of his struggle with Spengler's unflattering portrait of modern atomistic city-dwellers. Again, Walter Benjamin's groundbreaking reflections on modern popular culture undoubtedly pushed Adorno to meditate on the promise and blindness of newer cultural medias. However, I argued that Adorno's excessively bleak view of the unenlightening potential of modern popular culture, on display in the "culture industry" chapter of *Dialectic of Enlightenment* (1947), bore the imprint of his readings of Spengler's mockery of mass culture.

By emphasizing these continuities in modern German history, Adorno did not mean that the young West German republic was on the brink of repeating the fate of Weimar. This was not the case in 1950 when he republished his Spengler essay or in the late 1960s when he rejected the radical students' prediction of an imminent fascist coup. The warnings Adorno voiced were not about simple analogies between noticeably different political eras, but about structural and mental continuities. These continuities increased the chance that an alarming number of what *The Authoritarian Personality* called "*potentially fascistic*" individuals—individuals who would likely support authoritarian regimes should they gain popularity—walked the streets on both sides of the Atlantic.[8] I argued that Spengler's notion of Caesarism, despite its distortions, was one impetus that deepened Adorno's sensitivity to these continuities.

Finally, in chapter 3, I recounted how Adorno's repurposing of modern "German ideology," begun in the last years of the Weimar Republic, reached its peak in his and Horkheimer's *Dialectic of Enlightenment*. Characteristic of this most storied book of the Frankfurt School was its introduction of an anthropological perspective next to a Marxist one. This uneasy mix has usually, and not without justification, been explained by the inspiration the authors drew from Freud, Benjamin, Max Weber, or Ernst Cassirer. I argued that it was also the anthropological theories of Klages's *Spirit as Adversary of the Soul* (in particular its account of the prehistoric "Pelasgians") and Spengler's *Man and Technics* (which Adorno and Horkheimer

---

8. Theodor W. Adorno et al., *The Authoritarian Personality* (London: Verso, 2019), 1. Emphasis in the original. On Adorno's political perceptions and his relation to the student movement, see Fabian Freyenhagen, "Adorno's Politics: Theory and Praxis in Germany's 1960s," *Philosophy and Social Criticism* 40, no. 9 (2014): 867–93; Alex Demirovic, *Der nonkonformistische Intellektuelle. Die Entwicklung der Kritischen Theorie zur Frankfurter Schule* (Frankfurt: Suhrkamp, 1999).

at one point planned as a "springboard" for their own reflections) that stimulated *Dialectic of Enlightenment*'s notion of history as a never-ending maturation process, threatened from without by myths and from within by reason's own mythic origins.

Apart from anthropological scrutiny turning from a minor into a major motif, *Dialectic of Enlightenment* fitted smoothly into the trajectory of Adorno's path of thinking. However, it represented a drastic turn in that of Horkheimer's with its heavy pessimism toward Western civilization. It was not just that the book made strong assertions about reason's repressive side since pre-Socratic times. Occasionally it also came close to likening the social order of the New Deal United States to European totalitarianisms. Freud, Benjamin, Weber, and perhaps even Cassirer surely stimulated Adorno and Horkheimer's ponderings. With the help of underappreciated evidence such as correspondence, I demonstrated that one can also justifiably view *Dialectic of Enlightenment* as a critical rejoinder to Klages and Spengler, who, as Adorno wrote in an early draft of the book, "have shown more insight" than their invocation of "primordial powers" would allow one to assume.[9]

What is the present-day significance of this venture in intellectual history? How topical are Adorno's ideas in making sense of our own authoritarian populist conundrum, often expressed as the "age of Trump"? What, moreover, is the connection between what I have argued about Adorno's "gamble" with German ideology and the question of his contemporary relevance? These are the questions I wish to ponder in the remainder of this Epilogue.

A frequently highlighted downside of Adorno's critical theory—one occasionally associated with his fascination with *Zivilisationskritik* since Jürgen Habermas's and Axel Honneth's remarks in the 1980s—is his disproportionately gloomy assessment of modern Western society. This gloominess is most visible in *Dialectic of Enlightenment*, which, even when it is acknowledged that it was written

---

9. Theodor W. Adorno, "Geschichtsphilosophischer Exkurs zur *Odyssee*: Frühe Fassung von *Odysseus oder Mythos und Aufklärung*," in *Frankfurter Adorno Blätter*, vol. 5, ed. Rolf Tiedemann (Munich: edition text + kritik, 1992), 40.

in the darkest possible hour (Stalinism, World War II, and the Holocaust), resulted in an almost total equation of Western reason with instrumental calculation. Even if it is true that the book's rare optimistic moments came more from Adorno's, rather than Horkheimer's, hand, only in comparison to thinkers like Spengler and Klages do these moments appear optimistic.[10] From other perspectives—heartened by such recent examples as the Occupy Movement, Black Lives Matter, the Me Too campaign, and young people's climate marches as well as by "the very real empirical advances in individual freedom, morality, legality, and democracy that have been achieved in modernity"[11]—*Dialectic of Enlightenment* succumbs to a monolithic conception of history similar to that which Adorno criticized in Spengler and Klages. What George Friedman notes about Spengler's impact on *Dialectic of Enlightenment* also goes for Klages. Their impact "conditioned" the early Frankfurt School's "vision of the historical possibilities."[12]

It can be argued that one historical possibility that Adorno did not live to see, but to which his works and public interventions contributed in no small measure, was what Ronald Inglehart in 1977 dubbed the "silent revolution." This was a cultural shift that from the 1960s on gradually replaced exclusive nationalistic values and "us vs. them" dichotomies with an unprecedented tolerance of difference. Key factors behind this transformation, which largely vaccinated postwar generations against authoritarianism of all kinds, were a more humane upbringing for children, the spread of education, and the growing appeal of "postmaterialist" values of self-realization, all made possible by the material affluence of social democratic societies after World War II.[13]

---

10. On these rare glimpses of hope in *Dialectic of Enlightenment*, see Anson Rabinbach, *In the Shadow of Catastrophe: German Intellectuals between Apocalypse and Enlightenment* (Berkeley: University of California Press, 1997), 169–71.

11. Joel Whitebook, "Psychoanalysis and Critical Theory," in *The Routledge Companion to the Frankfurt School*, ed. Peter E. Gordon et al. (New York: Routledge, 2019), 44.

12. George Friedman, *The Political Philosophy of the Frankfurt School* (Ithaca, NY: Cornell University Press, 1981), 85.

13. Ronald Inglehart, *The Silent Revolution: Changing Values and Political Styles among Western Publics* (Princeton, NJ: Princeton University Press, 2016).

Given these historic changes brought about by the "silent revolution" in the past half century, one may rightly wonder whether Adorno's social criticism is not helplessly outdated. Further, are not today's readers of works like *Dialectic of Enlightenment* in danger of being carried away by Adorno's rhetorical charm and turned into organs of his pessimism, which is, as Leo Strauss once remarked, just what earlier happened to admirers of Martin Heidegger's existentialism? In Strauss's estimation, Heidegger's seductive writing style and personal charisma caused a "paralysis of the critical faculties" among less critical segments of his readers. Consequently, much of Heidegger's popularity reflected less sound judgment than lionizing of his "incipient *mythoi*" about Being.[14] An alternative to this celebratory mode is to stick to rigorous historicism and view Adorno's thought as little more than a product of its times. But this seems too rash to me, especially considering that the recent global tide of political authoritarianism has forced the "silent revolution" onto the defensive.[15] Another indication of Adorno's contemporaneity is the recent surge of interest in his ideas.

In the past decade or so, Adorno appears to have returned to shake the Frankfurt School tradition, guided for decades by the efforts of his most famous student, Habermas, to update critical theory, shaped in the dark interwar era, to fit the more hopeful postwar world. Notwithstanding Habermas's exceptional achievements in filling the "liberal-democratic deficit" of the early Frankfurt School, defending enlightenment against postmodernism and EU-technocrats, and acting as Germany's public conscience over the past seventy years, critics claim that in his hands the Frankfurt School tradition has come to resemble the Anglo-American liberal tradition of John Rawls and others. Habermas, critics complain, is too concentrated on abstract normative questions and too detached from deep historical analyses to explain why the world is moving toward inequality, nationalism, and xenophobia instead of global

---

14. Leo Strauss, "Kurt Riezler," In *What Is Political Philosophy? and Other Studies* (Glencoe, IL: The Free Press, 1959), 246.

15. Ronald Inglehart and Pippa Norris, "Trump and the Populist Authoritarian Parties: *The Silent Revolution* in Reverse," *Perspectives on Politics* 15, no. 2 (2017): 443–54.

justice and a fair distribution of economic resources. In this situation, many commentators have argued for Adorno's relevance in explaining these disturbing phenomena.

This raises the question: Was it, in part, Adorno's effort to harness Spengler's analysis of Caesarism for progressive ends that we have to thank for his critical virtues, virtues valued again today? Was it, in other words, partly Adorno's gamble with Spengler's analysis that today makes his critical theory, rather than an obsolete gloominess, an asset for understanding the present? It is with this question in mind that we should next take a brief look at attempts to read our present political predicament through an Adornoian lens.

Among recent commentators on Adorno's legacy, *The Authoritarian Personality* has been particularly appealing. Anxious to determine fascism's potential vogue in the postwar United States and to answer the pressing question "Could it happen here?", the study sought to identify a personality type suspicious of democratic principles, prone to excessive social conformism, and, most decisively, eager to "accept fascism if it should become a strong or respectable social movement."[16] Richard Wolin argues that even after seventy years the study still has a lot to teach us. It explains, he maintains, why certain people are more "susceptible to conspiracy theories and to claims that the system is rigged," and why these people are lured to political "movements that seek compensatory solace in emotionalism and scapegoating as opposed to the more laborious and mature, ego-centered approaches to political problem-solving." Wolin calls attention to contemporary authoritarians' indiscriminate hostility to all racial minorities and their distrust of liberal-democratic principles. Persuaded by racist images of populist rhetoric, they, much like Adorno and his coauthors diagnosed, replace rational thought and policy goals with libidinal cathexis by following demagogic political leaders such as Donald Trump, Marine Le Pen, and Viktor Orbán.[17]

---

16. Adorno et al., *The Authoritarian Personality*, 1.
17. Richard Wolin, "Our 'Prophet of Deceit': WWII-Era Social Scientists Explained Trump's Appeal," *The Chronicle of Higher Education*, October 30, 2016. See also Matthew C. MacWilliams, *The Rise of Trump: America's Authoritarian Spring* (Amherst, MA: Amherst College Press, 2016).

Further, while ours is no longer the state-regulated Ford-Keynesian capitalism of Adorno's day, his insights into authoritarianism may be even more relevant today, the time of what Samir Gandesha calls the "neoliberal personality." Since the late 1970s, the neoliberal marketization of social relations from healthcare to education has promised to create a world in which individuals "can exercise their capacity to articulate their own interests autonomously and rationally within the context of a genuine plurality of other such interests." But by undermining the allegedly bureaucratic welfare state, Gandesha argues, neoliberal capitalism has instead increased "a sense of social insecurity."[18] Our twenty-first-century society frequently announces, Gandesha continues, citing the Belgian psychoanalyst Paul Verhaeghe, "that anyone can make it if they just try hard enough, all the while reinforcing privilege and putting increasing pressure on its overstretched and exhausted citizens." However, the reality is that more and more "people fail, feeling humiliated, guilty and ashamed." What adds insult to injury, Verhaeghe laments, is that "we are forever told that we are freer to choose the course of our lives than ever before" and yet "the freedom to choose outside the success narrative is limited." It is no wonder, then, that those who cannot keep up "are deemed to be losers or scroungers, taking advantage of our social security system."[19] Instead of putting society on truly "free and rational foundations," Gandesha concludes, neoliberalism has instead generated a "surplus of aggression, humiliation and guilt" and strengthened "atavistic allegiances, xenophobic nationalism, racism and sexism."[20]

Even scholars less convinced by social-psychological explanations of authoritarianism have built on Adorno's legacy. According

---

18. Samir Gandesha, "'Identifying with the Aggressor': From the Authoritarian to Neoliberal Personality," *Constellations: An International Journal of Critical and Democratic Theory* 25, no. 1 (2018), 149, 151.
19. Paul Verhaeghe, "Neoliberalism Has Brought Out the Worst in Us," *The Guardian*, September 29, 2014.
20. Gandesha, "'Identifying with the Aggressor,'" 148–49. For more analyses combining psychology and critical economics, see the articles in *Critical Theory and Authoritarian Populism*, ed. Jeremiah Morelock (London: University of Westminster Press, 2018).

to Peter E. Gordon, Trumpism is less about the fury of uneducated, putatively authoritarian workers manipulated by news channels like Fox News than about the long-term negative bearing of the "culture industry," analyzed by Adorno and Horkheimer in *Dialectic of Enlightenment*, on critical thinking across the political spectrum. Rather than a malady of specific social groups ("losers of globalization") and explainable in economic and psychological terms, for Gordon Trumpism marks "another instance of the general pathology that is American political culture." Trumpism gives voice to "the thoughtlessness of the entire culture." The inability to genuinely experience and engage in self-reflection, hallmarks of mature personhood, plague not only authoritarian populists but often also so-called progressive circles, no matter how much the latter wish to demarcate themselves from the former.[21]

Max Pensky, for his part, joins Adorno and Alexis de Tocqueville in tracing the current authoritarian backlash to depoliticizing potentials inherent in "liberal democracy itself." Both Adorno and Tocqueville, Pensky suggests, saw in seemingly trivial everyday phenomena signs of more profound, but barely discernible, changes in societal control: the replacement of grassroots democratic activity with impersonal technocracy and atomistic consumerism. The neoliberal marketization and anesthetic lullabies sung by the entertainment industry, Pensky recognizes, have undoubtedly contributed to the deterioration of properly political existence and the rise of authoritarianism. He argues, however, that Adorno may be even more topical today as an interpreter of self-defeating tendencies of the "individualizing dynamic" unleashed by the liberal principle of (merely) formal equality.[22]

These assessments of Adorno's lasting relevance by Wolin, Gandesha, Gordon, and Pensky, it should be noted, hardly share Adorno's exaggerated worry about the decline of the individual. Nevertheless,

---

21. Peter E. Gordon, "The Authoritarian Personality Revisited: Reading Adorno in the Age of Trump," in Wendy Brown et al., *Authoritarianism: Three Inquiries in Critical Theory* (Chicago: University of Chicago Press, 2018), 68–69.

22. Max Pensky, "Radical Critique and Late Epistemology: Tocqueville, Adorno, and Authoritarianism," in Wendy Brown et al., *Authoritarianism: Three Inquiries in Critical Theory*, 93–94, 100, 102.

uniting their analyses is the view that Adorno helps us to see political authoritarianism—rather than merely as a crisis of political representation—as a sign of eroding conditions of democratic subjectivity itself. Remarkably, the problems highlighted by these scholars—the psychological effectiveness of populist propaganda, the manipulating medias of mass communication, and the decay of democratic virtues—are very much the same ones that Adorno drew attention to in Spengler's portrait of Caesarism. Although none of these scholars draws this connection between Adorno and Spengler, I would like to argue that it is visible in their recent Adornoian analyses of the "age of Trump."

For example, Gordon points out how the twenty-first-century media universe "prefers outrage to complexity and dismisses dialectical uncertainty for the narcissistic affirmation of self-consistent ideologies, each parceled out via its own private cable network." Echo chambers are not only a problem at the fringes of society. "Name just about any political position," Gordon mourns, "and what sociologists call 'pillarization'—or what the Frankfurt School called 'ticket' thinking—will predict, almost without fail, a full suite of opinions."[23] We should hear in these worries a distant echo of Spengler's warnings, over a hundred years ago, about "Caesars of the world-press,"[24] a warning that Adorno paid heed to during World War II and which came to inspire *Dialectic of Enlightenment*'s chapter on the culture industry.

Again, Pensky warns that the will to political self-determination is in danger of withering under democratic conditions that this same will once helped to establish. With its merely negative freedoms, liberal democracy ironically ends up creating individualistic consumers, anxious about material comforts and standing out from others, rather than citizens engaged in associational life and looking after the common good. Pensky credits Hannah Arendt's *Origins of Totalitarianism* (1951) for the insight that this urban atomization is "the kernel of loneliness at the heart of totalitarianism."[25] Spengler,

---

23. Gordon, "The Authoritarian Personality Revisited," 70.
24. Oswald Spengler, *The Decline of the West*, vol. 2, *Perspectives of World-History*, trans. Charles Francis Atkinson (New York: Knopf, 1994), 462.
25. Pensky, "Radical Critique and Late Epistemology," 94–95, 101.

however, had already in 1922 predicted that democratic ideals will perish "not from refutation, but from boredom," as modern urban "cavemen" are all too willing to give up those liberal rights that their grandparents fought for. Adorno, as we have seen, appreciated Spengler's diagnosis long before Arendt's book appeared.[26]

What about the legacy of Adorno's gamble with Klages? What about Adorno's attempt to place Klages's critique of Western "logocentrism" in the service of emancipation? Many critics have judged Adorno's worry over the ubiquity of instrumental reason as "hyperbolic," one with which *Dialectic of Enlightenment* in particular, it has been argued, "ran a bit wild."[27] I would like to propose, however, that something of Adorno's concern with instrumental reason and his plea for a more mimetic reason can be rescued when divorced from the exaggerating tone that he often succumbed to. One recent theorist in whose work Adorno's ideas—and thereby, the legacy of his struggle with Klages—are visible is the German philosopher Hartmut Rosa.

Bringing in Rosa may strike the reader as counterintuitive. For although Rosa advocates the Frankfurt School's emancipatory project, he rejects two core elements of Adorno's thinking. First, like the critics cited above, Rosa rejects Adorno's overly grim diagnosis of a modern life "damaged" by a rationality geared toward pragmatic efficiency and conceptual control. Unlike Adorno, who tended to find germs of freedom in only a few select works of art and philosophy, Rosa sees them in various realms of the modern world, from sports to popular music and work to friendships. Second, Rosa finds unsatisfying Adorno's negativist point of departure, according to which "he who wishes to know the truth about life in its immediacy must scrutinize its estranged form, the objective powers that determine individual existence even in its most hidden recesses."[28] For Rosa, too,

---

26. Spengler, *The Decline of the West*, vol. 2, 454.
27. Brian O'Connor, *Adorno's Negative Dialectic: Philosophy and the Possibility of Critical Rationality* (Cambridge, MA: MIT Press, 2004), 18, 67; Nancy Fraser and Rahel Jaeggi, *Capitalism: A Conversation in Critical Theory*, ed. Brian Milstein (Cambridge: Polity Press, 2018), 135.
28. Theodor W. Adorno, *Minima Moralia: Reflections from Damaged Life*, trans. E. F. N. Jephcott (London: Verso, 2000), 15.

it is imperative to criticize the ills of modern society. But "a vital critical theory," he adds, has to give expression to the hope that "a different mode of existence, another way of being in the world," is a real possibility. This hope indeed animated, Rosa emphasizes, Adorno's perusals of modern reified existence. But whereas Adorno rarely let himself express this hope in concrete terms, Rosa's notion of "resonance" is an attempt to spell it out more systematically.[29]

From Adorno's perspective, Rosa's trust in modern society's capacity to facilitate and safeguard oases of resonance might be guilty of hiding (to cite his words to Gehlen) "the dark side of reality with a veil of roses."[30] Yet, I believe that Rosa's idea of resonance, no matter how far his philosophical sensibility otherwise stands apart from Adorno's, is an attempt to keep alive and bring into sharper focus the idea of mimetic reason. Similarly, I see Rosa's diagnosis of "social acceleration" as an updated version of Adorno's scrutiny of instrumental reason. Both, moreover, are concerns that I believe go back to Adorno's early struggle with Klages. (I should emphasize that by this I do not mean that Rosa himself sees such a continuity between Adorno and Klages, any more than the scholars discussed earlier saw one between Adorno and Spengler.)

Echoing *Dialectic of Enlightenment*, Rosa claims that our late capitalist society is dependent on "dynamic stabilization." It is "structurally and institutionally compelled to bring more and more of the world under control and within reach, technologically, economically, and politically." It is forced "to develop resources, open markets, activate social and psychological potentials, enhance technological capabilities, deepen knowledge bases, improve possibilities of control, and so on." What this frenetic activity obscures, Rosa laments, is that the Enlightenment's goal of achieving autonomy has come to a standstill. "Wherever we stop to take a break, we lose ground against a highly dynamic environment, with which we are always in competition." Worse still, this rat race is accompanied by

---

29. Bjørn Schiermer, "Acceleration and Resonance: An Interview with Hartmut Rosa," *Acta Sociologica* (2020), 7. In addition to Adorno's mimesis, Rosa also mentions other similar notions of the early Frankfurt School: Benjamin's "aura," Marcuse's "eros," and Fromm's "love."

30. Adorno to Gehlen, January 15, 1969.

"the cultural principle of relentlessly expanding humanity's reach." The assumption that our life becomes more meaningful the more experiences we manage to have—in an increasingly self-conscious and competitive manner—has worked "its way deep into the tiniest pores of our psychological and emotional life."[31]

What this cultural principle fails to see, Rosa argues, is that autonomy, even if fully realized, does not on its own deliver what we expect from it. To a degree, the ability to control our environment is of course a precondition for good, nondamaged life. But by turning from a means to an end, Rosa argues, our desire for control threatens to eclipse the insight that truly resonant relationships to the world depend on them being not entirely under our control. While it is correct to say, he notes, that "experiences of alienation are rooted in a *lack of belief in one's own efficacy*," this diagnosis is one-sided. It puts too much emphasis on the "domination-oriented aspect of self-efficacy at the expense of its responsive, appealing, process-oriented dimension." It is, in other words, blind to "the 'pathic' side of successful relationships to the world." Rosa illustrates with several examples how "people frequently feel the least alienated (or the most 'with themselves') precisely when they *lose* control over themselves, their lives, or their circumstances." This happens, for example, when one falls "head over heels in love" or when one is "overpowered by a piece of music."[32]

Rosa illuminates his conception of a resonant relationship with an acoustic analogy of the harmony of two tuning forks vibrating at their own frequencies. The ideal manner of "vibrant human existence consists not in exerting *control* over things but in resonating with them, making them respond to us—thus experiencing *self-efficacy*—and responding to them in turn."[33]

---

31. Hartmut Rosa, *The Uncontrollability of the World*, trans. James C. Wagner (Cambridge: Polity Press, 2020), 8, 10.

32. Hartmut Rosa, *Resonance: A Sociology of Our Relationship to the World*, trans. James C. Wagner (Cambridge: Polity Press, 2019), 176–77. Emphasis in the original.

33. Rosa, *The Uncontrollability of the World*, 31; *Resonance*, chap. 5. Emphasis in the original. See also David Nirenberg and Ricardo L. Nirenberg, *Uncountable: A Philosophical History of Number and Humanity from Antiquity to the Present* (Chicago: University of Chicago Press, 2021).

This emphasis on the reciprocity of the subject and the world as a key to good life lies at the core of Adorno's thought. A resonant (in Adorno's terms mimetic) relationship rests on a delicate balance between control and unpredictability, self-determination and a certain kind of impressionability. In Adorno's works, however, such concerns appear most of the time only as glimpses amid examinations of life in its impoverished forms. Only rarely, as in the following passage from *Negative Dialectics*, does Adorno describe them more explicitly. "The reconciled condition would not be the philosophical imperialism of annexing the alien. Instead, its happiness would lie in the fact that the alien, in the proximity it is granted, remains what is distant and different, beyond the heterogenous and beyond that which is one's own."[34]

What is significant in this comparison of Adorno and Rosa is that with the concept of resonance Rosa is in my estimation rehabilitating that dimension of Adorno's thought that was nourished by the latter's wrestling with Klages. Commenting on Klages's condemnation of logocentrism, Michael Grossheim suggests that what instrumental reason—both as abstract classification and pragmatic means-ends calculation—overlooks "is the non-measurable atmospheric, everything that actually makes an impression on a person when he views the world with open eyes." A major deficiency that Klages diagnosed in the modern world, Grossheim stresses, was the general inability to be impressed, or moved.[35] Adorno appreciated aspects of Klages's diagnosis. This is not to say that he adopted Klages's ideas as his own. Far from it. *Everything hinges on how one understands this receptiveness or impressionability.* By venerating prehistorical "archaic images" as a remedy to logocentrism, Klages represented an extremely antisubjectivist and anti-Enlightenment position that had no room for emancipatory goals. Adorno always abhorred such antimodernism, familiar also from authoritarian religious orders, and the sacrifice of the individual that it entailed. When Adorno entered the philo-

---

34. Adorno, *Negative Dialectics*, 191.
35. Michael Grossheim, "'Die namenlose Dummheit, die das Resultat des Fortschritts ist.'—Lebensphilosophische und dialektische Kritik der Moderne," *Logos. Zeitschrift für systematische Philosophie* 3, no. 2 (1996), 114, 118.

sophical scene in Frankfurt in 1931, he was already unwavering about this. In matters of detail, he noted, critical theory might bear resemblance to Klages's theories "in a hundred characteristics." A decisive difference, however, remained. Klages's archaic images "describe their fatalistic orbit in the heads of human beings." Adorno's dialectical images, in contrast, are "instruments of human reason" that seek to liberate humanity from heteronomous forces.[36]

To use Rosa's terminology, Klages's understanding of resonance is banefully one-dimensional; something just befalls us from the outside without our having a say. This is a repressive, nonresonant relation. There is no harmony between two unique and independent voices but only a monologue, not two tuning forks but one.

Not long after the appearance of *Dialectic of Enlightenment* and *The Authoritarian Personality*, their provocative diagnosis of the West's authoritarian potential was given credence by Republican Senator Joseph McCarthy's attempts to expose alleged communist infiltration of branches of the US government. Among the victims of McCarthyism was the writer Thomas Mann, a figure celebrated during the war for his vocal opposition to Nazism. As a result of this defamatory campaign, Mann was forced to leave his Pacific Palisades home and move back to Europe, which he had left almost twenty years earlier. In California, both Mann and Adorno had been members of the exiled German community of artists and scholars, "Weimar on the Pacific." Mann's novel *Doctor Faustus* had benefited from Adorno's musical expertise, and Mann for his part had helped Adorno find a publisher for his aphoristic short essays, *Minima Moralia: Reflections from Damaged Life*.[37] Reporting on this irony of history that was McCarthyism to the not-so-surprised Adorno, Mann nevertheless wondered whether Adorno was too bleak regarding the future. With a reference to *Minima Moralia*, Mann regretted: "If there were only a single positive word, my honoured friend, that vouchsafed

---

36. Theodor W. Adorno, "The Actuality of Philosophy," trans. Benjamin Snow, in *The Adorno Reader*, ed. Brian O'Connor (Oxford: Blackwell, 2000), 36.

37. Ehrhard Bahr, *Weimar on the Pacific: German Exile Culture in Los Angeles and the Crisis of Modernism* (Berkeley: University of California Press, 2008), chap. 10.

even the vaguest glimpse of the true society." But "in this respect, and only this, your own reflections from damaged life say nothing."[38]

Adorno confirmed Mann's perception as accurate. Certain philosophical "asceticism with regard to any unmediated expression of the positive," a trait adopted from Hegel and Marx, "has become part of my very flesh and blood." And still, he added, "this truly is a case of asceticism, believe me, since the opposite impulse, a tendency to the unfettered expression of hope, really lies much closer to my own nature."[39]

Did this asceticism derive only from Hegel and Marx? Or, alternatively, from Jewish theology and its ban on making images of God, Freud's skepticism about civilization, or Arnold Schönberg's dissonant music? This conventional picture of Adorno is what I have tried to complicate in my reinterpretation of his intellectual biography. A good portion of Adorno's asceticism, I have sought to demonstrate, goes back to his preoccupation from the late Weimar era onward with Ludwig Klages's and Oswald Spengler's sullen diagnoses of the times, history, and the human condition.

---

38. Mann to Adorno, October 30, 1952, in *Theodor W. Adorno/Thomas Mann: Correspondence 1943–1955*, ed. Christoph Gödde and Thomas Sprecher, trans. Nicholas Walker (Cambridge: Polity Press, 2006), 93; see also 81.

39. Adorno to Mann, December 1, 1952, in *Correspondence 1943–1955*, 97.

Bibliography

Abromeit, John. *Max Horkheimer and the Foundations of the Frankfurt School*. Cambridge: Cambridge University Press, 2011.

Adorno, Theodor W. "The Actuality of Philosophy." Translated by Benjamin Snow. In *The Adorno Reader*, edited by Brian O'Connor, 23–39. Oxford: Blackwell, 2000.

Adorno, Theodor W. *Against Epistemology: A Metacritique. Studies in Husserl and the Phenomenological Antinomies*. Translated by Willis Domingo. Cambridge: Polity Press, 2013.

Adorno, Theodor W. *Aspects of the New Right-Wing Extremism*. Translated by Wieland Hoban. Cambridge: Polity Press, 2020.

Adorno, Theodor W. *Der Begriff des Unbewussten in der transzendentalen Seelenlehre*. In *Gesammelte Schriften, Bd. 1: Philosophische Frühschriften*, edited by Rolf Tiedemann, 79–322. Frankfurt: Suhrkamp, 1973.

Adorno, Theodor W. *Briefe und Briefwechsel—Bd. 4: Theodor W. Adorno—Max Horkheimer. Briefwechsel 1927–1969, Bd. I: 1927–1937*. Edited by Christoph Gödde and Henri Lonitz. Frankfurt: Suhrkamp, 2003.

Adorno, Theodor W. *Briefe und Briefwechsel—Bd. 4: Theodor W. Adorno—Max Horkheimer. Briefwechsel 1927–1969, Bd. II: 1938–1944*. Edited by Christoph Gödde and Henri Lonitz. Frankfurt: Suhrkamp, 2004.

Adorno, Theodor W. *Briefe und Briefwechsel—Bd. 5: Briefe an die Eltern, 1939–1951*. Edited by Christoph Gödde and Henri Lonitz. Frankfurt: Suhrkamp, 2003.
Adorno, Theodor W. "Cultural Criticism and Society." In *Prisms*, 17–34. Translated by Samuel Weber and Shierry Weber. Cambridge, MA: MIT Press, 1981.
Adorno, Theodor W. "The Curious Realist: On Siegfried Kracauer." In *Notes to Literature*, Vol. 2, 58–75. Translated by Shierry Weber Nicholsen. New York: Columbia University Press, 1992.
Adorno, Theodor W. *Die Transzendenz des Dinglichen und Noematischen in Husserls Phänomenologie*. In *Gesammelte Schriften, Bd. 1: Philosophische Frühschriften*, edited by Rolf Tiedemann, 7–77. Frankfurt: Suhrkamp, 1973.
Adorno, Theodor W. "Education after Auschwitz." In *Critical Models: Interventions and Catchwords*, 191–204. Translated by Henry W. Pickford. New York: Columbia University Press, 2005.
Adorno, Theodor W. "Free Time." In *Critical Models: Interventions and Catchwords*, 167–75. Translated by Henry W. Pickford. New York: Columbia University Press, 2005.
Adorno, Theodor W. "Freudian Theory and the Pattern of Fascist Propaganda." In *The Essential Frankfurt School Reader*, edited by Andrew Arato and Eike Gebhardt, 118–37. New York: Continuum, 1988.
Adorno, Theodor W. "The George-Hofmannsthal Correspondence, 1891–1906." In *Prisms*, 187–226. Translated by Samuel Weber and Shierry Weber. Cambridge, MA: MIT Press, 1981.
Adorno, Theodor W. *Gesammelte Schriften, Bd. 2: Kierkegaard. Konstruktion des Ästhetischen*. Edited by Rolf Tiedemann. Frankfurt: Suhrkamp, 1979.
Adorno, Theodor W. *Gesammelte Schriften, Bd. 10.2: Kulturkritik und Gesellschaft*. Edited by Rolf Tiedemann. Frankfurt: Suhrkamp, 1977.
Adorno, Theodor W. "Geschichtsphilosophischer Exkurs zur *Odyssee*: Frühe Fassung von *Odysseus oder Mythos und Aufklärung*." In *Frankfurter Adorno Blätter*, Vol. 5, edited by Rolf Tiedemann, 37–88. Munich: edition text + kritik, 1992.
Adorno, Theodor W. *Hegel: Three Studies*. Translated by Shierry Weber Nicholsen. Cambridge, MA: MIT Press, 1993.
Adorno, Theodor W. *History and Freedom: Lectures 1964–1965*. Edited by Rolf Tiedemann. Translated by Rodney Livingstone. Cambridge: Polity Press, 2008.
Adorno, Theodor W. "Husserl and the Problem of Idealism." In *Gesammelte Schriften, Bd. 20.1: Vermischte Schriften I*, edited by Rolf Tiedemann, 119–34. Frankfurt: Suhrkamp, 1986.
Adorno, Theodor W. "The Idea of Natural-History." In *Things beyond Resemblance: Collected Essays on Theodor W. Adorno*, 252–69. Translated and edited by Robert Hullot-Kentor. New York: Columbia University Press, 2006.
Adorno, Theodor W. *Kierkegaard: Construction of the Aesthetic*. Translated and edited by Robert Hullot-Kentor. Minneapolis: University of Minnesota Press, 1989.

Adorno, Theodor W. *Lectures on Negative Dialectics: Fragments of a Lecture Course 1965/1966*. Edited by Rolf Tiedemann. Translated by Rodney Livingstone. Cambridge: Polity Press, 2008.
Adorno, Theodor W. "The Meaning of Working Through the Past." In *Critical Models: Interventions and Catchwords*, 89–103. Translated by Henry W. Pickford. New York: Columbia University Press, 2005.
Adorno, Theodor W. *Minima Moralia: Reflections from Damaged Life*. Translated by E. F. N. Jephcott. London: Verso, 2000.
Adorno, Theodor W. *Nachgelassene Schriften. Abteilung 4: Vorlesungen. Bd. 12: Philosophische Elemente einer Theorie der Gesellschaft*. Edited by Tobias ten Brink and Marc Phillip Nogueira. Frankfurt: Suhrkamp, 2008.
Adorno, Theodor W. *Negative Dialectics*. Translated by E. B. Ashton. New York: Continuum, 2007.
Adorno, Theodor W. "Notizen zur neuen Anthropologie." In *Briefe und Briefwechsel—Bd. 4: Theodor W. Adorno—Max Horkheimer. Briefwechsel 1927–1969, Bd. II: 1938–1944*, edited by Christoph Gödde and Henri Lonitz, 453–71. Frankfurt: Suhrkamp, 2004.
Adorno, Theodor W. "On Kierkegaard's Doctrine of Love." *Studies in Philosophy and Social Science* 8, no. 3 (1939–1940): 413–29.
Adorno, Theodor W. *Ontology and Dialectics (1960/61)*. Edited by Rolf Tiedemann. Translated by Nicholas Walker. Cambridge: Polity Press, 2019.
Adorno, Theodor W. *Philosophy of New Music*. Edited and translated by Robert Hullot-Kentor. Minneapolis: University of Minnesota Press, 2006.
Adorno, Theodor W. "Remarks on *The Authoritarian Personality*." In *The Authoritarian Personality*, by Theodor W. Adorno, Else Frenkel-Brunswik, Daniel J. Levinson, and R. Nevitt Sanford, xli–lxvi. London: Verso, 2019.
Adorno, Theodor W. "Resignation." In *Critical Models: Interventions and Catchwords*, 289–93. Translated by Henry W. Pickford. New York: Columbia University Press, 2005.
Adorno, Theodor W. Review of *Charakterkunde der Gegenwart*, edited by Hans Prinzhorn. *Zeitschrift für Sozialforschung* 2, no. 1 (1933): 110–11.
Adorno, Theodor W. Review of *Das Problem des geistigen Seins*, by Nicolai Hartmann. *Zeitschrift für Sozialforschung* 2, no. 1 (1933): 110.
Adorno, Theodor W. Review of *Der Mensch und die Technik. Beitrag zu einer Philosophie des Lebens*, by Oswald Spengler. *Zeitschrift für Sozialforschung* 1, nos. 1–2 (1932): 149–51.
Adorno, Theodor W. Review of *La mante religieuse. Recherche sur la nature et la signification du mythe*, by Roger Caillois. *Zeitschrift für Sozialforschung* 7, no. 3 (1938): 410–11.
Adorno, Theodor W. "Spengler after the Decline." In *Prisms*, 51–72. Translated by Samuel Weber and Shierry Weber. Cambridge, MA: MIT Press, 1981.
Adorno, Theodor W. "Spengler nach dem Untergang: Zu Oswald Spenglers 70. Geburtstag." *Der Monat* 2, no. 20 (1950): 115–28.
Adorno, Theodor W. "Spengler Today." *Studies in Philosophy and Social Science* 9, no. 2 (1941): 305–25.

Adorno, Theodor W. "Was Spengler Right?" *Encounter* 26, no. 1 (1966): 25–29.
Adorno, Theodor W. "What National Socialism Has Done to the Arts." In *Essays on Music: Selected, with Introduction, Commentary, and Notes*, edited by Richard Leppert, 373–90. Translated by Susan H. Gillespie. Berkeley: University of California Press, 2002.
Adorno, Theodor W. "Wird Spengler recht behalten?" *Frankfurter Hefte* 10, no. 12 (1955): 841–46.
Adorno, Theodor W. "Zur Philosophie Husserls." In *Gesammelte Schriften, Bd. 20.1: Vermischte Schriften I*, edited by Rolf Tiedemann, 46–118. Frankfurt: Suhrkamp, 1986.
Adorno, Theodor W., Else Frenkel-Brunswik, Daniel J. Levinson, and R. Nevitt Sanford. *The Authoritarian Personality*. London: Verso, 2019.
Adorno, Theodor W., and Karl Kerenyi. "Mythologie und Aufklärung: Ein Rundfunkgespräch." In *Frankfurter Adorno Blätter*, Vol. 5, edited by Rolf Tiedemann, 89–104. Munich: edition text + kritik, 1992.
Adorno, Theodor W., and Lotte Tobisch. *Der private Briefwechsel*. Edited by Bernhard Kraller and Heinz Steinert. Vienna: Literaturverlag Droschl, 2003.
Anonymous. Review of *Kierkegaard: Konstruktion des Ästhetischen*, by Theodor W. Adorno. *Kölner Vierteljahrsschrift für Soziologie* 12 (1934): 198.
Assmann, Aleida. *Das neue Unbehagen an der Erinnerungskultur. Eine Intervention*. 3rd ed. Munich: C. H. Beck, 2020.
Bach, Jonathan, and Benjamin Nienass, eds. "Myths of Innocence in German Public Memory." Special issue, *German Politics and Society* 39, no. 1 (2021).
Baehr, Peter. *Caesarism, Charisma and Fate: Historical Sources and Modern Resonances in the Work of Max Weber*. London: Routledge, 2008.
Bahr, Ehrhard. *Weimar on the Pacific: German Exile Culture in Los Angeles and the Crisis of Modernism*. Berkeley: University of California Press, 2008.
Benhabib, Seyla. *Critique, Norm, and Utopia: A Study of the Foundations of Critical Theory*. New York: Columbia University Press, 1986.
Benjamin, Walter. *The Arcades Project*. Translated by Howard Eiland and Kevin McLaughlin. Cambridge, MA: Harvard University Press, 2002.
Benjamin, Walter. *The Correspondence of Walter Benjamin, 1910–1940*. Edited by Gershom Scholem and Theodor W. Adorno. Translated by Manfred R. Jacobson and Evelyn M. Jacobson. Chicago: University of Chicago Press, 1994.
Benjamin, Walter. *Gesammelte Briefe, Bd. 2: 1919–1924*. Edited by Christoph Gödde and Henri Lonitz. Frankfurt: Suhrkamp, 1996.
Benjamin, Walter. "Johann Jakob Bachofen." In *Selected Writings*, Vol. 3, edited by Howard Eiland and Michael W. Jennings, 11–24. Translated by Edmund Jephcott, Howard Eiland and Others. Cambridge, MA: The Belknap Press of Harvard University Press, 2002.
Benjamin, Walter. "Kierkegaard: The End of Philosophical Idealism." In *Selected Writings*, Vol. 2/2, edited by Howard Eiland, Michael W. Jennings, and Gary Smith, 703–5. Translated by Rodney Livingstone and Others. Cambridge, MA: The Belknap Press of Harvard University Press, 1999.

Benjamin, Walter. *One-Way Street*. Edited by Michael W. Jennings. Translated by Edmund Jephcott. Cambridge, MA: The Belknap Press of Harvard University Press, 2016.

Benjamin, Walter. "On the Concept of History." Translated by Harry Zohn. In *Selected Writings*, Vol. 4, edited by Howard Eiland and Michael W. Jennings, 389–400. Cambridge, MA: The Belknap Press of Harvard University Press, 2003.

Benjamin, Walter. *Origin of the German* Trauerspiel. Translated by Howard Eiland. Cambridge, MA: Harvard University Press, 2019.

Benjamin, Walter. "Paris, the Capital of the Nineteenth Century." In *Selected Writings*, Vol. 3, edited by Howard Eiland and Michael W. Jennings, 32–49. Translated by Edmund Jephcott, Howard Eiland and Others. Cambridge, MA: The Belknap Press of Harvard University Press, 2002.

Benjamin, Walter. "Review of Bernoulli's *Bachofen*." Translated by Rodney Livingstone. In *Selected Writings*, Vol. 1, edited by Marcus Bullock and Michael W. Jennings, 426–28. Cambridge, MA: The Belknap Press of Harvard University Press, 1996.

Benjamin, Walter. "Surrealism: The Last Snapshot of the European Intelligentsia." In *Reflections: Essays, Aphorisms, Autobiographical Writings*, 177–92. Translated by Edmund Jephcott. New York: Schocken Books, 1978.

Benjamin, Walter. "Theories of German Fascism: On the Collection of Essays *War and Warriors*, edited by Ernst Jünger." In *Selected Writings*, Vol. 2, Pt. 1, edited by Howard Eiland, Michael W. Jennings, and Gary Smith, 312–21. Translated by Rodney Livingstone and Others. Cambridge, MA: The Belknap Press of Harvard University Press, 1999.

Berlin, Isaiah. "Isaiah Berlin: In Conversation with Steven Lukes." *Salmagundi* 120 (Fall 1998): 52–134.

Berlin, Isaiah. "Memorial Address in St Mary's." In *Maurice Bowra: A Celebration*, edited by Hugh Lloyd-Jones, 16–21. London: Duckworth, 1974.

Bernstein, Jay M. "Negative Dialectic as Fate: Adorno and Hegel." In *The Cambridge Companion to Adorno*, edited by Tom Huhn, 19–50. Cambridge: Cambridge University Press, 2004.

Bishop, Paul. *Ludwig Klages and the Philosophy of Life: A Vitalist Toolkit*. New York: Routledge, 2017.

Bjurman, Lars, and Carl-Henning Wijkmark. Editorial remarks on *Dialectic of Enlightenment*'s Swedish translation, *Upplysningens dialektik: Filosofiska fragment*. Translated and edited by Lars Bjurman and Carl-Henning Wijkmark, 287–303. Gothenburg, Sweden: Daidalos, 1981.

Bock, Wolfgang. *Dialektische Psychologie. Adornos Rezeption der Psychoanalyse*. Wiesbaden, Germany: Springer, 2018.

Borchardt, Rudolf. *Pindarische Gedichte*. Munich: Deschler, 1929/1930.

Bowra, Cecil Maurice. "Sociological Remarks on Greek Poetry." *Zeitschrift für Sozialforschung* 6, no. 2 (1937): 382–99.

Brecht, F. J. Review of *Kierkegaard: Konstruktion des Ästhetischen*, by Theodor W. Adorno. *Kant Studien* 40 (1935): 327.

Breuer, Stefan. *Anatomie der konservativen Revolution*. Darmstadt, Germany: Wissenschaftliche Buchgesellschaft, 1993.
Breuer, Stefan. *Kritische Theorie: Schlüsselbegriffe, Kontroversen, Grenzen*. Tübingen, Germany: Mohr Siebeck, 2016.
Breuer, Stefan. "Materialistische Erkenntniskritik." In *Adorno Handbuch: Leben—Werk—Wirkung*, edited by Richard Klein, Johann Kreuzer, and Stefan Müller-Doohm, 430–36. 2nd ed. Berlin: J. B. Metzler, 2019.
Brunkhorst, Hauke. *Adorno and Critical Theory*. Cardiff: University of Wales Press, 1999.
Buchstein, Hubertus. "Otto Kirchheimer and the Frankfurt School: Failed Collaborations in the Search for a Critical Theory of Politics." *New German Critique* 47, no. 2 (2020): 81–106.
Buck-Morss, Susan. *The Origin of Negative Dialectics: Theodor W. Adorno, Walter Benjamin, and the Frankfurt Institute*. New York: The Free Press, 1977.
Cassirer, Ernst. *The Myth of the State*. New Haven, CT: Yale University Press, 1946.
Cassirer, Ernst. *The Philosophy of Symbolic Forms*, Vol. 2, *Mythical Thought*. Translated by Ralph Manheim. New Haven, CT: Yale University Press, 1955.
Charles, Matthew. "Secret Signals from Another World: Walter Benjamin's Theory of Innervation." *New German Critique* 45, no. 3 (2018): 39–72.
Claussen, Detlev. *Theodor W. Adorno: One Last Genius*. Translated by Rodney Livingstone. Cambridge, MA: Harvard University Press, 2008.
Clayton, John P. *The Concept of Correlation: Paul Tillich and the Possibility of a Mediating Theology*. Berlin: De Gruyter, 1980.
Davies, Peter. *Myth, Matriarchy and Modernity: Johann Jakob Bachofen in German Culture 1860–1945*. Berlin: De Gruyter, 2010.
Demirovic, Alex. *Der nonkonformistische Intellektuelle. Die Entwicklung der Kritischen Theorie zur Frankfurter Schule*. Frankfurt: Suhrkamp, 1999.
de Vries, Hent. *Minimal Theologies: Critiques of Secular Reason in Adorno and Levinas*. Translated by Geoffrey Hale. Baltimore, MD: Johns Hopkins University Press, 2005.
Dubiel, Helmut. *Theory and Politics: Studies in the Development of Critical Theory*. Translated by Benjamin Gregg. Cambridge, MA: MIT Press, 1985.
"Erinnerungen an Paul Tillich." In *Werk und Wirken Paul Tillichs: Ein Gedenkbuch*, 11–45. Stuttgart: Evangelisches Verlagswerk, 1967.
Fett, Othmar Franz. *Der undenkbare Dritte: Vorsokratische Anfänge des eurogenen Naturverhältnisses*. Tübingen, Germany: Edition Diskord, 2000.
Finkelberg, Margalit. *Greeks and Pre-Greeks: Aegean Prehistory and Greek Heroic Tradition*. Cambridge: Cambridge University Press, 2005.
Fleming, Paul. "The Secret Adorno." *Qui Parle* 15, no. 1 (2004): 97–114.
Fraser, Nancy, and Rahel Jaeggi. *Capitalism: A Conversation in Critical Theory*. Edited by Brian Milstein. Cambridge: Polity Press, 2018.
Frei, Norbert. *Adenauer's Germany and the Nazi Past: The Politics of Amnesty and Integration*. Translated by Joel Golb. New York: Columbia University Press, 2002.

Freud, Sigmund. *Civilization and Its Discontents*. Translated by David McLintock. London: Penguin, 2002.
Freyenhagen, Fabian. "Adorno's Politics: Theory and Praxis in Germany's 1960s." *Philosophy and Social Criticism* 40, no. 9 (2014): 867–93.
Friedman, George. *The Political Philosophy of the Frankfurt School*. Ithaca, NY: Cornell University Press, 1981.
Fromm, Erich. "Die sozialpsychologische Bedeutung der Mutterrechtstheorie." *Zeitschrift für Sozialforschung* 3, no. 2 (1934): 196–227.
Fromm, Erich. *The Working Class in Weimar Germany: A Psychological and Sociological Study*. Translated by Barbara Weinberger. Warwickshire, UK: Berg Publishers, 1984.
Fukuyama, Francis. *The End of History and the Last Man*. New York: The Free Press, 1992.
Gandesha, Samir. "'Identifying with the Aggressor': From the Authoritarian to Neoliberal Personality." *Constellations: An International Journal of Critical and Democratic Theory* 25, no. 1 (2018): 147–64.
Gandesha, Samir, Johan F. Hartle, and Stefano Marino, eds. *The "Aging" of Adorno's Aesthetic Theory: Fifty Years Later*. Milan: Mimesis International, 2021.
Gangl, Manfred. "The Controversy over Friedrich Pollock's State Capitalism." *History of the Human Sciences* 29, no. 2 (2016): 23–41.
Gangl, Manfred, and Gérard Raulet, eds. *Intellektuellendiskurse in der Weimarer Republik: Zur politischen Kultur einer Gemengelage*. 2nd ed. Frankfurt: Peter Lang, 2007.
Gasimov, Zaur, and Carl Antonius Lemke Duque, eds. *Oswald Spengler als europäisches Phänomen: Der Transfer der Kultur- und Geschichtsmorphologie im Europa der Zwischenkriegszeit 1919–1939*. Göttingen, Germany: Vandenhoeck & Ruprecht, 2013.
Gehlen, Arnold. *Urmensch und Spätkultur: Philosophische Ergebnisse und Aussagen*. Bonn: Athenäum, 1956.
Gödde, Christoph, ed. *Theodor W. Adorno und Alfred Sohn-Rethel: Briefwechsel 1936–1969*. München: text + kritik, 1991.
Gödde, Christoph, and Thomas Sprecher, eds. *Theodor W. Adorno/Thomas Mann: Correspondence 1943–1955*. Translated by Nicholas Walker. Cambridge: Polity Press, 2006.
Gordon, Peter E. *Adorno and Existence*. Cambridge, MA: Harvard University Press, 2016.
Gordon, Peter E., ed. "Adorno's *Aesthetic Theory* at Fifty." Special issue, *New German Critique* 48, no. 2 (2021): 1–220.
Gordon, Peter E. "The Authoritarian Personality Revisited: Reading Adorno in the Age of Trump." In Wendy Brown, Peter E. Gordon, and Max Pensky, *Authoritarianism: Three Inquiries in Critical Theory*, 45–84. Chicago: University of Chicago Press, 2018.
Gordon, Peter E. "Contextualism and Criticism in the History of Ideas." In *Rethinking Modern European Intellectual History*, edited by Darrin M. McMahon and Samuel Moyn, 32–55. Oxford: Oxford University Press, 2014.

Gordon, Peter E. *Migrants in the Profane: Critical Theory and the Question of Secularization*. New Haven, CT: Yale University Press, 2020.
Gordon, Peter E., Espen Hammer, and Axel Honneth, eds. *The Routledge Companion to the Frankfurt School*. New York: Routledge, 2019.
Gordon, Peter E., Espen Hammer, and Max Pensky, eds. *A Companion to Adorno*. Hoboken, NJ: Wiley-Blackwell, 2020.
Graf, Fritz. *Greek Mythology: An Introduction*. Translated by Thomas Marier. Baltimore, MD: Johns Hopkins University Press, 1993.
Grenz, Friedemann. "Ist die Soziologie eine Wissenschaft vom Menschen? Ein Streitgespräch zwischen Theodor W. Adorno und Arnold Gehlen." In *Adornos Philosophie in Grundbegriffen: Auflösung einiger Deutungsprobleme*, 224–51. Frankfurt: Suhrkamp, 1974.
Grimm, Marc. "Zur Aktualität Kritischer Theorie." *Zeitschrift für Politische Theorie* 8, no. 1 (2017): 113–21.
Grossheim, Michael. "'Die namenlose Dummheit, die das Resultat des Fortschritts ist.'—Lebensphilosophische und dialektische Kritik der Moderne." *Logos. Zeitschrift für systematische Philosophie* 3, no. 2 (1996): 97–133.
Grossheim, Michael, ed. *Perspektiven der Lebensphilosophie: Zum 125. Geburtstag von Ludwig Klages*. Bonn: Bouvier, 1999.
Habermas, Jürgen. "Nachwort" [Afterword]. In Max Horkheimer and Theodor W. Adorno, *Dialektik der Aufklärung*, 277–94. Frankfurt: Fischer, 1986.
Habermas, Jürgen. *The Philosophical Discourse of Modernity: Twelve Lectures*. Translated by Frederick G. Lawrence. Cambridge, MA: MIT Press, 1990.
Habermas, Jürgen. "Remarks on the Development of Max Horkheimer's Work." Translated by Kenneth Baynes and John McCole. In *On Max Horkheimer: New Perspectives*, edited by Seyla Benhabib, Wolfgang Bonss, and John McCole, 49–65. Cambridge, MA: MIT Press, 1993.
Habermas, Jürgen. *The Theory of Communicative Action*. Vol. 1, *Reason and the Rationalization of Society*. Translated by Thomas McCarthy. Boston: Beacon Press, 1984.
Habermas, Jürgen. "Walter Benjamin: Consciousness-Raising or Rescuing Critique." In *On Walter Benjamin: Critical Essays and Recollections*, edited by Gary Smith, 90–128. Cambridge: MIT Press, 1988.
Hansen, Miriam Bratu. "Benjamin's Aura." *Critical Inquiry* 34, no. 2 (2008): 336–75.
Hansen, Miriam Bratu. *Cinema and Experience: Siegfried Kracauer, Walter Benjamin, and Theodor W. Adorno*. Berkeley: University of California Press, 2011.
Harrington, Anne. *Reenchanted Science: Holism in German Culture from Wilhelm II to Hitler*. Princeton, NJ: Princeton University Press, 1996.
Hawley, George. *Making Sense of the Alt-Right*. New York: Columbia University Press, 2017.
Hegel, Georg Wilhelm Friedrich. *Lectures on the Philosophy of World History. Introduction: Reason in History*. Translated by H. B. Nisbet. Cambridge: Cambridge University Press, 1975.

Hegel, Georg Wilhelm Friedrich. *Phenomenology of Spirit*. Translated by A. V. Miller. Oxford: Oxford University Press, 1977.
Herf, Jeffrey. *Reactionary Modernism: Technology, Culture, and Politics in Weimar and the Third Reich*. Cambridge: Cambridge University Press, 1986.
Herodotus. *The Histories*. Translated by Aubrey de Sélincourt. New York: Penguin Books, 2003.
Hobsbawm, Eric. *The Age of Extremes: The Short Twentieth Century, 1914–1991*. London: Abacus, 1994.
Hohendahl, Peter Uwe. *The Fleeting Promise of Art: Adorno's Aesthetic Theory Revisited*. Ithaca, NY: Cornell University Press, 2013.
Hölderlin, Friedrich. *Poems and Fragments*. Translated by Michael Hamburger. Cambridge: Cambridge University Press, 1980.
Hölscher, Uvo. "Strömungen der deutschen Graezistik in den zwanziger Jahren." In *Altertumswissenschaft in den 20er Jahren: Neue Fragen und Impulse*, edited by Hellmut Flashar, 65–85. Stuttgart: Franz Steiner Verlag, 1995.
Homer. *The Iliad*. Translated by Robert Fagles. New York: Penguin Books, 1991.
Homer. *The Odyssey*. Translated by Robert Fagles. New York: Penguin Books, 1996.
Honneth, Axel. "Anthropologische Berührungspunkte zwischen der Lebensphilosophischen Kulturkritik und der 'Dialektik der Aufklärung.'" In *21. Deutscher Soziologentag 1982. Beiträge der Sektions- und ad hoc-Gruppen*, edited by Friedrich Heckmann and Peter Winter, 786–92. Opladen, Germany: Westdeutscher Verlag, 1983.
Honneth, Axel. *Pathologies of Reason: On the Legacy of Critical Theory*. Translated by James Ingram. New York: Columbia University Press, 2009.
Horkheimer, Max. "Authority and the Family." In *Critical Theory: Selected Essays*, 47–128. Translated by Matthew J. O'Connell. New York: Continuum, 1972.
Horkheimer, Max. "Begriff der Bildung." In *Gesammelte Schriften, Bd. 8: Vorträge und Aufzeichnungen 1949–1973*, edited by Gunzelin Schmid Noerr, 409–19. Frankfurt: Fischer, 1985.
Horkheimer, Max. "Diskussion über die Aufgabe des Protestantismus in der sekularen Zivilisation." In *Gesammelte Schriften, Bd. 11: Nachgelassene Schriften 1914–1931*, edited by Gunzelin Schmid Noerr, 345–405. Frankfurt: Fischer, 1987.
Horkheimer, Max. "Diskussionen über die Differenz zwischen Positivismus und materialistischer Dialektik." In *Gesammelte Schriften, Bd. 12: Nachgelassene Schriften 1931–1949*, edited by Gunzelin Schmid Noerr, 436–92. Frankfurt: Fischer, 1987.
Horkheimer, Max. *Eclipse of Reason*. New York: Continuum, 2004.
Horkheimer, Max. "Egoism and Freedom Movements: On the Anthropology of the Bourgeois Era." In *Between Philosophy and Social Science: Selected Early Writings*, 49–110. Translated by G. Frederick Hunter, Matthew S. Kramer, and John Torpey. Cambridge, MA: MIT Press, 1993.

Horkheimer, Max. "Einführung in die Philosophie der Gegenwart." In *Gesammelte Schriften, Bd. 10: Nachgelassene Schriften 1914–1931*, edited by Alfred Schmidt, 169–333. Frankfurt: Fischer, 1990.

Horkheimer, Max. "Eine neue Politik der Linken." In *Gesammelte Schriften, Bd. 14: Nachgelassene Schriften 1949–1972, Notizen*, edited by Gunzelin Schmid Noerr, 365. Frankfurt: Fischer, 1988.

Horkheimer, Max. "The End of Reason." *Studies in Philosophy and Social Science* 9, no. 3 (1941): 366–88.

Horkheimer, Max. "Montaigne and the Function of Skepticism." In *Between Philosophy and Social Science: Selected Early Writings*, 265–311. Translated by G. Frederick Hunter, Matthew S. Kramer, and John Torpey. Cambridge, MA: MIT Press, 1993.

Horkheimer, Max. "On the Problem of Truth." In *Between Philosophy and Social Science: Selected Early Writings*, 177–215. Translated by G. Frederick Hunter, Matthew S. Kramer, and John Torpey. Cambridge, MA: MIT Press, 1993.

Horkheimer, Max. Preface to *The Authoritarian Personality*, by Adorno et al., lxxi–lxxiv. London: Verso, 2019.

Horkheimer, Max. "The Rationalism Debate in Contemporary Philosophy." In *Between Philosophy and Social Science: Selected Early Writings*, 217–64. Translated by G. Frederick Hunter, Matthew S. Kramer, and John Torpey. Cambridge, MA: MIT Press, 1993.

Horkheimer, Max. Review of *Jahre der Entscheidung I Teil: Deutschland und die weltgeschichtliche Entwicklung*, by Oswald Spengler. *Zeitschrift für Sozialforschung* 2, no. 3 (1933): 421–24.

Horkheimer, Max. "Wissenschaft und Krise. Differenz zwischen Idealismus und Materialismus. Diskussionen über Themen zu einer Vorlesung Max Horkheimers." In *Gesammelte Schriften, Bd. 12: Nachgelassene Schriften 1931–1949*, edited by Gunzelin Schmid Noerr, 349–97. Frankfurt: Fischer, 1985.

Horkheimer, Max. "Zur Emanzipation der Philosophie von der Wissenschaft." In *Gesammelte Schriften, Bd. 10: Nachgelassene Schriften 1914–1931*, edited by Alfred Schmidt, 334–419. Frankfurt: Fischer, 1990.

Horkheimer, Max, and Theodor W. Adorno. *Dialectic of Enlightenment: Philosophical Fragments*. Translated by Edmund Jephcott. Stanford, CA: Stanford University Press, 2002.

Hughes, H. Stuart. *Oswald Spengler: A Critical Estimate*. New Brunswick, NJ: Transaction Publishers, 1992.

Hulatt, Owen. *Adorno's Theory of Philosophical and Aesthetic Truth*. New York: Columbia University Press, 2016.

Hullot-Kentor, Robert. "Back to Adorno." In *Things beyond Resemblance: Collected Essays on Theodor W. Adorno*, 23–44. New York: Columbia University Press, 2006.

Hullot-Kentor, Robert. "Critique of the Organic: Kierkegaard and the Construction of the Aesthetic." In *Things beyond Resemblance: Collected Essays on Theodor W. Adorno*, 77–93. New York: Columbia University Press, 2006.

Immanen, Mikko. *Toward a Concrete Philosophy: Heidegger and the Emergence of the Frankfurt School*. Ithaca, NY: Cornell University Press, 2020.
Inglehart, Ronald. *The Silent Revolution: Changing Values and Political Styles among Western Publics*. Princeton, NJ: Princeton University Press, 2016.
Inglehart, Ronald, and Pippa Norris. "Trump and the Populist Authoritarian Parties: The Silent Revolution in Reverse." *Perspectives on Politics* 15, no. 2 (2017): 443–54.
Jay, Martin. *Adorno*. Cambridge, MA: Harvard University Press, 1984.
Jay, Martin. *The Dialectical Imagination: A History of the Frankfurt School and the Institute of Social Research, 1923–1950*. Boston, MA: Little, Brown and Co., 1973.
Jay, Martin. "Introduction to a Festschrift for Leo Löwenthal on His Eightieth Birthday." In *Permanent Exiles: Essays on the Intellectual Migration from Germany to America*, 101–6. New York: Columbia University Press, 1986.
Jay, Martin. *Marxism and Totality: The Adventures of a Concept from Lukács to Habermas*. Berkeley: University of California Press, 1984.
Jay, Martin. *Reason after Its Eclipse: On Late Critical Theory*. Madison: University of Wisconsin Press, 2016.
Jenemann, David. *Adorno in America*. Minneapolis: University of Minnesota Press, 2007.
Jones, William David. *The Lost Debate: German Socialist Intellectuals and Totalitarianism*. Urbana: University of Illinois Press, 1999.
Kauders, Anthony D. *Der Freud Komplex. Eine Geschichte der Psychoanalyse in Deutschland*. Berlin: Berlin Verlag, 2014.
Keum, Tae-Yeoun. *Plato and the Mythic Tradition in Political Thought*. Cambridge, MA: The Belknap Press of Harvard University Press, 2020.
Klages, Ludwig. *Der Geist als Widersacher der Seele: Erstes bis Viertes Buch* [The spirit as adversary of the soul: Books one through four]. In *Sämtliche Werke, Bd. 1*, edited by Ernst Frauchiger, Gerhard Funke, Karl J. Groffmann, Robert Heiss, and Hans Eggert Schröder. Bonn: Bouvier Verlag, 1969.
Klages, Ludwig. *Der Geist als Widersacher der Seele: Fünftes Buch* [The spirit as adversary of the soul: Book five]. *Sämtliche Werke, Bd. 2*, edited by Ernst Frauchiger, Gerhard Funke, Karl J. Groffmann, Robert Heiss, and Hans Eggert Schröder. Bonn: Bouvier Verlag, 1966.
Klages, Ludwig. "Die Grundlagen der Charakterkunde." In *Sämtliche Werke, Bd. 4*, edited by Ernst Frauchiger, Gerhard Funke, Karl J. Groffmann, Robert Heiss, and Hans Eggert Schröder, 191–428. Bonn: Bouvier Verlag, 1976.
Klages, Ludwig. "Mensch und Erde." In *Sämtliche Werke, Bd. 3*, edited by Ernst Frauchiger, Gerhard Funke, Karl J. Groffmann, Robert Heiss, and Hans Eggert Schröder, 614–30. Bonn: Bouvier Verlag, 1974.
Klages, Ludwig. *Vom kosmogonischen Eros*. In *Sämtliche Werke, Bd. 3*, edited by Ernst Frauchiger, Gerhard Funke, Karl J. Groffmann, Robert Heiss, and Hans Eggert Schröder, 353–497. Bonn: Bouvier Verlag, 1974.

Klages, Ludwig. "Vom Traumbewusstsein." In *Sämtliche Werke, Bd. 3*, edited by Ernst Frauchiger, Gerhard Funke, Karl J. Groffmann, Robert Heiss, and Hans Eggert Schröder, 155–238. Bonn: Bouvier Verlag, 1974.

Klein, Richard, Johann Kreuzer, and Stefan Müller-Doohm, eds. *Adorno Handbuch: Leben—Werk—Wirkung*. 2nd ed. Berlin: J. B. Metzler, 2019.

Kracauer, Siegfried. "Der enthüllte Kierkegaard." In *Werke, Bd. 5.4: Essays, Feuilletons, Rezensionen*, edited by Inka Mülder-Bach, 486–91. Berlin: Suhrkamp, 2011.

Kramer, Andreas, and Evelyn Wilcock. "'A Preserve for Professional Philosophers': Adornos Husserl-Dissertation 1934–37 und ihr Oxforder Kontext." *Deutsche Vierteljahrsschrift für Literaturwissenschaft und Geistesgeschichte* 73 (October 1999): 115–61.

Kuhn, Helmut. Review of *Kierkegaard: Konstruktion des Ästhetischen*, by Theodor W. Adorno. *Zeitschrift für Ästhetik und allgemeine Kunstwissenschaft* 28, no. 1 (1934): 102–9.

Kühne-Bertram, Gudrun. *Aus dem Leben—zum Leben: Entstehung, Wesen und Bedeutung populärer Lebensphilosophien in der Geistesgeschichte des 19. Jahrhunderts*. Frankfurt: Peter Lang, 1987.

Lebovic, Nitzan. *The Philosophy of Life and Death: Ludwig Klages and the Rise of a Nazi Biopolitics*. New York: Palgrave Macmillan, 2013.

Lepenies, Wolf. *Melancholy and Society*. Translated by Jeremy Gaines and Doris Jones. Cambridge, MA: Harvard University Press, 1992.

Levin, Thomas Y. "For the Record: Adorno on Music in the Age of Its Technological Reproducibility." *October* 55 (Winter 1990): 23–47.

Lonitz, Henri, ed. *The Complete Correspondence, 1928–1940: Theodor W. Adorno and Walter Benjamin*. Translated by Nicholas Walker. Cambridge, MA: Harvard University Press, 1999.

Löwith, Karl. Review of *Kierkegaard: Konstruktion des Ästhetischen*, by Theodor W. Adorno. *Deutsche Literaturzeitung* 4 (1934): 28.

Lukács, Georg. *History and Class Consciousness: Studies in Marxist Dialectics*. Translated by Rodney Livingstone. London: Merlin Press, 1971.

Lukács, Georg. *The Theory of the Novel: A Historico-Philosophical Essay on the Forms of Great Epic Literature*. Translated by Anna Bostock. London: Merlin Press, 1971.

Lunn, Eugene. *Marxism and Modernism: A Historical Study of Lukács, Brecht, Benjamin, and Adorno*. Berkeley: University of California Press, 1982.

Macdonald, Iain, and Krzysztof Ziarek, eds. *Adorno and Heidegger: Philosophical Questions*. Stanford, CA: Stanford University Press, 2008.

MacWilliams, Matthew C. *The Rise of Trump: America's Authoritarian Spring*. Amherst, MA: Amherst College Press, 2016.

Mali, Joseph. "The Reconciliation of Myth: Benjamin's Homage to Bachofen." *Journal of the History of Ideas* 60, no. 1 (1999): 165–87.

Marchand, Suzanne L. *Down from Olympus: Archaeology and Philhellenism in Germany, 1750–1970*. Princeton, NJ: Princeton University Press, 1996.

Marx, Karl, and Friedrich Engels. *The German Ideology*. In *Collected Works*, Vol. 5, 19–539. London: Lawrence and Wishart, 1976.
Mazower, Mark. *Dark Continent: Europe's Twentieth Century*. New York: Penguin, 1998.
McCole, John. *Walter Benjamin and the Antinomies of Tradition*. Ithaca, NY: Cornell University Press, 1993.
Merlio, Gilbert, and Daniel Meyer, eds. *Spengler ohne Ende: Ein Rezeptionsphänomen im internationalen Kontext*. Frankfurt: Peter Lang, 2014.
Michels, Robert. *Political Parties: A Sociological Study of the Oligarchical Tendencies of Modern Democracy*. Translated by Eden Paul and Cedar Paul. New York: The Free Press, 1962.
Mitchell, Leslie. *Maurice Bowra: A Life*. Oxford: Oxford University Press, 2009.
Mörchen, Hermann. *Adorno und Heidegger: Untersuchung einer philosophischen Kommunikationsverweigerung*. Stuttgart: Klett-Cotta, 1981.
Morelock, Jeremiah, ed. *Critical Theory and Authoritarian Populism*. London: University of Westminster Press, 2018.
Morgan, Marcia. "Adorno's Reception of Kierkegaard: 1929–1933." *Sören Kierkegaard Newsletter* 46 (2003): 8–11.
Mosse, George L. *The Crisis of German Ideology: Intellectual Origins of the Third Reich*. New York: Grosset & Dunlap, 1964.
Müller-Doohm, Stefan. *Adorno: A Biography*. Translated by Rodney Livingstone. Cambridge: Polity Press, 2009.
Murray, Gilbert. *Five Stages of Greek Religion*. New York: Columbia University Press, 1925.
Nirenberg, David, and Ricardo L. Nirenberg. *Uncountable: A Philosophical History of Number and Humanity from Antiquity to the Present*. Chicago: University of Chicago Press, 2021.
Norton, Robert. *Secret Germany: Stefan George and His Circle*. Ithaca, NY: Cornell University Press, 2002.
O'Connor, Brian. *Adorno's Negative Dialectic: Philosophy and the Possibility of Critical Rationality*. Cambridge, MA: MIT Press, 2004.
Owen, David. "Nietzsche and the Frankfurt School." In *The Routledge Companion to the Frankfurt School*, edited by Peter E. Gordon, Espen Hammer, and Axel Honneth, 251–65. New York: Routledge, 2019.
Pauen, Michael. *Dithyrambiker des Untergangs: Gnostizismus in Ästhetik und Philosophie der Moderne*. Berlin: Akademie Verlag, 1994.
Pausanias. *Description of Greece*, Vols. 1–5. Translated by W. H. S. Jones. Cambridge, MA: Harvard University Press, 1989.
Pensky, Max. "Radical Critique and Late Epistemology: Tocqueville, Adorno, and Authoritarianism." In *Authoritarianism: Three Inquiries in Critical Theory*, by Wendy Brown, Peter E. Gordon, and Max Pensky, 85–124. Chicago: University of Chicago Press, 2018.
Piketty, Thomas. *Capital in the Twenty-First Century*. Translated by Arthur Goldhammer. Cambridge, MA: The Belknap Press of Harvard University Press, 2014.

Plessner, Helmut. *Levels of Organic Life and the Human: An Introduction to Philosophical Anthropology*. Translated by Millay Hyatt. New York: Fordham University Press, 2019.
Pollock, Friedrich, ed. *Frankfurter Beiträge zur Soziologie*. Vol. 2, *Gruppenexperiment: Ein Studienbericht*. Frankfurt: Campus, 1955.
Pollock, Friedrich. "Is National Socialism a New Order?" *Studies in Philosophy and Social Science* 9, no. 3 (1941): 440–55.
Pollock, Friedrich. "State Capitalism: Its Possibilities and Limitations." *Studies in Philosophy and Social Science* 9, no. 2 (1941): 200–225.
Prutsch, Markus J. *Caesarism in the Post-Revolutionary Age: Crisis, Populace and Leadership*. London: Bloomsbury, 2020.
Rabinbach, Anson. *In the Shadow of Catastrophe: German Intellectuals between Apocalypse and Enlightenment*. Berkeley: University of California Press, 1997.
Raulet, Gérard. "Secularization, Myth, Anti-Semitism: Adorno and Horkheimer's *Dialectic of Enlightenment* and Cassirer's *Philosophy of Symbolic Forms*." Translated by Ladislaus Löb. In *The Early Frankfurt School and Religion*, edited by M. Kohlenbach and Raymond Geuss, 171–89. London. Palgrave, 2004.
Reichardt, Tobias. *Recht und Rationalität im frühen Griechenland*. Würzburg, Germany: Königshausen & Neumann, 2003.
Richards, Robert J. *The Romantic Conception of Life: Science and Philosophy in the Age of Goethe*. Chicago: University of Chicago Press, 2002.
Riesman, David. *The Lonely Crowd: A Study of the Changing American Character*. New Haven, CT: Yale University Press, 2001.
Roberts, David. *Art and Enlightenment: Aesthetic Theory after Adorno*. Lincoln: University of Nebraska Press, 1991.
Röder, Brigitte, Juliane Hummel, and Brigitta Kunz. *Göttinnendämmerung: Das Matriarchat aus archäologischer Sicht*. Königsfurt, Germany: Krummwisch, 2001.
Rosa, Hartmut. *Resonance: A Sociology of Our Relationship to the World*. Translated by James C. Wagner. Cambridge: Polity Press, 2019.
Rosa, Hartmut. *The Uncontrollability of the World*. Translated by James C. Wagner. Cambridge: Polity Press, 2020.
Rose, Gillian. *The Melancholy Science: An Introduction to the Thought of Theodor W. Adorno*. London: Macmillan Press, 1978.
Ruehl, Martin A. "Aesthetic Fundamentalism in Weimar Poetry: Stefan George and His Circle, 1918–1933." In *Weimar Thought: A Contested Legacy*, edited by Peter E. Gordon and John P. McCormick, 240–72. Princeton, NJ: Princeton University Press, 2013.
Schelsky, Helmut. *Rückblicke eines "Anti-Soziologen."* Opladen, Germany: Westdeutscher Verlag, 1981.
Schiermer, Bjørn. "Acceleration and Resonance: An Interview with Hartmut Rosa." *Acta Sociologica* (2020): 1–7.
Schmid Noerr, Gunzelin, and Eva-Maria Ziege. Introduction. In *Zur Kritik der regressiven Vernunft: Beiträge zur "Dialektik der Aufklärung,"* edited by

Gunzelin Schmid Noerr and Eva-Maria Ziege, 5–10. Wiesbaden, Germany: Springer, 2019.
Schnädelbach, Herbert. *Philosophy in Germany, 1831–1933*. Translated by Eric Matthews. Cambridge: Cambridge University Press, 1984.
Schopf, Wolfgang, ed. *Theodor W. Adorno/Siegfried Kracauer: Correspondence, 1923–1966*. Translated by Susan Reynolds and Michael Winkler. Cambridge: Polity Press, 2020.
Shelmerdine, Cynthia W., ed. *The Cambridge Companion to the Aegean Bronze Age*. Cambridge: Cambridge University Press, 2008.
Shotwell, James T. "Spengler." In *The Faith of an Historian and Other Essays*, 221–29. New York: Walker, 1964.
Skidelsky, Edward. *Ernst Cassirer: The Last Philosopher of Culture*. Princeton, NJ: Princeton University Press, 2008.
Sohn-Rethel, Alfred. *Intellectual and Manual Labor: A Critique of Epistemology*. Translated by Martin Sohn-Rethel. London: Macmillan Press, 1978.
Sombart, Werner. *Why Is There No Socialism in the United States?* Translated by Patricia M. Hocking and C. T. Husbands. London: Macmillan, 1976.
"Special Section on Carl Schmitt and the Frankfurt School." *Telos* 71 (1987): 37–109.
"Special Section on Frankfurt School and Nietzsche." *Constellations: An International Journal of Critical and Democratic Theory* 8, no. 1 (2001): 127–47.
Spengler, Oswald. *The Decline of the West*. Vol. 1, *Form and Actuality*. Translated by Charles Francis Atkinson. New York: Knopf, 1994.
Spengler, Oswald. *The Decline of the West*. Vol. 2, *Perspectives of World-History*. Translated by Charles Francis Atkinson. New York: Knopf, 1994.
Spengler, Oswald. *Man and Technics: A Contribution to a Philosophy of Life*. Translated by Charles Francis Atkinson. London: Allen & Unwin, 1932.
Spengler, Oswald. "Pessimismus." In *Reden und Aufsätze*, edited by Hildegard Kornhardt, 63–79. Munich: C. H. Beck, 1937.
"Spenglerheft." *Logos. Internationale Zeitschrift für Philosophie der Kultur* 9, no. 2 (1920–1921): 133–295.
Stauth, Georg. "Critical Theory and Pre-Fascist Social Thought." *History of European Ideas* 18, no. 5 (1994): 711–27.
Stauth, Georg, and Bryan S. Turner. "Ludwig Klages (1872–1956) and the Origins of Critical Theory." *Theory, Culture & Society* 9 (1992): 45–63.
Stern, Alexander. "Guilt and Mourning: Adorno's Debt to and Critique of Benjamin." In *A Companion to Adorno*, edited by Peter E. Gordon, Espen Hammer, Max Pensky, 51–66. Hoboken, NJ: Wiley-Blackwell, 2020.
Stern, Fritz. *The Politics of Cultural Despair: A Study in the Rise of the Germanic Ideology*. Berkeley: University of California Press, 1961.
Stone, Ronald H. *Professor Reinhold Niebuhr: A Mentor to the Twentieth Century*. Louisville, KY: Westminster/John Knox, 1992.
Strauss, Leo. "Kurt Riezler." In *What Is Political Philosophy? and Other Studies*, 233–60. Glencoe, IL: The Free Press, 1959.

Thies, Christian. *Die Krise des Individuums: Zur Kritik der Moderne bei Adorno und Gehlen*. Reinbek, Germany: Rowohlt, 1997.
Thucydides. *History of the Peloponnesian War*. Translated by Rex Warner. New York: Penguin Books, 1974.
Tiedemann, Rolf. Editor's afterword. In Theodor W. Adorno, *Gesammelte Schriften, Bd. 20.2: Vermischte Schriften II*, 813–32. Frankfurt: Suhrkamp, 1986.
Tiedemann, Rolf. Editor's note. In Theodor W. Adorno, *Ontology and Dialectics (1960/61)*, edited by Rolf Tiedemann. Translated by Nicholas Walker. Cambridge: Polity Press, 2019.
Tiedemann, Rolf. "'Gegenwärtige Vorwelt': Zu Adornos Begriff des Mythischen (I)." In *Frankfurter Adorno Blätter*, Vol. 5, 9–36. Munich: text + kritik, 1992.
van Reijen, Willem, and Jan Bransen. "The Disappearance of Class History in 'Dialectic of Enlightenment': A Commentary on the Textual Variants (1947 and 1944)." In Max Horkheimer and Theodor W. Adorno, *Dialectic of Enlightenment: Philosophical Fragments*. Translated by Edmund Jephcott, 248–52. Stanford, CA: Stanford University Press, 2002.
Villa, Dana. "Weber and The Frankfurt School." In *The Routledge Companion to the Frankfurt School*, edited by Peter E. Gordon, Espen Hammer, and Axel Honneth, 266–81. New York: Routledge, 2019.
Wasserstrom, Steven M. *Religion after Religion: Gershom Scholem, Mircea Eliade, and Henry Corbin at Eranos*. Princeton, NJ: Princeton University Press, 1999.
Weber, Max. "Science as a Vocation." In *From Max Weber: Essays in Sociology*, edited and translated by H. H. Gerth and C. Wright Mills, 129–56. New York: Oxford University Press, 1958.
Weiß, Volker. Afterword. In Theodor W. Adorno, *Aspects of the New Right-Wing Extremism*, 42–63. Translated by Wieland Hoban. Cambridge: Polity Press, 2020.
Weiß, Volker. *Die autoritäre Revolte: Die Neue Rechte und der Untergang des Abendlandes*. Stuttgart: Klett-Cotta, 2018.
Wellmer, Albrecht. *The Persistence of Modernity: Essays on Aesthetics, Ethics and Postmodernism*. Translated by David Midgley. Cambridge: Polity Press, 1991.
Wesel, Uwe. *Der Mythos von Matriarchat: Über Bachofens Mutterrecht und die Stellung von Frauen in frühen Gesellschaften*. Frankfurt: Suhrkamp, 1999.
Wheatland, Thomas. *The Frankfurt School in Exile*. Minneapolis, University of Minnesota Press, 2009.
Whitebook, Joel. "Psychoanalysis and Critical Theory." In *The Routledge Companion to the Frankfurt School*, edited by Peter E. Gordon, Espen Hammer, and Axel Honneth, 32–47. New York: Routledge, 2019.
Wiggershaus, Rolf. *The Frankfurt School: Its History, Theories, and Political Significance*. Translated by Michael Robertson. Cambridge: Polity Press, 1994.
Wilcock, Evelyn. "Adorno in Oxford 1: Oxford University Musical Club." *Oxford Magazine* 127 (1996): 11–13.

Wilcock, Evelyn. "Adorno in Oxford 2: A Merton Circle." *Oxford Magazine* 143 (1997): 10–12.
Wohlfarth, Irving. "Walter Benjamin and the Idea of a Technological Eros: A Tentative Reading of *Zum Planetarium*." *Benjamin Studies* 1, no. 1 (2002): 65–109.
Wolin, Richard. *Walter Benjamin: An Aesthetic of Redemption*. Berkeley: University of California Press, 1994.
Woods, Roger. *The Conservative Revolution in the Weimar Republic*. New York: Palgrave Macmillan, 1996.
Zuidervaart, Lambert. *Truth in Husserl, Heidegger, and the Frankfurt School: Critical Retrieval*. Cambridge, MA: MIT Press, 2017.

INDEX

Abromeit, John, 20, 57n75
Adenauer, Konrad, 74–75
Alternative for Germany Party, 5
Anders, Günther, 3
antisemitism: *Dialectic of Enlightenment* and, 119; George and, 9; Heidegger and, 17; Klages and, 9, 14, 29, 38–39, 66; New Right and, 5; Night of the Broken Glass and, 82, 110, 130. *See also* racism
archaic image: Adorno's critique of, 31, 41, 172–73; Bachofen and, 40, 127; Benjamin and, 14; *Dialectic of Enlightenment* and, 143, 148; Jung and, 40; Klages and, 14, 29, 40, 127, 140, 172–73
Arendt, Hannah, 112, 168–69

Bachofen, Johann Jakob, 40, 42–44, 125–28, 131, 139, 140n64

Benjamin, Walter: Adorno's critique of, 14, 41, 53–55, 108–9, 159; Adorno's debt to, 6, 12, 23–25, 33–36, 69, 124, 137, 158; Bachofen and, 44; capitalism and, 53; Cassirer and, 134–35; dialectical image and, 36, 39–40; *Dialectic of Enlightenment* and, 25, 112, 118, 121, 154–55, 161–62; domination of nature and, 35–37, 112; Horkheimer and, 66, 118; Jewish theology and, 6, 23, 25, 40; Jung and, 54; Jünger and, 41; Klages and, 14, 33, 37–41, 53–54, 158–59; Marxism and, 12, 36, 158; mass culture and, 108–9, 112, 160–61; National Socialism and, 36; reception of, 36–37; reification and, 39; Schmitt and, 41
Bergson, Henri, 29, 100
Berlin, Isaiah, 17–19, 86, 132

Bernstein, Jay M., 58, 63, 93
Black Lives Matter, 163
Bloch, Ernst, 35, 158
Borchardt, Rudolf, 21, 128, 130, 132, 142
Bowra, Cecil Maurice, 132–33
Brecht, F. J., 56
Breuer, Stefan, 31, 50, 52–53, 120
Buchstein, Hubertus, 92
Buck-Morss, Susan, 12, 20

Caesarism: Adorno and, 25, 74–75, 78–88, 93–102, 107–9, 115, 148, 159–61, 165, 168; Bonapartism and, 79, 97; capitalism and, 94, 160; Gramsci and, 79; Horkheimer and, 113–15, 148–49; Marxism and, 97–98; Napoleonism and, 79–80; National Socialism and, 80–81, 87n53; Schmitt and, 79; Spengler and, 25, 74–75, 78–89, 93–98, 130, 159–60, 165; totalitarianism and, 79–80, 82, 87n53; Weber and, 93
Caillois, Roger, 137n59
capitalism: Adorno and, 3, 34, 41, 46, 49, 53–54, 86–88, 91–98, 107, 120, 137, 145, 159–60; Benjamin and, 53; Caesarism and, 94, 160; democracy and, 83, 166; development of, 62, 67–68, 78, 90–96, 160; Ford-Keynesian form of, 3, 163, 166; Horkheimer and, 57, 64, 67–69, 93, 113–15; Klages and, 29, 31, 37, 42, 45–46; Lukács and, 35, 57; Marxism and, 41, 87, 97–98; neoliberal form of, 166–67; phenomenology and, 49, 62–64, 67–68; Pollock and, 78, 91–94, 113, 160; Spengler and, 86, 107, 115; Weber and, 93, 119
Cassirer, Ernst, 71, 73, 126, 130n43, 133–37, 154–55, 161–62
Christianity, 34, 140n64, 141, 144. *See also* Judeo-Christianity
chthonic worldview, 29, 39, 130, 138–39, 142–43, 153
Claussen, Detlev, 20

conservative revolutionary movement: Adorno and, 12, 21, 26, 155; anti-communism of, 10, 77; as forerunner of Nazism, 10, 12; Klages and, 10, 155; *Lebensphilosophie* and, 10–11; New Right and, 16, 26; Nietzsche and, 22; rise of, 6; Spengler and, 10, 77, 86, 155; traditional conservatism and, 10. *See also* critique of civilization; radical conservatism
constellation, 31, 34, 36, 41, 53–57, 60. *See also* dialectical image
constitutive subjectivity: Adorno and, 22, 24–25, 32, 46–48, 51–52, 55, 59–61, 63, 145; capitalism and, 46; Husserl and, 52, 63; Kant and, 59; Klages and, 24–25, 145. *See also* identity thinking; logocentrism
Cornelius, Hans, 59
Cosmics, 9, 126. *See also* George, Stefan; Klages, Ludwig
Counter-Enlightenment, 10, 157
critique of civilization, 6, 12, 14, 17–21, 26, 44, 70, 137, 157–58, 162. *See also* conservative revolutionary movement; radical conservatism
cultural morphology: Adorno and, 15, 75–77, 86, 89–90, 160; Horkheimer and, 115n119, 149; Spengler and, 7, 15, 24, 72, 75–77, 80, 98–99
culture industry: Adorno and, 4–5, 25, 79, 83, 101–2, 107–112, 115, 161; *Dialectic of Enlightenment* and, 25, 79, 83, 101–2, 108–12, 161, 167–68; twenty-first century and, 5, 167–68. *See also* mass culture

Decline of the West, The (Spengler): Adorno's youth and, 94–96, 100–101; Apollonian antiquity and, 7, 76; Caesarism and, 25, 74–75, 78–89, 93–98, 106, 159–61; cultural morphology of, 7, 24–25, 72, 75–76, 80; Faustian West and, 7, 75–77, 80, 150–52; Weimar Republic and, 80–81, 93–95

democracy: Adorno and, 2, 24–25, 74, 80–83, 110, 158, 167–69; capitalism and, 83, 166; Cassirer and, 71, 73; Gehlen, 2–3; Homer and, 127, 133; inherent defects of, 79, 89; Klages and, 14, 24; Napoleons and, 79; right-wing populism and, 5–6, 165–69; the silent revolution and, 163–64; Spengler and, 24–25, 74, 77–78, 80–81, 88–89, 100–101, 158–60, 168–69; subjectivity and, 83, 167–69; United States and, 83, 91–92, 102–3, 159, 167–68; Weimar Republic and, 71–73, 80–81, 159–61; West Germany and, 74, 83–85, 161
demythologization, 18, 128, 133, 138n59, 142–47, 151
Descartes, Rene, 49
dialectical image, 36, 39–40, 54–55, 173. *See also* constellation
Dialectic of Enlightenment (Horkheimer and Adorno): domination of nature and, 120, 125, 140–44, 153; mimetic reason and, 148, 154; Pelasgians and, 138, 140–48, 161–62; philhellenism and, 125, 127–33
Dilthey, Wilhelm, 11, 57
disenchantment, 25, 39, 119–20, 122, 135
domination of nature: Adorno and, 22, 28, 35, 46, 50, 64, 112, 130n44, 151n99; Benjamin and, 35–37, 112; *Dialectic of Enlightenment* and, 120, 125, 140–44, 153; Horkheimer and, 130n44, 149, 151–52; Kierkegaard and, 34; Klages and, 18, 37, 50, 64, 140; Spengler and, 18, 125, 149–50, 151n99

Eisenstein, Sergei, 9
Engels, Friedrich, 44, 68, 97
ethnonationalism, 4
existentialism, 33–34, 47, 56, 71, 105
expressionism, 6, 112

Fichte, Johann Gottlieb, 68
Frankfurt discussion, 51, 56–57

Frenkel-Brunswik, Else, 102, 160
Freud, Sigmund: Adorno and, 5, 12, 23, 25, 35, 75, 89, 103–5, 137, 158, 160, 174; *Dialectic of Enlightenment* and, 25, 118–19, 121–22, 154–55, 161–62; Horkheimer and, 23, 104, 113–14; Klages and, 38, 122; repression and, 6, 25, 103, 119; Spengler and, 106–7
Freyer, Hans, 10
Friedman, George, 13, 78, 83, 100–102, 108, 123, 163
Fromm, Erich, 23, 44, 89, 104, 170n29
Fukuyama, Francis, 4, 26

Gandesha, Samir, 166–68
Gehlen, Arnold, 1–3, 21, 107, 156–57, 170
George, Stefan, and the George Circle: Adorno and, 9, 15, 21, 122, 129, 132; antisemitism and, 9; Bachofen and, 126; Bowra and, 132; Goethe and, 8; Hölderlin and, 8; influence of, 8–9, 21, 129; Klages and, 8–9, 29, 126, 132; philhellenism and, 8, 126, 129, 132
German Youth Movement, 8, 37–38
Goebbels, Joseph, 82, 110
Goethe, Johann Wolfgang von, 8–9, 125–26, 131
Gordon, Peter E., 27n67, 51, 105–6, 166–68
Gramsci, Antonio, 79
graphology, 38–39, 86
Grimm, Marc, 5
Grossheim, Michael, 31, 109n102, 146, 172

Habermas, Jürgen: Adorno and, 3–4, 6, 12, 22, 26, 162, 164; Benjamin and, 36; *Dialectic of Enlightenment* and, 3, 119, 124n29, 147n88; Klages and, 26n66
Hartmann, Heinz, 100
Hartmann, Nicolai, 45, 51–52, 130n43
Hegel, Georg Wilhelm Friedrich, 28, 33, 54–63, 68–69, 113, 147n88, 158–59, 174

Heidegger, Martin: Adorno and, 13, 16–17, 21, 23–24, 51–52, 55–57, 130n43, 138n59, 164; antisemitism of, 17; *Being and Time* of, 23–24, 51, 56–57, 130n43, 138n59; *Black Notebooks* of, 16–17; Cassirer and, 71, 73; Hegel and, 57; Hitler and, 73; influence of, 51, 56–57; Klages and, 16–17; Spengler and, 16–17
Heraclitus, 145
Herf, Jeffrey, 10
Herodotus, 139
Hesse, Hermann, 9
Hindenburg, Paul von, 9
Hitler, Adolf, 8, 10, 18n47, 73, 81, 84–85, 95, 97, 104, 113, 117, 159. *See also* National Socialism
Hobbes, Thomas, 152
Hofmannsthal, Hugo von, 10
Hölderlin, Friedrich, 8, 148
Holocaust, 22, 72, 74, 86, 163
Homer: Adorno and, 47, 124n29, 131–32; Borchardt and, 128; Bowra and, 132–33; *Dialectic of Enlightenment* and, 18, 30, 116, 124n29, 127–28, 132–33, 140–48, 150–54; interwar reactionaries and, 127–28, 131–32; Klages and, 139–41; Nietzsche and, 125–27; Pelasgians and, 139; pre-Socratics and, 47, 64, 145
Honneth, Axel: Adorno and, 3, 6, 12, 22, 26, 162; *Dialectic of Enlightenment* and, 3, 13, 30, 120–21, 123, 146–47
Horkheimer, Max: Adorno's debt to, 23, 57–58, 158; Adorno's disagreement with, 41–42, 49, 57–58, 61n85, 64–69, 89, 114, 147; Adorno's impact on, 113–15, 148–49; *The Authoritarian Personality* and, 102–3; Benjamin and, 66, 118; Caesarism and, 113–15, 148–49; capitalism and, 7, 64, 67–69, 93, 113–15; cultural morphology and, 115n119, 149; Freud and, 23, 104, 113–14; Fromm and, 23, 89, 104; Hegel and, 57, 68–69, 113; Husserl and, 67–68; Klages and, 14n36, 41–42, 58, 66–69; *Lebensphilosophie* and, 69; Marxism and, 57, 113, 130n44, 158; National Socialism and, 67, 151–52, 154; Niebuhr and, 113; Nietzsche and, 130n44; pessimistic turn of, 20, 113–115, 130n44, 162; Pollock and, 91–93, 113–14; Sohn-Rethel and, 46, 63–68; Spengler and, 113–15, 148–49, 154; Tillich and, 113; totality and, 57, 68–69; Weber and, 93, 122
Hughes, H. Stuart, 7, 99–100
Hullot-Kentor, Robert, 54–56, 124n29
Humboldt, Wilhelm von, 125
Husserl, Edmund: Adorno and, 29, 35, 48–53, 55n71, 61–64, 66–67, 100, 145; categorial intuition and, 61, 67; constitutive subjectivity and, 52, 63; Hegel and, 61–63; Horkheimer and, 67–68; Kant and, 62; Klages and, 29–30, 100; Spengler and, 100

identity thinking: Adorno and, 22, 46, 51, 60, 64, 66, 120, 151; *Dialectic of Enlightenment* and, 146–47; Klages and, 50, 64–66, 120; neo-Hegelianism and, 57; phenomenology and, 51–52; Sohn-Rethel and, 64–66, 151. *See also* constitutive subjectivity; logocentrism
immanent critique, 19, 55, 60–63, 78, 147–48
Inglehart, Ronald, 163–64
instrumental reason: Adorno and, 4, 22, 157, 169–70; *Dialectic of Enlightenment* and, 119–20, 140–41, 146, 163, 169; Klages and, 50, 141, 172; Rosa and, 170–71; Spengler and, 149–50; Weber and, 119

Jaeger, Werner, 129
Jay, Martin, 12–13, 20, 110, 117–18, 153, 158
Jewish theology: Adorno and, 2, 6, 23, 57n75, 158, 174; Benjamin and, 6,

23, 25, 40; *Dialectic of Enlightenment* and, 25
Judeo-Christianity, 29, 38, 140. *See also* Christianity
Jung, Carl Gustav, 40, 54, 126, 137n59
Jünger, Ernst, 10, 21, 41

Kafka, Franz, 36
Kant, Immanuel, 2, 11, 35, 47, 59, 62, 64–65, 151, 158
Kantorowicz, Ernst, 9, 132
Keum, Tae-Yeoun, 135–36
Kierkegaard, Søren: Adorno and, 31–35, 43, 47–48, 53–57, 63, 105–7; as idealist, 33–34, 63; Plato and, 43, 47; revival of, 33
Kirchheimer, Otto, 92
Klages, Ludwig: antisemitism of, 9, 14, 29, 38–39, 66; antisocialism of, 14; archaic image and, 14, 29, 31, 40, 127, 140, 173; Bachofen and, 40, 44, 126–27, 139; Benjamin and, 14, 33, 37–41, 53–54, 158–59; Bergson and, 29–30, 100; Caillois and, 137n59; capitalism and, 29, 31, 37, 42, 45–46; chthonic worldview and, 29, 39, 130, 138–39, 142–43, 153; conservative revolutionary movement and, 10, 155; democracy and, 14, 24; *Dialectic of Enlightenment* and, 13–15, 18, 24, 30–32, 109n102, 120–25, 129–31, 137–48, 154–55, 161–63; domination of nature and, 18, 37, 50, 64, 140; dream consciousness and, 40; dual metaphysics of, 8, 11, 15, 29, 38, 120, 130, 138n59; Freud and, 38, 122; George and, 8–9, 29, 126, 132; German Youth Movement and, 37–38; graphology and, 38–39, 86; Heidegger and, 16–17; Hegel and, 56n71, 58; Homer and, 139–41; Horkheimer, and, 14n36, 41–42, 58, 66–69; Husserl and, 29–30, 100; identity thinking and, 50, 64–66, 120; influence of, 6–10, 39; instrumental reason and, 50, 141, 172; Kracauer and, 43; *Lebensphilosophie* and, 11, 29, 45, 50, 147, 158–59; logocentrism and, 8, 25, 29–30, 51, 58, 64, 69, 100, 122, 130, 138–39, 142, 158, 169, 172; mass culture and, 109n102; National Socialism and, 10, 39, 67; *Negative Dialectics* and, 22, 24–25, 28–32, 48, 159; Pelagians and, 125, 138–49, 161; phenomenology and, 50–52, 145; Plato and, 37; pre-Socratics and, 49–50, 68, 145; racism and, 38–39; reification and, 37; Rosa and, 169–73; Spengler and, 10, 86, 149–50; Weber and, 29, 119
Kommerell, Max, 9
Korsch, Karl, 98
Kracauer, Siegfried, 19, 35, 42–45, 47, 59, 123, 129
Kuhn, Helmut, 56

Lebensphilosophie: Adorno and, 11, 53, 69, 158–59; conservative revolutionary movement and, 10–11; *Dialectic of Enlightenment* and, 146–47; Horkheimer and, 69; Klages and, 11, 29, 45, 50, 147, 158–59; as philosophical vogue, 11–12; politics of, 11, 16; rehabilitation of, 16; Spengler and, 11, 86, 152–53
Lebovic, Nitzan, 16, 38, 43
Le Pen, Marine, 165
Lepenies, Wolf, 1–2, 156–57
Levin, Thomas Y., 108, 109
Levinson, Daniel J., 102, 160
logocentrism: chthonic worldview and, 130, 138; Klages and, 8, 25, 29–30, 51, 58, 64, 69, 100, 122, 130, 138–39, 142, 158, 169, 172; Pelagians and, 139, 142; Western philosophy as, 8, 29, 37. *See also* constitutive subjectivity; identity thinking
Löwenthal, Leo, 66, 105
Löwith, Karl, 56
Lukács, Georg: Adorno and, 6, 12, 35, 57–58, 69, 98, 119, 157–58, 160; capitalism and, 35, 57; Hegel and, 6, 57; Kant and, 64–65; Marxism and,

Lukács (*continued*)
6, 12, 35, 57, 64–65, 119, 157–58, 160; reification and, 6, 64–65, 119; Sohn-Rethel and, 64–65; totality and, 57; Weber and, 119

Machiavelli, Niccolò, 81, 89, 107
Maistre, Joseph de, 17, 86
Mali, Joseph, 39, 127
Mann, Thomas, 106, 173–74
Marcuse, Herbert, 57, 170n29
Marx, Karl, and Marxism: Adorno and, 6, 12, 14, 18, 23, 25, 35, 41, 50, 58, 69, 75, 86–89, 94–98, 118–20, 134, 137, 145–46, 151–52, 157–61, 174; Benjamin and, 12, 36, 158; Berlin and, 17; Bloch and, 35, 158; Caesarism and, 97–98; capitalism and, 41, 87, 97–98; *Dialectic of Enlightenment* and, 14, 117–20, 145–46, 151, 161; Hegel and, 57–58, 68–69; Horkheimer and, 57, 113, 130n44, 158; Lukács and, 6, 12, 35, 57, 64–65, 119, 157–58, 160; New Left and, 12, 36, 157; Pollock and, 91–94, 158, 160; Sohn-Rethel and, 64–66, 131, 137, 158–59; Spengler and, 7, 86, 97–98; totality and, 57, 68–69
mass culture: Benjamin and, 108–9, 112, 160–61; Gehlen and, 2; Klages and, 109n102; Spengler and, 25, 74, 82–83, 101–2, 107–112, 160–61, 168. *See also* culture industry
matriarchy, 44, 126, 139, 143
McCarthy, Joseph, and McCarthyism, 102, 173
McCole, John, 37, 39
Me Too, 163
Michels, Robert, 88, 98
mimetic reason: Adorno and, 24, 28, 32, 60–63, 70, 147, 154, 158–59, 169–70; *Dialectic of Enlightenment* and, 148, 154; *Negative Dialectics* and, 24–25, 28, 70, 158, 172; resonance and, 170–73
Möller van der Bruck, Arthur, 10, 21

Mörchen, Hermann, 13
Müller-Doohm, Stefan, 21, 33
Murray, Gilbert, 131–32
Musil, Robert, 9
Mussolini, Benito, 97

National Democratic Party, 5
National Socialism: Adorno and, 5, 42, 44–45, 47, 73, 81, 84–87, 92, 95, 110–11, 148, 159; Benjamin and, 36; Caesarism and, 80–81, 87n53; conservative revolutionary movement and, 10, 12; *Dialectic of Enlightenment* and, 135–36; Horkheimer and, 67, 151–52, 154; Klages and, 10, 39, 67; racism and, 135–36; Spengler and, 10, 77, 154, 160. *See also* Hitler, Adolf
Nazis and Nazism. *See* Hitler, Adolf; National Socialism
Neumann, Franz, L., 92
New Left, 4, 12, 36, 157, 161
New Right, 4–5, 16, 26
Niebuhr, Reinhold, 95–96, 105, 110, 113
Nietzsche, Friedrich: Adorno and, 15, 22, 58, 122, 127–29; conservative revolutionary movement and, 22; *Dialectic of Enlightenment* and, 15, 122, 127–28; Homer and, 125–27; philhellenism and, 125–31; Spengler and, 72, 99; *völkisch* epigones of, 127–28, 131
Night of the Broken Glass, 82, 110, 159
non-identical, 25, 35, 60

Occupy Movement, 163
O'Connor, Brian, 59, 69n111, 169
Orbán, Viktor, 165

Parmenides, 49–50, 145
Pauen, Michael, 31, 108, 123, 147
Pausanias, 139
Pelasgians, 125–26, 138–49, 161
Pensky, Max, 167–68
phenomenology, 45, 49–52, 61–64, 67, 145. *See also* Heidegger, Martin; Husserl, Edmund

philhellenism: Adorno and, 125, 127–33; Bachofen and, 125–28, 140n64; Bowra and, 132–33; *Dialectic of Enlightenment* and, 125, 127–33; George and, 8, 126, 129, 132; *Goethezeit* and, 125–26, 131; Klages and, 138–43; Nietzsche and, 125–31
physiognomy and, 11, 98–101
Pindar, 21, 128, 142
Plato, 28, 33, 37, 43, 47, 49–50, 151
Pollock, Friedrich, 78, 84–85, 91–96, 113, 119, 158, 160
preponderance of the object, 35, 60, 66
pre-Socratics, 46–47, 49–50, 64–65, 68, 70n111, 145–46, 162
Proust, Marcel, 36
Prutsch, Markus J., 80
psychoanalysis. *See* Freud, Sigmund

racism: Adorno and, 104; Alternative for Germany Party and, 5; Klages and, 38–39; National Socialism and, 135–36; right-wing populism and, 4, 165. *See also* antisemitism
radical conservatism, 3, 6, 11, 16, 18, 77, 94, 152, 158. *See also* conservative revolutionary movement; critique of civilization
Raulet, Gérard, 134
reification, 6, 34, 37, 39, 64–65, 119, 137n59, 170
Reinhardt, Karl, 129
resonance, 170–73
Riesman, David, 106
right-wing populism, 4–6, 162–69
Roberts, David, 151n99
Rosa, Hartmut, 169–73
Rose, Gillian, 12, 20
Rousseau, Jean-Jacques, 125
Ruehl, Martin A., 129
Ryle, Gilbert, 48

Sanford, R. Nevitt, 102, 160
Scheler, Max, 45, 52, 130n43
Schelling, Friedrich, 68
Schelsky, Helmut, 3

Schmitt, Carl, 10, 13, 41, 79
Schönberg, Arnold, 6, 23, 175
Schopenhauer, Arthur, 72, 114
Schröder, Hans Eggert, 39
Schuler, Alfred, 9
sexism, 5, 166
Shotwell, James T., 90
Simmel, Georg, 9
Skidelsky, Edward, 135
Sohn-Rethel, Alfred: Adorno and, 46–47, 51, 63–66, 131, 137, 145, 151, 158–59; *Dialectic of Enlightenment* and, 145–46, 151; Horkheimer and, 46, 63–64, 66, 68; identity thinking and, 64–66, 151; Klages and, 46–47, 51, 65–66; Lukács and, 64–65; Marxism and, 64–66, 131, 137, 158–59; pre-Socratics and, 46, 64–66, 70n111, 131, 145–46, 151, 159
Sombart, Werner, 88, 98
Spengler, Oswald: Arendt and, 168–69; *The Authoritarian Personality* and, 25, 78–79, 83, 101–7, 160–61; Bergson and, 100; Caesarism and, 25, 74–75, 78–89, 93–98, 130, 159–60, 165; capitalism and, 86, 107, 115; conservative revolutionary movement and, 10, 77, 86, 155; cultural morphology and, 7, 15, 24, 72, 75–77, 80, 98–99; cyclical theorists and, 78, 81, 89, 160; democracy and, 24–25, 74, 77–78, 80–81, 88–89, 100–101, 158–60, 168–69; *Dialectic of Enlightenment* and, 15, 18, 24, 78–79, 83, 95, 108–11, 115, 123–25, 130–31, 137, 148–55, 160–63; domination of nature and, 18, 125, 149–50, 151n99; early critics of, 72–73, 76, 86, 90, 96, 99–100, 111–12, 124; Freud and, 106–7; Heidegger and, 16–17; Hobbes and, 152; Horkheimer and, 113–115, 148–49, 154; Husserl and, 100; influence of, 6–7, 10, 72, 75, 80, 94; instrumental reason and, 149–50; Klages and, 10, 86, 149–50; *Lebensphilosphie* and,

Spengler (*continued*)
11, 86, 152–53; Marxism and, 7, 86, 97–98; mass culture and, 25, 74, 82–83, 101–2, 107–112, 160–61, 168; Michels and, 88, 98; National Socialism and, 10, 77, 154; *Negative Dialectics* and, 149–50; Nietzsche and, 72, 99; physiognomy and, 11, 98–101; political writings of, 77; Pollock and, 78, 93–96, 160; Sombart and, 88, 98; Weber and, 93
Spirit as Adversary of the Soul, The (Klages): Adorno's planned review of, 19, 31, 41–53, 66–67, 123; antisemitism and, 38, 66–67; Benjamin and, 37, 39; *Dialectic of Enlightenment* and, 120, 129–30, 138–48, 154–55, 161–62; logocentrism and, 8, 25, 29, 37, 130, 158; Pelasgians and, 125, 138–48, 161
Stalin, Joseph, and Stalinism, 4, 80, 113, 116–17, 162–63
state capitalism. *See* Pollock, Friedrich
Stauth, Georg, 14n36
Stoics, 81
Strauss, Leo, 71, 73, 164
Surrealism, 36, 39

Thalheimer, August, 97
Thies, Christian, 94
Thucydides, 139
Tiedemann, Rolf, 14–16, 20, 32, 121n14
Tillich, Paul, 33, 57, 95–96, 105, 110, 113, 138n59
Tocqueville, Alexis de, 167

totality, 28, 33, 57–58, 68–69
Trakl, Georg, 112
Trump, Donald, 6, 162, 165, 167–68

Verhaeghe, Paul, 166
Villa, Dana, 122
völkisch, 39, 44, 131, 140n64

Weber, Max: Adorno and, 25, 29, 93, 118–22, 137, 154–55, 161–62; capitalism and, 93, 119; *Dialectic of Enlightenment* and, 25, 93, 118–22, 154–55, 161–62; disenchantment and, 25, 119; Horkheimer and, 93, 122; Klages and, 29, 119; Lukács and, 119; Pollock and, 93, 119; Spengler and, 93
Weiß, Volker, 5, 85
Wellmer, Albrecht, 14, 120, 154
Wiggershaus, Rolf, 13
Wilamowitz-Moellendorf, Ulrich von, 127
Winckelmann, Johann Joachim, 125
Wittgenstein, Ludwig, 23, 29
Wohlfarth, Irving, 37
Wolf, Friedrich August, 125
Wolfskehl, Karl, 9
Wolin, Richard, 20, 66, 165, 167–68
working through the past, 4, 74, 84–87, 90, 159–61

Xenophanes, 128, 142

Zetkin, Clara, 97
Zuidervaart, Lambert, 51